The American Option
and yes, I almost became an American

By Philip Morgan Cheek

"This is a war of the unknown warriors. The whole of the warring nations are engaged, not only soldiers, but the entire population, men women, and children. The fronts are everywhere, villages, factories, schools, shops..."

—Winston Churchill 1940

"The people of Britain would become protagonists in their own history."

—From The Peoples War,
by Angus Calder, 1969

Brick Tower Press

© Philip Morgan Cheek, 2005

Cheek, Philip Morgan
The American Option (and yes, I almost became an American)
Includes Bibliography, Index and Glossary

ISBN 1-883283-40-X, First Edition, December 2005

Library of Congress
        Control Number: 2005935311

The American Option
and yes, I almost became an American

By Philip Morgan Cheek

Dedication:
For my mother and the lonely women of wars

Brick Tower Press
New York

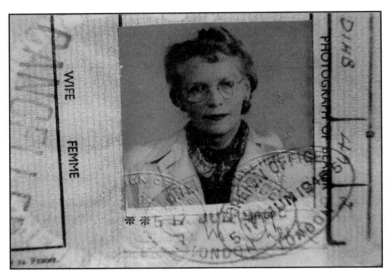

Gwendoline Mary Morgan Cheek
A woman of London, 1939 to 1945
"...It's my son, my mother began, he's going to America..."

CONTENTS

LIST OF ILLUSTRATIONS

In Appreciation

Of all the sources used to relate my story as an evacuee to America side-by-side with the events of World War II, most were hunted down in libraries. Others, I came upon by chance in unlikely places in England, America and New Zealand. Some, private persons, seemed curious about a project highlighting the plight of children and women in wars apparently spawned by a school reunion. It was not, however, my first idea and which, initially, had focussed upon The Montclair Kimberley Academy in New Jersey, U.S.A., and its benevolent role in accepting British wartime evacuees as students. This drew interest from the present headmaster, Dr Peter R. Greer. Regrettably, of the five original students I have been able to trace only myself and so now, almost by default, the tale encompasses both the forced and voluntary mass movement of millions.

Lucky intelligence came through the owner of a Taipa Bay tourist lodge in the very far north of New Zealand, member of a lay study group monitoring the development and maybe the proliferation of alternative weaponry. There, over months, the book took shape. In a virtual garden of Eden new tools of terror incongruously dovetailed into the main theme, the protection of the national lifeblood. Children.

New York Times' news cuttings popped up at opportune moments providing insight into adolescent bewilderments and the story of the Oradour-sur-Glane massacre in 1944 France. Chelsea Military Antiques, London, confirmed the inscription on The Hitler Youth Movement daggers in one last telephone call on the subject. A lodge guest introduced me to Helga Tiscenko's book, *Strawberries with the Führer*. A London Times story, *A Schizoid Nation*, neatly came up about the time I was attempting to disseminate fact and myth about American mores, philosophies and decorums which I'd been obliged to learn and try to use. Kate Bolland, Royal Liver Assurance (pronounced Lyver), breathed life and credibility into the lore that sprung the name Liverpool. Christina (Tina) Tippit Brown, a "daughter" of the American Revolution, was timely with her Westport, Connecticut, Historical Society's newsletter recounting the set-piece commemoration: *The British Are Coming*. As sponsors, the Society had re-enacted Fairfield County's own beachhead resistance of other times on its very own Compo Beach. But I'd already done it in a different guise on September 15th 1940 on a Boston "beachhead" and was, on that day, welcomed.

My thanks to William Brown, husband of Tina, both Broadway writers, for photographs plus a great shot of American and British flags together on their Westport home's flagstaff, and to Skip and Audreta (Dreta) Pape of Fort Collins, Colorado, for photographs of my American "family." They and my own parents were to finally meet postwar on a chilly afternoon at Niagara Falls in 1947. For the rest, I have used the amateur snaps of boyhood and youthful times when the click of a camera shutter meant adventure. Captain George Bonwick, a Battle of the Atlantic veteran, earns my gratitude for technical opinion. Gillian Ennis, editor, *The Sea* newspaper, Missions To Seafarers, pulled out of a hat the identity of the flowering weed that flourished on London's wartime rubble not seen by Londoners, it was said, since the Great Fire of 1666.

The People's War was the first book I delved into for the explicit, obscene, and piteous detail depicting the European terror of the 1930's and 1940's. Surviving copies of Montclair Academy's student-produced newspaper of the day, the *Montclair News*, provided glimpses of social and political comment by the school's eighteen-year-olds before they were gathered up for college—or the military draft. I thank you all and now you, the reader.

PMC

Prologue

London, September 11th 2001 around 1300, GMT.

Two passenger aircraft had gone into the New York World Trade Center towers—one plane per tower. Both towering structures were already at ground level, or Ground Zero, as it would be termed.

In London, I'd pushed the ON button of the TV to get the 1 p.m. world news. I believed I'd selected the right channel, but obviously hadn't. It was showing some kind of *Towering Inferno* movie with even more horrific special effects. Perhaps, like nameless others, I had begun to tire of movies that appeared to depend on a cacophony of gratuitous noise and computerized, virtual reality images to capture a new century's unique audience. I was about to change channels. But then, what was our familiar news reader doing in such a movie? Oh, I decided, some cynical director had hijacked an Orson Welles' technique and hired our friendly newscaster for enhanced credibility. Was nothing sacred? No, it seemed, not even a 1940's Walter Winchell. This kind of scorn lasted for ten seconds at the most. Mesmerised, I did not change channels; I sank into a chair and in that way I saw and listened and was thus introduced to a new world order of supreme savagery and waste with America as epicenter.

On my calling cards I describe myself as a sailor and writer. The writer bit refers to a large number of continuing attempts to get manuscripts published by some publisher who will finally recognise their great worth in historical or literary circles. That hasn't happened yet. However, since 1999 I'd been collaborating with an old school pal and his wife in their production of a screenplay based on a story I'd given him. En-route, via New York, either to or from some ship or other, I would stop over at their Westport, Connecticut home and our proposed film would feature in a fairly flexible agenda of brunches, chat and chess.

Year 2001 was to be marked by a class reunion at our school in New Jersey, The Montclair Kimberley Academy and we would never forget that we belonged to the Class of "46. In it, in 1940, I met Bill—William F. Brown. We were 13 and 12 respectively. The school was then called just Montclair Academy. In later years I would meet Bill's wife, Tina, co-writer of our movie.

A year after the barely believable events of September 11th 2001 I confess that, at the time, I seriously debated the attractions of

New York–September 11, 2001
"...introduced to a new world order of supreme savagery and waste..."

the school reunion compared to the uncertainty of a scheduled landing at J.F. Kennedy Airport, or anywhere else. I was booked to fly on October 4th, leaving enough time, before the reunion hi-jinks on the 20th for other visits in Los Angeles, Denver and New York. But I am mean when it comes to forfeiting seats in anything—outside a life or death situation. So I let two cancelling deadlines go by while confusion conveniently reigned among the booking clerks. Further out, flight controllers and a shocked Pentagon continued to deliberate over closing or opening airspace for the likes of school reunionists in economy or maybe high powered business types in club class.

For Bill and me, our re-acquaintance, following my departure from the Academy in 1942 and his own graduation in 1946, would happen many, many years hence. There was World War II and the Korean War to work through, each of us, in our different roles, involved in both. Ladies in our marriages would claim our attention and concentrate the mind. Both his Montclair and finally Princeton days would fade naturally into those proper little slots of memory which can be re-opened on demand, but not so often when a war has intervened; when lives can be brutally changed or wherein satisfying achievement and excitement may not be duplicated in peaceful times.

1   Leisurely Haste–An Escape From War

Chelsfield, Kent, England–June 2nd 1940.

" **A**ll right Philip, have you made your mind up yet, what's it to be, go to America or stay here with your mother until peace comes?"

It was my father speaking, on short leave from his ship. He, my mother and I were seated in the living room of our small, semi-detached bungalow somewhere in southern England. Everywhere in wartime was, "somewhere in England." No one must know what part. But the farms, hedgerows and the beaten earth paths across paddocks were but a stone's throw from our front gate. I would walk along them going to school and knew every turn and small depression. Even the outcrops of prehistoric chalk would convey a feeling of progress toward my destination. Either to school or to the small country, Chelsfield Railway Station... Oops, you see how difficult it is to avoid careless talk!

My father's words and their sequence curiously summed up the relationship which then existed between me and my parents. And, amidst the talk of those times, there was no doubt as to the ultimate arrival of peace or on whose terms it would be made.

The use of my full Christian name was significant too. Shortening it to anything else was not then a fashion and never would be contemplated by them. The story went how, when they'd been trying different names for their sound, appearance or to placate some pushy family member prior to the Christening, my mother had chosen Philip since it could not be messed up. My godfather gave me Arthur and my mother won with Morgan. With my father's name there was no contest of course, but with Morgan thoughtfully incorporated I would later have a choice. In subsequent years, living in Australia, I soon realised there was no name which Australians could not do over, to make it sound more matey. Mateship in that land, of course, being a religion of sorts.

Then there had been the matter of choice given to me. Despite a most imminent invasion by German, S.S. shock troops and the disgusting *kultur* they espoused and would bring with them to our beaches to pollute our air and daily life, my parents had always given me choices. Of course, they were training me to make wise judgements. I doubt if they had read a book on how to raise a balanced individual but, while we lived with certain basic Victorian and religious values, both parents, and particularly my mother, layered on a goodly supply of self reliance and motivation. I was very much the third member of our team and would be heard as well as seen. Now, I was being asked if I wanted to go to America.

Finally, the alternative option—"...or stay here with your mother?" was, as I now suspect sixty-four years on, both a stern attempt to overcome emotion and a kind of expressionless hope that I would choose America. And this, despite that for as long as I can remember, the final words from my sailor father as he departed for another voyage had always been: "Now look after Mother, Philip." Sometimes, similar exhortations would appear in letters he would write to me: "Take care of Mother, Philip," or, "study hard, so mother and dad can be proud of you." But I never studied hard until I went to sea myself and then I crammed, frantically.

This day was also my mother's birthday, her fortieth. Both parents were as old as the year, my father just squeezing in before Christmas. Born Gwendoline Mary Morgan in one of those Victorian homes in a crescent of identical ones in the port city of Newport, South Wales, she'd been one of four sisters. From number thirteen, Clytha Crescent, she would attend school daily until aged sixteen while on Sundays the whole family would attend the Alma Street, Wesleyan chapel morning and evening. Eventually she would leave home to live in Cardiff's YWCA hostel and find employment in the *Western Mail* newspaper's retail stationery department from which female employees were invited to leave should they contemplate marriage.

Around this time, through the accident of looking back in the street one day, she met my father—also looking back. "Haven't I seen you somewhere," were the words she would attribute to my father who had apparently seen her in the *Western Mail's* shop. Over a span of years, building up the sea time for his third and final qualification as Master of a foreign-going steamship in the British Merchant Service, he would occasionally pop in to buy workbooks while attending the *Neptune Nautical Academy,* in Charles Street and sweating before an oncoming exam. My mother would forever recall the period, before leaving her job and marrying, as her happiest in the single state. She never tired of recounting both girl escapades, charity "do's" or the disciplined kindliness and moral security afforded by the world-wide youth fellowship—and the benign rule of Miss Souter, matron, Young Women's Christian Association.

My father, born Seth Stanley Cheek six months earlier than my mother, could officially call himself a Victorian. He'd arrived on December 3rd 1899 at home, in the town of Neath, South Wales in the county of Glamorganshire. He had been one of four brothers.

I, on the other hand, for better or for worse, first saw the patterned, papered walls of a nursing home in Cardiff, the Welsh capital city, from the white enameled iron bedstead provided for my mother. I have a picture of her in it looking twice as old as some of the sepia snapshots that had preceded her confinement. Early child-hood memories carry a vague suggestion that I had been a difficult birth for a woman so small and, since I fall into the category of "only child" the cause of my being sole and solitary heir seems clear. Brothers and sisters were put on hold, indefinitely. From all of which it will be seen that I am a Welshman born though not bred. The breeding part of my upbringing, after the age of seven, was all han-dled, with a good deal of care and wisdom, in England.

At seven, therefore, I arrived with my parents at the second of their several matrimonial homes. There, my father would repair for the few hours of shore leave typically permitted by Britain's post-Great War merchant marine instead of wasting time in train travel twixt London and South Wales. Inevitably, vestiges of my Celtic roots were preserved if only by my parents' occasional visits to their respective families in either Cardiff or Newport.

With my father more often than not at sea for months at a time, I probably got to know the grandparents on my mother's side better since grandfather had been in sailing ships of the Chilian nitrate trade and had signed on in the then composite rank of "second Mate and Bosun." One imagines it would have been one of the more active roles in a four-master and this certainly came through to me during visits to the old Newport home. There I would sit at the square deal table at which we ate and he, in his stuffed, leather armchair by the fire might recount, with the gusto of an ancient mariner, an impossible passage around Cape Horn.

But Sarah Ann Harris, of the whitewashed, Full Moon cottage in the tiny village of Ponthir, had put paid to all that and Fred Morgan "swallowed the anchor" for her, leaving me with an early her-itage of the sea. It would be reinforced, from time to time by his passing over to me relics of his sailing days such as a sailmaker's "palm" plus a few discoloured needles, a tin whistle, a mandolin and an early edition of *Bowditch*, the compiler of America's bible of astronomical navigation, carefully covered in white duck canvas. Except for the palm and nee-dles, which form part of my own sea-going kit today, these icons have since fallen victim to my parents' changes of address and my father's delight in the big clear-outs that accompanied every move.

By then, of course, I was myself well into my own sea career. If my ship was berthed in Cardiff I would visit my grandfather, taking along some of the ship's issue of rum-soaked, plug tobacco off which he would shave slivers of the solidified leaf with a very sharp knife and eco-nomically mix with some cheaper brand. I was miffed once when he did similar with some Christmas cigars. In the attic, three floors up where my mother and her sisters once would have slept, the dusty floors were covered with newspapers on which herbs were drying. It was rumoured that even tea leaves were mixed in. At times, his pipe smoke failed to convince that the mixtures were, as he claimed, health providing.

Despite all, I would listen, with rapt attention to his analysis of the family tree. Aided by yellowing news cuttings, grandfather Morgan would explain the ramifications of marriage settlements, deedpol skullduggery and 18th century hand-shake deals that had allowed our line to be somehow diverted from the great house of Tredegar with its association with Sir Henry Morgan[1], late of Risca. Henry it was who, in the 1640's, playing fast and loose with the King of Spain's treasure ships in the Caribbean, had turned buccaneer. He flew his flag in assorted ships and prizes—coloured black, having on it a skull and crossed bones in white. It must have been an arresting signal. Redeemed by King Charles II after capturing Panama, knighted and made deputy governor of Jamaica, a substantially enlarged Royal Privy Purse "gifted" from Spanish gold, just may have had some knock-on effect. My grandfather's tobacco mix and an upright life kept him going until ninety. I like that story and, many years into the future, I would recognise certain tendencies which, whether hereditary or not, would colour my existence in satisfying shades.

On my father's side, he had an elder brother, my Uncle Fred, who had become captain some ten years before my father's first command in 1940. My father would say he had followed his brother to sea in 1915 at age fifteen as there was not a great deal of career choice in Neath, near Swansea, at that time. He had left Gnoll School at the mandatory age having collected the usual volumes of the day presented to him and others as prizes for good attendance or sport and had tried his luck first sorting nails in an ironmongers shop, then measuring customers in a bespoke tailoring shop. At some point, in 1915, his widowed mother saved the day by buying him, as she had for Uncle Fred, a navigating apprenticeship with the Ellerman and Bucknall Steamship Co., Ltd., of London. It would become a career in which he would surpass himself despite two sinkings in 1917 then desperate, unemployed days, the reward of many, in the post-war Great Depression. He would fare slightly better in World War II.

I was still struggling with my father's question and near impossible choices, England or America for my war—or for life. Who could know? Growing up to the age I then was in the only child environment and a father in the British Merchant Navy, now made choosing a difficult and even responsible business. Who would now look after my mother?

"Now don't worry about your mother," said my father, correctly reading my thoughts."She will be going to America too, as soon as another passage can be booked in another ship." It seemed he did not want us to travel together in the *Baltrover*, the ship he had served in as chief officer for eight years on the London/Baltic run. He had swapped eighteen month voyages for ten day ones at less wages

1 *The Way of the Pirate* by Robert Downie, page 167, Brick Tower Press, 2005.

so that my mother, at least, could enjoy something like a normal marriage and all three of us a civilised homelife. Just the thought of a real voyage in the beloved ship I used to visit when at her usual berth in The Pool of London, that short stretch of barge-strewn River Thames between Tower Bridge and London Bridge, was almost enough to tip the scales toward America.

My first voyage in the ship had been quite short, one of the ten day trips at aged ten convalescing after a bloodier than normal extraction of my tonsils and adenoids. Medical opinion of the day favoured the double whammy. On board, I'd slept on the settee in my father's cabin which had been at the after end of the boat deck and was seasick for the first time. A steward would bring up from the dining saloon ice cream in stainless steel dishes and Martha, the long-serving senior stewardess, would look in now and then with a book or magazine from the ship's library and I would munch king-sized, Cadbury's nut-milk chocolate as I peered through the porthole at small coasters and barges in the Kiel Canal.

There had been excursions ashore in the company of two jolly ladies from my father's table in the dining saloon. There was the occasion when my father had hired one of those bicycle rafts and we peddled like mad across the stretch of water between German Danzig and Polish Zoppot. This lighthearted devilment on a sunny day, of crossing a frontier on water forbidden on land to those without special visas into the Polish corridor, must have somehow compensated for the morbid evidence of the Nazi march to war only another three years away. Then, the peace treaty that gave to landlocked Poland access to the sea and just about every other treaty designed to preserve a post-armistice peace, would be swept away along with many of their signatories. That voyage had been a schoolboy's dream come true but it had still been in peacetime, albeit a disappearing one. At age ten I recognised no threat.

Now, June 2nd, Britain had been at war for nine months, but not total war...not yet. We were about to end the Bore War or Phoney War as coined by American journalists, when little of war affected most people. Perhaps only the shrill whistles of irate Air-Raid Wardens spotting a light chink in our domestic blackout arrangements, would remind us that life had changed. Much, of course, had been happening on the diplomatic front and upon the sea where instant war had already been felt with the sinkings among our merchant fleets, each loss being a separate defeat. They were tempered by a surprise silver lining naval success off Uruguay, South America. There, the stalking of Germany's pocket battleship, *Graf Spee*, by three outgunned, lesser ships of the Royal and New Zealand Navy, became the renowned Battle of the River Plate ending with an ignominious scuttling and wasteful suicide of the German captain.

Not much was happening in France where a British Expeditionary Force of two divisions plus all the armour that could be rustled up, had been dispatched in support of the French. The propaganda fronts, however, were very active.

My father, still serving in the *Baltrover* for the Norwegian campaign designed to forestall the country's invasion by Germany, carried troops and stores for an army belatedly landed on a frozen shore. He then fell ill with bronchitis, a legacy of years amid Baltic winter conditions standing on fog-drenched navigating bridges where sweat would turn to ice. Discharged from Southampton General Hospital he discovered that his ten years seniority for captain had gone for nought in a company whose personnel and industrial policies proved little different from many others of the period. Ships' officers, with their captains, had been two a penny during almost the whole of the inter-war years' accursed economic depression. With ineffectual trade union support for a re-appointment to his ship after recovery, excluded from the company's limited medical cover, hospital bills to pay, miniscule savings, us to clothe and feed and me, to be educated to some degree, my father opted for the Royal Naval Reserve. It paid a wage. Britain's navy, scaled down by, with hindsight, naive peace treaties, had begun to induct Merchant Navy officers who would soon man the new convoy escort craft being constructed with near desperate haste at acquired sites in Britain and along Canada's great rivers. And so, 213 of the relatively tiny 850 gross tons, Flower class corvettes were born (105 in Canada), without which the German U-boat menace might never have been reduced to manageable levels—and its ultimate demise.

My father was initially stationed on one of the many south coast, island forts built during the Napoleonic wars against France. Now, these strange garrisons, protruding above the inshore waters where seabirds nested and bred, which had become objects of some curiosity to children building sand castles on nearby beaches, came into their own again. They would contribute to the continuous boom defense system for the protection of Portsmouth Harbour and the great naval base within. Steel cable, linking several mooring buoys for flotation and with a steel net suspended, could be opened and closed, like doors, by a tug.

German mine-laying submarines may have found the challenge of attempting to nudge past the nets during opening and closing of the boom sections irresistible. A tug could disappear in a flash after striking a misplaced or newly-laid mine. My father was put in charge of one of these booms and so realised his ten year ambition for independent command in which he'd been thwarted in more peaceful times.

During May and June, 1940, I would visit the nearby Chelsfield Railway Station and wonder at the scruffy appearance of soldiers leaning out of windows, grabbing cups of tea and sandwiches from members of the Women's Voluntary Services. It was a one-way experience for the soldiery who were London-bound from the many landing points they'd managed to reach in near scarecrow disarray along Britain's south coast. Their reappearance in England heralded the great evacuation from Dunkirk. We would soon learn how these dog-tired men represented the remnants of our defeated Expeditionary Force. We would also learn why, via cautious press announcements.

Initially sent to France to bolster the much-vaunted Maginot Line in northern France, the BEF's unpreparedness for a French military and political collapse in the wake of Leopold, the Belgian King's capitulation, had led to our men's rearguard scramble to escape encirclement. Success in averting the greater calamity, that of wholesale deportation into prisoner of war camps, would be achieved with the greater part of the force reaching the French beaches of Dunkirk. There, the now legendary embarkation of men into ships, pleasure-craft or smaller, in which to reach England's shore, would be aided by the German High Command's inability to follow up its advantage due to Hitler's inexplicable intervention or God's more plausible one. Almost all tanks, armoured transport, field guns and fuel but not, as it later showed, the men's fighting spirit, would be

Returning from Dunkirk to fight another day
(*Courtesy:* Hutchinson & Co., Ltd., Publishers, U.K.)

17

left in France. Sacrificing, on the other hand, is perhaps not the same as losing battles through incompetence. So I knew, as I stood on platform one of Chelsfield Railway Station watching the trains go by, that things were different now.

My father, enjoying his day or two's break from a new command, was saying: "Now, come and look at this map a minute Philip." He began to open the folds of a largish motor touring map that was beginning to disintegrate at the creases. Pointing to a town he'd already ringed around using one of those indelible marking pencils one needed to lick first, he said: "Just here, see? That's where you'll be living—if you decide on America."

This statement had, of course, been preceded by intermittent references to an invitation which had come with a letter some days before from an American family I already knew about. I hadn't taken it all very seriously. I was absorbed with my latest woodworking project at Beckenham Technical College and had designed and half made a table rack for books. The project was a test of how to make joinery cuts near invisible when put together. As it was, the class were able to attend the school woodwork shop only once every two weeks. The policy of dispersing school children around parents' homes on alternate days to lessen the death toll if a school was bombed, had already begun. Special radio programmes for schools were devised by the British Broadcasting Corporation which began at 10:30 each morning. Our accompanying teacher, say, for history would synchronise with a BBC history programme beamed out on a Tuesday. Then, not even "Lord Haw Haw," (the British traitor, William Joyce), would know which parents' home we were using for history that day. The government policy was to save our lives not help us to pass exams.

"Also, Philip, you will do better at school and then be well ahead of everyone else when the war is over." My father was still pointing with the pencil at the circle which encompassed a town called Montclair and it was in a state called New Jersey. Then he reached for the family photo album, apparently already unearthed in preparation for this more serious discussion with son and heir. My mother hurriedly disappeared toward the kitchen to prepare our evening meal. He turned up photographs of people I'd already learned were our "pseudo-American family."

Christmases in my brief life up till then, had always been accompanied by an annual greetings card more original and decorative than most of what we could find in our town. And there were always snapshots and a proper letter enclosed from these great but distant friends of my parents who had a son and a daughter and who grew taller with each year's photo. Well, naturally, they were friends of my mother too, because they were friends of my father. She had not met them and would do so only after the war had ended. But wasn't that the way of things with families? Their family name was Sheldon.

The American Option

The relationship with my father went back as far as the Great War of 1914-1918, so-called because the maniacal first European-wide conflict had then been considered to have been the greatest of all time. There would never be another war to earn the title "Great" would there? The world could rest in peace. But, as my father was flattening out the well-used motoring map on his old sea chest, that sometimes doubled as a coffee table, and an arresting smell of something nice cooking in the kitchen floated by, mental pictures of dishevelled soldiers on trains passing through our railway station, flashed back.

As things were to turn out, the Great War would keep its greatness in terms of senseless waste if only for the fact that this second war, with the French now out of it and exclusively enveloping us, would try to be less cavalier with life on the battle-fronts when, as they would, expand to the world's four corners. Over the twenty years between the wars life had somehow become more meaningful to our army generals and even more meaningful to an air force honed on Great War aerial dog fights—and pilots without parachutes.

The newer Royal Air Force, flying its biplane fighters into the second show, had a man, R.J. Mitchell, designer of the Spitfire who'd thrown the Air Ministry a lifeline in 1937. Even then, it was diffidently grabbed. Only later in the war would I learn that in 1940, as I was preparing to leave my homeland, it had been the RAF with its first workhorse monoplane fighter, the Hawker Hurricane, and finally with the still barely credited Spit, that had effectively turned the tables on Luftwaffe plans to soften us up prior to an invasion. In London, Winston Churchill, Prime Minister at last on May 10th, with his war cabinet, but not families like ours, now believed in its inevitability; perhaps a few weeks away. Thus, the most junior of our armed forces ensured our national survival until the great Congress of America enabled that country's leader, President Franklin D. Roosevelt, to become our chief ally in arms.

Back home, our very few "Brylcreem Boys," as fighter pilots were dubbed after the stabilising properties of that renowned brand of hair preparation had, thanks to their plain joy of flying; their verve; their very personalised sacrifices plus the significant margin that our development of radar had provided them with, totally upset the Germans steeped in euphoria and self-gratification. And the "Brylcreem Boys" all had parachutes this time round. And "Mae West" inflatable lifejackets—if any should find himself in the "drink."

As the pages of the photograph album were turned, I recognised the images which the popular Eastman Kodak folding camera would have produced. Holiday snaps, children in bathing suits, my father even, standing at the end of a lakeside jetty looking very youthful, a very tasteful brick chalet-style home, a boy in a wide check sports jacket cradling a black spaniel, a girl in a white frock posing with the same black spaniel, the mother and father in separate shots. I had often wondered who they were; why they seemed to have become important to my family which, by comparison with these people's large motor cars in the backgrounds of some photos, appeared more affluent than mine by that one comparison. We had no car.

"If you decide you would like to go to America," my father was saying, "this lady will be a sort of auntie to you, like your auntie Lillian whom you like a lot. Her name is Elinor and this will be your Uncle Roy. This is Audreta, whom you've heard me speak of from time to time and this is Harold who's about three years older. You, are about six months younger than Audreta so you'll have to watch your P's and Q's," he finished, giving me a quizzical glance. I gazed upon the photograph of the girl. She looked nice, in the natural way. I wouldn't be so afflicted by self-consciousness with her, I thought. My one previous experience with the opposite sex had materialised during a Chelsfield village school play. I'd played the part of a woodsman and the girl, Maureen Denslow, had some part I cannot remember. It proved a very advanced affair to my way of thinking and involved me in the surreptitious purchase of a bottle of scent which I wished to keep from my mother. How the finance was managed I cannot recall.

"Dad, how did these people come to be in the photo album; who are they really? Are they relatives of Nanna when she was working as chef in big houses in Canada and America?" In the previous century my grandmother, on my father's side, had been one of the great Victorian lady travellers who'd packed their portmanteaus and boxes and taken passage in the comparatively frail, wet sailing ships of the era—and returned to tell their tales.

"Well," my father replied, "it was like this. I met Elinor Crane, as she then was, toward the end of the Great War. She had a sort of second job, working for the United Services Club in New York City, a volunteer, to make things go, get the armed services and the merchant marine to talk to one another, that kind of thing. Me, and the second 'Sparks'..er, wireless operator to you, often visited the club while our ship was in port. Elinor, who of course we'd already met on previous visits to New York, would invite some of us to her parent's home at weekends—if the ship was in long enough. We would get slap-up home cooking, plenty of chat, listen to gramophone records and return to our ships. Then there was Cora, or Cody as she became affectionately known to the family after marrying Harold. She was a great one was Cody, full of bluff, direct humour and opinion. Harold was Burberry's man in New York—you know, the famous raincoat of that name."

"Oh, and that's why you always call your raincoat 'my Burberry?'"

"Exactly. And sometimes we would end up in her folks' apartment on Long Island, with Elinor and her boyfriend, Roy Sheldon."

The American Option

"How old were you then, Dad?"

"Oooh...about eighteen, nineteen, at a guess."

"And you remained friends between the wars, until now?"

"Well, I hope we'll always be friends. Anyway, Elinor got married to Roy eventually about the time Gwen, your mother and I got married in 1925. You came along, Harold, named after Harold Nash, came along....and then Audreta."

"And you never sort of lost touch then?"

"No, never. Roy came out of the American army—not entirely unscathed. I was torpedoed twice as you know and got home both times. Friendships forged in the shadow of a terrible war seldom fade. You may understand that one day Philip."

Perhaps, for the first time ever, I was beginning to comprehend the significance of those recurring Christmas cards. Sometimes they would contain hand-written verse by Roy Sheldon himself plus photos with dates or explanation on the back of the Velox printing paper, always in Elinor's neat and typical American script: "Aug. 5, 1928...here's you, Stanley, looking too dressed up for the lake, ha!" "Sept. 16, 1937....This is Harold and Audreta paddling their first canoe...Lake Mohawk." Photos that always seemed to have been taken by Elinor. Photo identities of a family I would soon call my own. It may have been the picture of Audreta, in her white cotton frock, looking serious, hair tied severely back with a ribbon, that decided me. She might need some taking care of I considered! I carefully extracted the picture from the album's black page and placed it, for the time being, between the pages of *Gulliver's Travels*. Jonathan Swift was current required reading for English literature. Now, I wondered, at whose house would the class be gathering tomorrow?

And so, a boyhood sense of adventure, uncertainty, the location map, the photo of an American junior high school student of uncertain age in virgin white and her elder brother, who would become my big brother, saw the scales bump down for my personal American odyssey. I was twelve and a quarter.

I was reassured that my mother would not be left alone in England for long. Our twin families, separated only by a formidable ocean, the Atlantic, would soon be together for the duration of what would become the latest, most threatening armed conflict on the face of the planet. It was a pity of course, that the book rack could not now be completed in all its perfection of hair-line joinery. I would come back and finish it after the war was over. Then, I would use up the scholarship for the architecture and draughting courses I'd narrowly won before the balloon had gone up on the previous September 3rd. My mother had, on one occasion, commented that my brains appeared to be more in my fingers than my head. But then I supposed that could also have meant becoming a pianist, a surgeon or a cat burglar. At any rate, there seemed no room in my mind at that time for the possibility that things would not be comfortably the same after my visit by sea to our American

Harold & Audreta Sheldon—1939
"...she might need some taking care of..."

"family" in New Jersey.

On that basis, therefore, I put aside all other reservations about leaving my mother, school and friends in England and, like the grown-up I felt I almost was, I gave my decision to my parents in soldierly fashion.

2   Churchill and the Pack Ice of Politics

Or ought it to be described as a sailor-like fashion? Because now, with the big decision made, my mother's birthday flowers from my father and I, in the largest vase and the prospect of us attending a local picture theatre after our dinner, I was intent upon going over in my mind what I would pack for my most important voyage yet.

But, going to "the pictures" would be fun. I would weigh up the necessities destined for my sea-bag later, in bed. The main, and only feature that evening was *Gone With The Wind* at The Commodore cinema in the nearest big town to us, Orpington. We had seen it on its first release just before war had begun the previous year. It was the grandest and first big colour epic filmed by Technicolour. David O. Selznick, the director, had achieved a kind of immortality with his four and a quarter hour film, the longest run ever. It was also about America and I believed I now needed to know about how the people there behaved and did things. So the film had returned to the town's cinema at rather an apt time I thought. No one, of course, could be exactly green about American culture and comedy. Fred Astaire and Ginger Rogers, Judy Garland and Mickey Rooney, Katherine Hepburn and Spencer Tracey, Stan Laurel and Oliver Hardy, Jimmy Cagney, George Raft, Bogart had all seen to that. Now, there was Clark Gable matched with our own Vivienne Leigh!

At the cinema, there would also be a Pathé-Gazette newsreel narrated with the graphic and precise diction of the day. The usual intermission on this evening, however, would come two hours into the film as it was so long. My father or I would then be able to intercept the girl with the tray of ice cream in blocks and tubs plus wooden spoons and cigarettes and book matches as she progressed steadily up and down the aisles with a tiny torch affixed to the tape that supported the tray around her neck. Her uniform was standard, nationwide and I, for one, thought these members of the cinema staff looked rather good in their black dresses, white lace aprons and white lace caps. They recalled the waitresses nicknamed "nippies," in branches of the ubiquitous Lyon's Corner House cafés whose corner sitings cleverly gave the shops two frontages embellished with a large, gold-embossed J. Lyons & Co., Ltd. over the door—for ease of spotting by tea and bun-starved Londoners.

Unfortunately, the theatre organ would not be playing in the interval, we had read in the paper, due to the tighter schedule. Never mind, we agreed, we couldn't have everything. We parroted the now popular cliché: "Don't yer know there's a war on," and laughed ridiculously. My mother really wanted to see the film again so we hurried up with our meal.

After seeing the film and the newsreel giving us what details of the battle fronts were then permitted, we decided to walk home by a route that took in a fish and chip shop being also the shorter way. This would take us along Orpington High Street, Sevenoaks Road and then up the winding Goddington Lane, picking our fish and chips out of the hole we made in the newspaper wrapping. If we passed anybody they might, as unobtrusively as possible, sniff the air and wonder where the fish shop was! But there was a shortage of newspapers for recycling to the nation's fish shops which, tradition-ally, they used for the outer wrapping. Newsprint, that once arrived regularly by sea from Canada, dictated both the size of the daily newspapers and therefore, indirectly, fish shop supply. The contents needed to be eaten with more speed before the reduced newspaper insulation left everything cold. The joke about people buying a meal plus something to read was less of a joke during the war when cen-sorship meant that one needed to read every available newspaper—salt and vinegar-stained or not.

Both war, domestic news and a few ads, had to be crammed onto four broadsheet pages, reduced from a peacetime thirty two. *The Daily Sketch* was our only tabloid format and that paper, with *The Illustrated London News*, took care of most of the photo-journalism. Shipping space was already becoming desperately tight and intended for food and war material only. The German U-boat blockade to starve us had already begun.

If the weather was fine our fish and chip route was more enjoyable. In winter we would wait at the bus-stop by the brick and concrete communal air-raid shelter. If it was snowing or sleeting, the self-disciplined queue of people lined up in the lee of the shelter and thought it would be a jolly good idea if the local council readapted the structure after the war to a proper bus shelter. Such air-raid shel-ters were meant to be effective only against bomb blast not direct hits. Opposite, on a road traffic roundabout, stood the white obelisk memorial to the first World War dead. It was in use on Britain's November 11th Armistice Day. Wreaths of blood-red, replica pop-pies, symbols of mindless Great War slaughter among real ones of the Flanders battlefields, would lay about its base. The town's small uniformed detachments of men and women paraded. Veterans would dress tidily and some women wore the medals of their absent men-folk, glittering after an early morning clean with the metal polish usually kept for front-door fittings. For *this* war's medals it was too early.

Ultimately, June 2nd, with its decision-making and small family celebration went with the wind. Next day I had serious matters to think of and serious work to do. Leaving our small bungalow at 38 Malvern Road, I crossed over to where the hard-packed earth farm track, lined with the flowering may tree, led to the little country railway station. From there I travelled two stops to Petts Wood. A short walk past shops to a suburban street and I was at the parents' house of one of my schoolmates. This home had been chosen for that day's history class. About twelve of us were present and, a few minutes before 10:30 the family wireless was switched on for the scheduled BBC's History-For-Schools programme. After an hour and half of this sort of tuition we needed a rest and someone produced tea and Marmite sandwiches.

After a good deal of chatter and going to the single toilet in the house, the Beckenham College's teacher assigned to this particular house for the day, successfully marshalled us all back into the living room for a session of fractions and other arithmetical horrors. By around 2:30 p.m. both the owners of the house, who'd provided its use for the week to the Board of Education, and us, had had enough and we all said thank you and went our various ways. It was necessary for us to get back to our homes early as people were preparing for their nights in shelters.

Ours was looking pretty comfortable about then, I remember. The curved, corrugated steel sections, standing in the earth like four letter j's upside down to form the walls and roof of our Anderson shelter, had arrived sometime in April. Men had come to dig out a square hole in the chalk of our garden, away from the house and then erect the steel sections and bolt on the front and rear sheets. The work left to us was to shovel all the chalk and earth back over the structure, plus as much as we could filch from the surrounding garden. The result became a mound with our imaginative blast wall curving in front of the entrance. For the first time we felt there may have been a purpose in living where we did, on prehistoric, calcified sea organisms. With barely a foot of top-soil in a garden that struggled to produce flowers from the packets of seed my father still kept sowing, our reward was a perfectly dry, damp-proof air-raid shelter. Our bones, following a direct hit with a bomb having our names on it, might have improved the quality of the chalk thereabouts in succeeding millennia

The shelter itself, as an idea, had progressed from the Whitehall desk of Sir John Anderson, epitome of the civil servant. As an interesting mix of personal traits he is worth a digression. It may show how thoroughly accidental can be the preservation of civilian lives from an enemy bent upon killing just them, without wasting bombs on military targets. For everyone believed the first "troops" in the front line would be the civilian populations of big cities where preparations to survive, rather than resist attack was the priority.

Home secretary and minister of home security in the Chamberlain government, Anderson was an expert in control mech-

"...our reward was a perfectly dry, damp-proof air-raid shelter..."

anisms with an aptitude for repression. In combating Irish Nationalists, he had employed a quasi-military arm of the Royal Irish Constabulary, whose khaki, relieved only by black belts and caps, earned them the sobriquet, "Black and Tans." He repressed the General Strike. As governor general of Bengal he'd repressed restless natives and invented regional machinery for civil defense. Chamberlain recognised this unique talent to repress things and got him to perfect arrangements whereby a panicking population might be repressed in the event of air raids.

Gaining the second highest marks ever in the Civil Service examination, (his paper on political science was poor), Angus Calder provides this portrait: "Before the computer was perfected, he would have been a tolerable substitute. Early in 1940, probably no cabinet minister had a lower public appeal. His formal, uncompromising manner never infused warmth, humour or general sympathy. Alleged, by one or two admirers, to have a streak of dour humour, the wit was as dry and fine as invisible dust. While discussing air-raid shelters with King George, he absent-mindedly responded to the King's remarks with: 'But my dear man...' The King roared with laughter. Anderson remained passive. Who else, with centralised planning in its rudimentary state, could have so calmly confronted the enormous statistics of the war economy–and coped."

Anderson, not deputy prime minister Attlee, was Churchill's heir-apparent in the wartime coalition government in the event of the latter's death–perhaps in an air accident. So, thank you Sir John, for our sturdy Anderson shelter!

On four, two-feet wide bunks, top and bottom, the springing was steel lattice. My mother made mattresses to fit the narrower width since foam was a thing of the future, and we could heat the interior and boil water on a candle in a large upturned flower pot with a hole in its base. I modified a spare bicycle lamp and hooked it into a bolt hole, left surplus in the roof flanges during construction, then wired up a switch screwed into wood near the entrance for our emergency lighting. Wireless communication came via my latest and most improved crystal set. My youthful imagination and enthusiasm visualised that with sufficient tinned food, water and the occasional bottle of milk from our United Dairies milkman, my mother and I could remain underground for a month!

This somewhat juvenile estimate of our position and resources was coupled with my great desire to possess a 22-calibre rifle. The weapon would provide for both our defense and a last ditch stand against invading Germans if they made the really bad mistake of coming. My martial spirit had its genesis in the German propaganda machine and the new British government under Mr Winston S. Churchill, for soon after he'd taken charge of our destinies he had wasted no time at all in urging us to fight on the beaches and anywhere else, for that matter. Therefore we would. We could not know then by just how narrow a political and personal margin he had won the Prime Ministership. In Conservative Party ranks there were those who still hoped that Hitler was just a political figure temporarily off his trolley. Certain doors remained open for diplomatic "moves" to arrange peace terms favourable to Great Britain and the Empire. Some still say that, but for our continued alliance and support to a France rapidly facing defeat in the field, we might have reached an "accommodation."

In the weeks preceding my fatalistic decision to accept the invitation to go to America, our government, like the French, had been in secret turmoil. Our four-page newspapers had dutifully jazzed up our exploits by land, sea and air and had been sparse in their reporting of who was saying what to whom in cabinet circles, because they *had no news*. John Lukacs (American, 1999) explains in his book, *Five Days In London—May 1940*, just why Hitler came closest to winning *his* war in the days May 24th to 28th inclusive.

Lukacs writes: *"Great Britain could not have won the war in May 1940 but Churchill was the one who did not lose it."* He also explains why, in the War Cabinet, members were behaving almost like bulls and toreadors in a bull ring (my description) and why there was a virtual clampdown on their utterances—until more than fifty years had passed. An enlightened world would then learn just how close to Armageddon we had come in Britain during the five days of political in-fighting and gambling for the highest stakes ever in the modern world. One of the stakes being the United States of America as a future ally in kind as well as mind.

I shall recap briefly something of the momentous events which preceded and immediately followed Churchill's return to power from years in the political wilderness. It is intended as a backdrop to the general evacuation of children to the British dominions overseas and then, on a more limited scale, to America.

Primarily, it was seen as a life or death way of getting the nation's young lifeblood to the wider Empire, because there *was* a price to pay in a number of tragic ship sinkings. But in Canada, South Africa and far off Australia and New Zealand, something of Britain's culture and heritage would endure if the motherland was over-run and destroyed beyond recognition. The Polish state and Jewish populations had already become role models for bestiality. They would be systematically rubbed out by men with a scholarly culture overlaid with the brutish indoctrination of the German National Socialist Party. One writer has described the overseas evacuation programme as sending the crown jewels to safety although Hitler would say, in a slightly different context: "He who possesses the youth possesses the future."

The first great population movement to those country locations reasonably safe from the threat of bombing had already occurred by June 2nd 1940 and, too, my own preparations for leaving home.

Germany's monster aerial bombing aircraft of the Great War, the dirigible airship, named after Count Zeppelin, killed 1,410 civilians in about 100 raids on London and the provinces. This figure would be the tally for just one Luftwaffe raid at the commencement of the London blitz. A pre-war presumption had been that Germany would start bombing our cities at once, continuing for perhaps 60 days non-stop.

Certain 1917-1918 figures assumed each ton of high explosive dropped would cause 50 casualties. Whilst the assumption proved misleading, in a first frightening attack by Germany's known massive fleet of aircraft on cities, they still might kill 500,000 people and injure twice that figure. In the event, the actual casualty rate per ton proved to be about 17. Our civil administration therefore planned in the light of errors while still imagining the unthinkable and their pessimism erred, as it happened, on the right side.

Planning for a nation-wide evacuation of children, mothers with babies, the infirm and homeless, had begun as early as 1934. One of the chief principles of the policy was to remove from potential battle areas, so far as was possible, civilians inessential to military operations who could jam up military planning and divide priorities. During the war's course, London and provincial cities within bombing range, were evacuated three times. The first, September 1st 1939, totalled 1,473,000. Many would return home by Christmas when the expected, instant bombing of cities failed to materialise.

The Chamberlain government which, at the 1938 Munich conference, had stalled Hitler's territorial grabs with the sacrifice of Czechoslovakia, declared war on September 3rd. The period of grace helped our air-force build up its fighter strength along with the further development of our east coast radar screen. Beyond that, the prime minister had been unable to influence events. Quoted, during the Munich crisis, he declared: "How horrible, fantastic, incredible it is that we should be digging trenches and trying on gas masks here, because of a quarrel in a far-away country between people of whom we know nothing."

He had grown out of touch with consensus thinking that, in the inter-war years of developing aviation and air travel, just about everyone acknowledged how close we all were to everyone else. No country was so far-away that its behavioural effect on a neighbouring state could be ignored. The Chamberlain era and the muddling through that somehow saved our bacon, endured until late 1940 when the prime minister died from cancer. His term in office had become a sad one, marked by military miscalculation, disaster and both good and bad luck.

When, in 1939, he brought back into government Winston Churchill as First Lord of the Admiralty, the navy ran up a signal: "Winston is back!" For it was he, in that same 1914 role, with Admiral Lord Fisher as First Sea Lord, who had transformed the Royal Navy from coal to oil-burning ships just before the Great War. A "First Lord" is a political posting. Fisher, as First Sea Lord, was the professional sailor. Scapegoated for his earlier visionary, yet failed Dardanelles campaign to bring the war to a speedier end, Churchill had reverted to army rank—for his was the military mind. The two men enjoyed an uneasy relationship. Now, months spent on the Western Front as colonel gave him the insight he needed into what trench warfare was all about. He formed some definite opinions. Out of government but returning to the House of Commons as a back-bench member of parliament, he assumed the mantle of political soothsayer. It would be his long-term, between-the-wars role, intermittently sustained, attending his Woodford, Essex constituents; by his brick-laying hobby and writing the mammoth history of his family, the Dukes of Marlborough.

His namesake, John Churchill, the 1st Duke (1650-1722) might have considered building walls a trifle naff, but then times and energy outlets change. And I have seen all Winston's walls at Chartwell, his home, and I can report they are highly professional, the pointing perfect and there would have been work for him in New York City when the skyscrapers were going up. In the new role he excelled. He would make controversial visits to Germany, then return warning various governments in power of Hitler's contemptuous disregard of postwar peace treaties by secretly rearming. Few believed him. Now, they did. Down the years that tale has been well told. Weapons inspectors had not been invented, but there would be abundant archival evidence that he'd tried, without stint, to do his country a service. Soon, it would sanction his greatest contribution. In the cabinet. In the government.

As First Lord, 1940 edition, he oversaw the disappointing

Norwegian campaign to secure the country against German invasion. Notwithstanding, when Chamberlain lost his party's confidence in the war's progress and stepped down, no other minister of government could enlist sufficient support. Chamberlain handed in his resignation to King George VI and Churchill moved, albeit symbolically, into number 10 Downing Street, official home of Great Britain's prime ministers, on May 10th. Characteristically, on compassionate grounds, for no more reliable explanation has been offered, he continued to live at Admiralty House wherein lie the apartments of The First Lord of the Admiralty, in The Mall, down the road from Buckingham Palace. At that house he would call to present his already well-known credentials to the occupants residing. Chamberlain, then ill, stayed on at "number ten."

The beginning of the war had coincided with my first term at Beckenham Technical College whereat the brains in my fingers were to have been developed further. During the first months of my second term after the Christmas holidays I was getting immersed into the kind of expanded, third dimensional technical drawings associated with blueprints. Along with that went the intricacies of lettering and signwriting, working with metal and, as already mentioned, various projects in carpentry and joinery. I was also introduced to the mysteries of the slide rule and logarithms. Where all this was to lead I hadn't a clue. My education, career leanings and my commitment to serious study had, for long been a source of nagging worry to my parents. I seemed to spend a lot of time building models of ships in which my father had served, drawing pictures of his latest, the *Baltrover*, and I was also getting into small steam engines, crystal wireless sets and an imaginative land irrigation system.

One day in February, with the River Thames still frozen over during the great freeze-up of the century, my mother felt an appointment with an industrial psychologist might help with the problem of how I would eventually earn money and eat. The ice conditions were playing havoc with the electrified lines into London but I dimly recall having got to the address and to the meeting. A lady guided me through a series of exercises where one had to sort out tricky word comparisons and make sense from them. That would determine my IQ. There were audio, vision and colour blindness tests and how rapidly I could discern a number from a page of coloured dots. Having acquired a residual deafness in one ear after recovering from measles without my ever realising it, she informed me of the fact there and then and ruled out careers in the army, navy and air-force unless a manpower shortage made things desperate. Turning to the positive side she concluded that I would do very well in any job which involved meeting people and in that category she listed shops, door-to-door sales, gas or electric meter readers and fitting people with new reading spectacles.

My mother went into shock from the news of my deafness.

The American Option

"How could you possibly have not known, and not told us before this?" she exclaimed, mortified that I was no longer the perfect specimen she had reared with such care through peace, economic depression and now war. I explained, mystified by her horrified look, that I couldn't remember being any different. I said that in any case, it had always been an advantage.

"An advantage! How can you say such a thing?! "said my mother in protest and visibly upset.

"Yes, well...if I have trouble getting to sleep at night through noise all I do is turn over on my good side."

My careers, psychoanalyst and my school work did teach me one thing: whatever experiences one collects will invariably come in useful in unexpected ways. As already explained, daily attendance at the College proper ceased as the fear of gas and high explosive bombing re-introduced a second phase of wholesale evacuation back to safer rural areas. It also brought chaos to the education system which would become a permanent feature of a five year, eight month war.

The German armies ended the "phoney war" by a sweep into Denmark, Belgium and Holland in April 1940. They then breached the French Maginot Line at Sedan in the beginning of May with an armoured dash through the "impenetrable" Ardennes Forest. Lukacs, in his *Five Days*....quotes a remark overheard in an expensive London grill-room: "How could Leopold surrender.....such a nice boy. I'm terribly shocked by it......He was at Eton." But disbelief at the turn of events was more widespread. People were numbed by both censored and leaked news; unable to grasp they were in danger....much like rabbits in a car's headlights. "A mood of panic gripped upper-class circles" since they had greater access to information and could better distill truth from fantasy. General Ironside, chief of the general staff, is quoted as saying to Anthony Eden, formerly Chamberlain's foreign minister until 1938 when he resigned over appeasement policies: "This is the end of the British Empire." But a post-war world would have to wait for Great Britain to give the bigger chunks away by negotiation and consent as a standard bearer for a diverse ethnic morality called democracy.

In Westminster's corridors of power it is now clear from Lukacs's *Five Days*...that Churchill was embroiled in a battle of wits and intrigue to ensure his survival even after his historic, climb back into government. He would endure four days of secretive struggle with members of his war cabinet before establishing what would become, later in the year, during the Battle of Britain, his unassailable hold on power. By then, his credibility as the very best war leader to emerge since Elizabeth the First addressed her sailors at Tilbury, with the Spanish armada in the offing, was assured. As then, the uncertainties associated with an English Channel crossing, would un-nerve our enemies and one man in particular sitting atop a mountain near Berchtesgarden, Bavaria. Moats did that to some people didn't they?

About then, however, in addition to Hitler, a man who occupied Churchill's sharp attention was Lord Halifax, Chamberlain's foreign minister, and retained until he was appointed ambassador to Washington. Anthony Eden moved to fill the gap. Halifax is described as presenting something of a shadowy figure little known to the man-in-the-street, austere and with a warmth matching religious conviction. In the war cabinet it would be his voice which, for Churchill's ears, would be exasperatingly raised in favour of utilising certain unofficial diplomatic channels to propose mediation with Hitler even at so late a stage. At cabinet meetings Halifax would quietly return again and again to his latest conversations with Italy's ambassador, Giuseppe Bastianini concerning the employment of Mussolini as intermediary in a negotiated peace with Hitler. Understandably, for those who knew him not even well, this line was anathema to Churchill. Great Britain, in a European-wide settlement, would be in deadly danger of becoming a mere satellite of a German-dominated European continent.

In the five days of which John Lukacs writes, Churchill's room for manoeuvre was surprisingly circumscribed by Halifax's somewhat unusual conversational relationship with King George VI. Queen Elizabeth, on the other hand, is said to have been reserved in her opinion of Churchill. An awareness of this and the knowledge that the King and Lord Halifax between them could jointly have opposed him and even caused his removal from the premiership, would not have made for relaxed War Cabinet sessions. It would not have been in Churchill's nature voluntarily to walk on eggshells in that manner at least. And what was his nature?

From *The People's War* by Angus Calder (1969), we have this interesting appraisal:
"The man who found himself 'walking with destiny' on May 10th 1940, was a man of action and a man of war" and, this from Lord Halifax's diary: "His, is the most extraordinary brain, Winston's, to watch functioning that I have ever seen.....a most curious mixture of a child's emotion and a man's reason." The child had assembled a collection of nearly fifteen-hundred toy soldiers. The man, enjoyed playing with real ones. In time of peace, emotion and reason were at odds; in time of war, man and boy were one. His hero had been the first Duke of Marlborough, his own family line, who had defeated the French at Blenheim in 1704. Winston, himself, came to earth prematurely in a cloaks and rest-room to which his mother had been rushed while attending the St. Andrew's Ball at Blenheim. The manicured lawns and carefully tended paths and statuary of Blenheim Palace would be his childhood playground. It is still a perfect place in summer to hold vintage Bentley car meetings and launch hot-air balloons. His mother was the American socialite, Jeanette (Jennie)

The American Option

Jerome and his father, Lord Randolph Churchill, had held a variety of 19th century cabinet posts notably chancellor of the exchequer, handling the finances of the nation.

After his planning of the 1916 Dardanelles campaign disastrously failed due to naval signalling mix-ups, he left the government and took up military rank once more as colonel and found himself in the trench warfare of the Western Front. He complained, about that time, that: "War, which used to be cruel and magnificent, has now become cruel and squalid. In fact, it has been completely spoilt. It is the fault of democracy and science. Instead of a small number of well-trained professionals championing their country's cause with ancient weapons and a beautiful intricacy of archaic manoeuvres, we now have whole populations, including even women and children, pitted against one another in brutish, mutual extermination." But, he added, if the rules were to change in 1940, he would abide by them.

He owed his position not to his ancestry, but to the processes of parliamentary democracy–and thus to the people. All his people, including even women and children, were his soldiers when the invader threatened and bombs fell. His imagination resolved contradictions. His supreme asset, of course, had always been his domination over words. His familiarity with the English language enabled him to survive Harrow. Just. Then, as soon as he'd found wars to fight in such as Kitchener's Sudan campaign or the Cuban War, he found a style to describe them and side-tracked into journalism for the Boer War. From Gibbon and Macaulay he learned a prose style–processional, sprightly in rhythm, sombre yet ironic in utterance.

From his doctor and confidant, Lord Moran: "Without that feeling for words he might have made little enough of his life. For, in judgement, skill in administration, in knowledge of human nature, he does not at all excel." There was nothing spontaneous about his speeches which ranged from crushing ripostes to unexpected questions in Parliament. They would all have been previously recruited then drilled into action should the occasion for them ever arise. From one admirer: "There was no charm of voice, no facility of gesture......just that extraordinary rhetoric, half laboured, half instinctive–that nonetheless held his hearers."

3　America–De Facto Ally

During the crucial five days–when "Great Britain could not have *won* the war in May 1940 but that Churchill was the one who did not *lose* it," Lord Halifax would have experienced something of Churchill's "extraordinary brain" functioning. On May 28th he suffered a further war cabinet meeting at which Halifax again voiced his theories on tactical conciliation ostensibly to keep the Empire intact.

In the government of national unity, comprising members of all three major political parties, Tory, Labour and Liberal, which Churchill had formed to fight the war, its general cabinet, of which the war cabinet was an entity, included Labour and Liberal Party supporters of his "stand-and-fight" principles.

Some hours after the war cabinet meeting had irresolutely ended, Churchill convened a meeting with the *whole* cabinet and exacted a vote on his proposed conduct of the war. He won overwhelming support and, possibly to Halifax's chagrin and dismay, individual ministers left their chairs and came to him and patted his shoulder. The alternative, sacking a foreign minister influential in royal circles, would have been meat for press greyhounds. It would have produced frissons in a so-called united government and in a national morale showing the first few cracks. Lord Halifax, personal confidant of the King, partaker of tea on Buckingham Palace lawns, nonetheless bowed to the brain with the "most curious mixture of a child's emotion and a man's reason." In this way, Churchill saved Britain, Europe and western civilisation. His "We shall fight on," declaration, despite what might occur at Dunkirk, which so upset Halifax, became the hinge on which our fate hung. Churchill would go on to "play with real soldiers" and become the greatest statesman of the age.

While this best-kept secret of the war, Churchill's battle of will and wit with Lord Halifax, was unfolding in the upstairs cabinet room at number 10 Downing street, with all the drama of the TV series, *The West Wing*, my mother was into her "war work," as she called it.

"Now, I may not be home for tea," she might say as we prepared to go our ways after breakfast...me to someone's house for a school session; she to her war work. "We're doing such-and-such school this afternoon, fitting and supplying new gas masks and demonstrating the way to put them on. It shows up the tendencies some children have for asthma, you see. Some women yesterday, just tore them off after a few seconds. Don't know how *they're* going to get on, I'm sure. I've put something on a plate with a plate on top in the pantry (domestic refrigerators were not in general use) in case you get peckish before I get back," she concluded.

When war had started my mother had allowed herself to be recruited into the local Air-Raid Precautions unit and had been issued with a silver badge stamped ARP to wear when engaged on whatever duties came up. Angus Calder, *The People's War*, claims 1937 as the earliest date when an Air-Raid Wardens' Service was created and, by 1938 some 200,000 citizens had been recruited. Police and local government were trained in anti-gas measures.

Inevitably by then, fears were publicised. Unlike The Great War, youth did not go off whistling patriotically to foreign parts shouldering a rifle. Thus, British people, well before the balloon went up, saw any new war in terms of his own living room smashed, his mother crushed to death, his children maimed, neighbours' corpses in familiar streets, a sky black with bombers with crosses on their wings and the air poisoned with gas. My mother was "in" to gas at that time. Manuals and pamphlets were kept in the dining room which we rarely used until my father came home.

An entirely new social survey organisation called Mass Observation, (MO), employing voluntary observers among people in assorted walks of life, found a surprising number of Britons contemplated killing their families if war broke out. People recalled, from the cinema newsreels of the time, frightful scenes from the pitiless Italian bombing of Abyssinians then Spaniard against Spaniard in Spain where a mercenary German air force came of age shooting up practice targets—vehicles with red crosses on their roofs.

For the 1938 Munich crisis ARP services were mobilised—with an allocation of ten wardens per square mile in London. They became actively engaged directing the digging of trenches in parks; converting cellars; requisitioning basements and siting barrage balloons. Thirty-eight million gas masks were issued to men, women and children—none for babies until later when a contraption into which mothers pumped air with a bellows came on stream. A light rub with a cake of Pears Soap was a recommended aid to ensure the flexible, plastic window remained free of condensation. In the streets, the tops of the red post office pillar boxes got a coating of a yellowish gas detector paint. Local Gas Identification Squads emerged from street cleaners. Gas types were lung irritants, tear gases, sneezing gases and blister gases. Smells from floor polish, mustard, musty hay, bleaching powder, horseradish, geraniums and peardrop boiled sweets would become false alarms! Large numbers of papier-mâché coffins were ordered, snakes in the London Zoo were put to death and, as homes were disrupted a holocaust of stray pets occurred.

Outside veterinary surgeries the slain lay in heaps. ARP wardens, I remember, who manned underground posts and patrolled the suburban blackout, wore a blue battle dress uniform and had a steel helmet and carried, slung over their shoulder a more advanced type of gas mask in a canvas bag. The police whistle, blown angrily if a chink of light stole out to compromise the blackout, was handy in a top pocket. Civilian respirators, by comparison, were fairly simple affairs with their horrible-smelling rubber, air-tight masks with replaceable filters to breath through. The smell of the thing was enough to make some people want to vomit. They were issued in cardboard boxes with a cord to hang around the neck when walking. But as the war dragged on, the prospect of gas as a weapon and asthmatic attacks from the masks, diminished. Most adults left them at home. Children still carried them to school along with their books, under penalty. I don't recall my mother ever having a "tin hat," but as a gas specialist, she carried her cardboard box around.

Sometimes I would go to the small railway station to meet my father arriving on leave, still captain of his navy, boom-defense tug. He would be carrying his service gas mask and a blue-painted Royal Navy steel helmet slung around various parts of his Lieutenant Commander's uniform. I was very proud to accompany him in this rig since, in the Merchant Navy, during peacetime, uniform was only worn aboard ship. The quick-change from ship to shore "gear" was always a feature of home or shore-going. Once, I couldn't understand some returning businessman remarking to a companion within our hearing: "Uniform...really old boy! Just a bit too showy for this little place, don't you think?" Fortunately for the civilian, and knowing my father, he would have been restrained from a direct riposte by the uniform.

Some Merchant Navy captains and officers, and ratings, for whom service at sea provided them with no uniform or who preferred civilian attire, would wear the Merchant Navy (MN) badge. Hopefully, this would entitle those of obvious military age to stares of approval and not scorn in trains, buses or in the street.

The manner in which the British people took to war was chock full of idiosyncratic comment and behaviour and sometimes just quixotic as fitted the moment. To Churchill, their peril was beyond comprehension and was moved to confess: "We will come through in triumph, but may lose our tail feathers."

From John Lukacs: "By May 23rd the majority of people did not know how catastrophic the situation in their army was and refused to recognise how close Hitler had already come to ultimate victory. And too, the British martial spirit was not unwavering. On May 23rd, when Churchill and Halifax would have been verbally feignting like duelists, London life was proceeding with every outward appearance of peacetime normality. Vera Brittain, novelist, noted: "Iron railings, of course, have gone from the parks for armaments yet the beauty of summer scents and sounds maintain an illu-

sion of peace, as though watching the funeral of European civilisa-
tions elegantly conducted." Women were selling flags for Animal
Day as news of the Belgian surrender was broadcast on the 1 p.m.
news.

The atmosphere finally descended into a quiet fatalism, of
waiting for the inevitable. (Invoking, once more, the rabbit in a car's
headlight analogy.) There would be instances of violent criticism of
the French and uneasy fluctuation of moods, even to a few younger
housewives saying that if Hitler came at least they'd have their hus-
bands back.

The French, for their part, were suspicious of British aims.
Certain of Chamberlain's Germanophile inclinations were also shared
by the Royal Family–German in its origins–and high civil servants
of influence. More astoundingly, Germany's apparent unhindered
advance into France was suspected as being a part of some British
strategy!

In France, by May 23rd, 250,000 troops of the British
Expeditionary Force, were already encircled, trapped by the German
twin sweeps through the Ardennes Forest and surrendered Belgium.
Yet, on the same day, Hitler's interventionist HALT order which
enabled the force to reach Dunkirk, denied General Heinz Wilhelm
Guderian his historic chance of winning World War II almost in a
morning. The fate of Britain and the outcome of World War II had,
by then depended on two things. The divisions between Halifax and
Churchill (now resolved) and the success, still to come, of Operation
Dynamo–getting back in and then out of Dunkirk–in anything that
floated!

There must also be something about an encircled army
which, so far as the British are concerned, appears to spark not
despondency but saucy improvisation. Take this passage from
Dunkirk, co-authored by Lt. Colonel Ewan Butler and Major J.S.
Bradford, British Expeditionary Force, in 1955. The recollections of
each were sharp and eyewitness accounts prolific. Scene: A little
group of infantry isolated from the main force outside Arras, France,
under a sergeant. A bleak road; bleak landscape...anything, the
sergeant thought, to stop the German tanks. "Then, he saw a little
pub by the roadside and an idea struck him. The door, locked,
yielded to the sergeant's rifle butt. In the bar was a dresser covered
with plates and more in the cupboard below. The sergeant and his
men carried them to the road and there laid the innocent china, face
downwards, in a complicated pattern. Then they got down in a ditch
and waited. An hour later six enemy tanks came nosing down the
road and halted at the sight of this unorthodox 'minefield.' Their
crews disembarked and came forward cautiously to inspect this new
device. The sergeant's men shot every one of them and, advancing,
set fire to the crewless tanks." If you see what I mean?

On British farms, girls who had signed up for the Land Army

were ashamed to wear their uniforms of corduroy breeches and green sweaters, because no one knew who they were. "People say we look like out-of-work cowboys!" Earlier, in Scotland, large stocks of highly inflammable whisky created a headache for the civil defense authorities and a hangover for an island's inhabitants. A succession of local authorities refused to have the stocks in their area. Eventually, a shipload worth a million pounds sailed for America to dump this forerunner of the current nuclear waste problem. But the ship went aground in fog on the island of Barra. There, delighted Hebrideans claimed the wreck as treasure trove–and a sure gift from Providence. In post-war years a film was made of this exploit. Title? *Whisky Galore.*

After the Munich peace moves had run their manipulative course it is said that about one in three civilians felt a second "Munich" would be better than war. These people had been comforted by the testimony of astrologers and spiritualists that peace would be preserved.

As an unreal month of May drew to a close the war was accelerating and a more fatalistic attitude began to supplant moods of panic and despondency among all three classes in British society. While the whole structure of national belief still rocked a mood of "let's get it over with then," seeped through, Americans working in London provided an unexpected fillip when it was announced on May 17th that they had formed their own contingent within the Local Defense Volunteers (LDV) later to be called The Home Guard. And, not to be outdone by our "Brylcreem Boys" in Hurricanes and Spitfires, their own famed Tiger Squadron was already on ops and highly visible with a painted, razor-toothed tiger covering the engine cowling. "Dammit," we thought, "our American cousins are in this from the word go. So, here goes mate!"

On May 13th Churchill made his "blood, sweat, toil and tears" speech as being all he had to offer and Queen Wilhelmina of The Netherlands, rang King George asking for air cover for her still-fighting army. The King said: "Message passed to everyone concerned," and went back to bed. He remarked later: "It is not often one is rung up at that hour, especially by a Queen. But, in these days anything may happen, and far worse things too." The Dutch Royal Family arrived in England that evening aboard a Royal Navy destroyer.

On May 28th, after vanquishing Halifax with wit and words, Churchill let go again with his "We shall fight on the beaches, in the fields on the landing grounds, we shall never surrender...." from which Halifax and other advocates of "reason" would surely have got their final message and America, perhaps its first, regarding its own vital interests. But on May 26th, with a national disaster in the offing a national day of prayer had been celebrated in Westminster Abbey. The Royal Family and highest personages of the Empire remaining in London, attended at 10 a.m. and there is little doubt their prayers were fervent. As May turned into June, 225,000 of the 250,000 men originally sent to France arrived back in England with the odd rifle. Churchill: "A colossal military disaster...wars are not won by evacuation..." A general view was expressed thus: "Now we know where we are. No more bloody allies." Then, King George, in a letter to his mother expressed himself succinctly: "Personally, I feel happier now that we have no allies to be polite to and to pamper...."

However, in June, 1940, not only were we alone, but virtually unarmed. Sir Oswald Mosely, leader of the British Union of Fascists, was imprisoned along with his wife, in Holloway Prison and allowed to employ other prisoners as servants. For the Home Guard there were rifles from the Crimean War and the Indian Mutiny sprinkled among pick-axes, crowbars and 6-foot spears. Workers in factories turned out coshes and knives after completing a day's shift duty. A mixture of resin, petrol, tar and a fuse in a bottle somehow had been termed a "Molotov Cocktail," after the Russian foreign minister and used with great effect by the gallant Finns in the winter struggle against the Russian army. Those would be hurled against invading tanks on our beaches. Other harassing measures were 3-foot cube concrete blocks as tank traps, to be dragged across roads, "pill boxes," wheel locking devices on buses and the removal of rotor arms from the distributor caps of car engines. This would immobilise available transport if we were overrun.

All of these activities were either in sight or being discussed by everyone as we waited for—we knew not what and we began to use our Anderson air-raid shelter intermittently. The blitz, proper, had not begun, but we were getting limited night raids by German aircraft testing London's defenses. They, in turn, would be driven off by our fighter aircraft and anti-aircraft barrages or discouraged by the increasing numbers of barrage balloons anchored by their sharp steel wires and height-controlled by winches. Our village was nicely in line for the jettisoned bomb loads of Dornier aircraft escaping back to Germany or to captured French airfields.

Each morning I would try to attend the classes at private houses. My mother and I would emerge from the nicely earthed-up Anderson shelter with the beginnings of summer flowers on top and breath in the fragrances of our quite attractive garden. It was turning out to be a flaming month of June and, by the time we had eaten breakfast one day in the house, temperatures were well up into the 60's and would perhaps reach 90 degrees Fahrenheit by 2 p.m. Above, the blue sky, would be painted with white aircraft vapour trails like tangled spaghetti as Spitfires grappled with our enemy accompanied by the rattle of cannon fire. On earth, I decided that shrapnel, collected from roads and fields, might be a good souvenir to take with me to America. Accordingly, on that day, I collected or swapped with other pupils, a goodly selection of the stuff. By the time I reached home later, my gas mask container was about full of some interesting, razor-sharp shapes plus an expended cannon shell from one of our Hurricanes or Spits. That would really floor my new buddies when I got to a school in America.

With the invasion imminent, as we thought, schools and local authorities were about to face the second mass movement of people out of the cities and into rural areas. The same categories of evacuee that had gone in September, but then returned home during the Phoney War, were gathered up

"....tangled spaghetti as Spitfires grappled..."
Courtesy: Royal Mail

anew. Again, it was decided by consent who would go to foster homes. I was swept up in my school's preparations such as medical examination, documentation, issue of identity discs, photographic record, final class achievement reports –to ensure a smooth transition to some other school. My mother, however, became busy collecting and completing the necessary paperwork for my leaving England altogether.

My father had, by mid-July, talked his way out of his navy commission, totally disenchanted with the "system," as he called it. In fact, a growing disgust with the amateurish, unseamanlike qualities of elderly, senior naval officers hauled out of retirement, began to intrude into our home. Admirals, who had worked up their rank during a peacetime regime that, say, existed on the "China station," or the "West Indies station," proved, in many cases, to be out of touch with certain practicalities. The intake of inductees from the merchant marine who had benefited from more general training, might be compared with a naval officer specialist in gunnery or catering pronouncing on navigation and nautical astronomy.

"I am fed up with that lot," said my father one memorable day near the end of June–meaning, of course, the Royal Navy. "I'm going to look up Jack Watts. Everyone knew that no one could exit the navy in wartime except via a court martial. But my father would kick any system if he wished. And now he wished.

Jack Watts was a shipowner and businessman who had been a passenger on the *Baltrover* in 1936. My father, chief officer then, and Jack Watts had hit it off, as people do. He went to see him and, in late July 1940, my father was in a North Atlantic convoy, master of a Canadian Great Lakes steamer, the *Yorktown*. It seems it was one hell of a voyage, with the navigating bridge structure almost over the anchor hawsepipes. My mother was never able to return his naval uniform to naval stores. But now, he would be wearing *four* gold rings around his cuffs instead of two and a half and from then on he never wore anything less.

The American Option

Notwithstanding that my father's days in the United Baltic Corporation were a thing of the absolute past, my mother sought the advice of the head of the passenger department at the company's Fenchurch Street address, London. My father's former ship, the *Baltrover*, following a refit after the Norwegian campaign, when he had fallen sick, was now on Furness Withy's Atlantic run. Her 250 or so passenger accommodation would not, one feels, have been booked out. Her speed was limited to around 13 knots with a sub on her tail. The conversation with the passenger department manager might typically have gone something like this:

"Yes, I think so," Mr Pettifer said kindly to my mother, sitting in his office, "We can get your son on an August sailing to an east coast of America port. He's not fourteen yet is he?"

"No, just twelve," confirmed my mother.

"Hah, nicely under-age. He will rate as a child, for the fare. The fact you will not be accompanying him can be worked out, I think......"

"I er, don't quite see...."

"We will make Mr Huggins, the chief officer, a guardian. Very kind man, he served under your husband I believe. So, that's no problem."

"How much will you want, Mr Pettifer, we don't have much and his clothes for the trip and all........"

"Well...I've discussed it with the directors. We think twelve pounds will cover it nicely. We must leave the matter of getting him to Liverpool and then being received on the ship's arrival to you, of course but, didn't I hear something about you having friends in New York or somewhere? We received a wireless message from Captain Cheek in the *Yorktown* a few days ago saying something about a family going to meet your son, when the port is known."

"Yes, that would be right. I can't thank you enough, Mr Pettifer, for all the help and advice...being we're on our own now, Philip and me. And he's a good boy."

"Well, we used to see enough of him aboard the old ship before the war. I suppose he'll want to follow the sea as a career also, when he comes of age?" The passenger manager was about to rise from behind his desk.

"Yes, well," my mother smiled "...he'll have to do better at school first. Like other children, he's missed quite a few lessons."

"Goodbye then, Mrs Cheek...but call me, please, any time you need our advice on any matter...oh, and we congratulate Captain Cheek on his first command. It's rather nice really, your son will know almost everyone on board our ship, er like old friends."

"Goodbye, Mr Pettifer."

Maybe they said different things, of course. The only corroborating evidence is that twelve pounds went out of my parents' savings account leaving it virtually empty until a new half-monthly wage allotment from my father's new employer arrived. For my father had not consciously gone to war. A war had simply enveloped his livelihood, our bread and butter—in peace *or* war. The nation's merchant marine was a civilian occupation and first in any firing line whatever a crew's preference. There had been no Phoney War for merchant sailors. Anticipating Chamberlain's dutiful observance of existing treaty obligations to Poland, Grand Admiral Dönitz, chief of the German navy's U-boat arm, had positioned his boats at key points. Perhaps an hour or two after the British ultimatum had been received in Berlin at 11 a.m., September 3rd 1939, the Anchor Line's passenger ship *Athenia* had been torpedoed north of Ireland with great loss of life. Germany had drawn first blood, against civilians, not the military. Churchill, with oratory that imported so many new phrases into our common currency, spoke in Manchester:

"Come then, let us to the task, to the battle, to the toil—each to our part, each to our station. Fill the armies, rule the air, pour out the munitions, strangle the U-boats, sweep the mines, plough the land, build the ships, guard the streets, succour the wounded, uplift the downcast—and honour the brave. There is not a week, nor a day, nor an hour to lose."

But, of course, there had already been lost weeks; months; years until, on May 7th 1940, Leo Amery, an ex-minister of considerable standing and a notorious bore, surpassed himself from the floor of the House of Commons. Quoting Oliver Cromwell's address to the Long Parliament when he thought it no longer fit to conduct the affairs of the nation, Amery opened up another dyke protecting Chamberlain's supposed indispensibility:

"You have sat too long here for any good you have been doing," he shouted. "Depart, I say, and let us have done with you. In the name of God, go." Words that effectively ended the Chamberlain government.

Hitler would hope for a peace without an invasion and was encouraged by Churchill's subsequent government who kept open unofficial channels of negotiation. Thus, a dithering Hitler gave the RAF and British ground forces a further precious month of grace—June 16th to July 16th. My mother returned from London that day with my passage ticket in her handbag and a rumour that invasion orders had been given. On July 19th Hitler once more made a peace overture from the Reichstag. Within the hour, it is said, it was rejected out of hand by Churchill via the BBC. When August 1st dawned, people in Hampshire and Somerset were picking up yellow leaflets dropped from German aircraft. They read: "LAST APPEAL TO REASON, etc..." and they were happily recovered and later auctioned—for the Red Cross.

4 An Option Taken Up

*" There may be dark days ahead and war can no longer be confined
to the battlefield. But, we can only do the right thing as we see
the right, and reverently commit our cause to God. If, one and all,
we keep resolutely faithful to it, ready for whatever service or sacrifice it may
demand, then, with God's help, we shall prevail. May He bless and keep us
all."*

Those words, haltingly delivered by the King at 6 p.m. on
September 3rd 1939 and broadcast to the Empire, are still occasionally quoted in wireless programmes and newspaper or magazine articles. They appeared, in some context or other, in an August, 1940
news item. By then it was clear that we were up against it and yellow
leaflets were not going to change anything. For a start, yellow was
the wrong colour. The Belgian surrender in early May followed by
the French capitulation of June 18th had made most people see a
bright colour red.

The blue skies over Kent in August, became partially
obscured by larger amounts of tangled spaghetti. The vapour trails
ranged from one horizon to the other as the first air battle of the war
escalated with the frenzied tactics of aerial dog-fights reminiscent,
apart from speed, of the Great War over the Western Front. Each
pilot of bomber or fighter pitted his senses and skill against, for the
most part, just one other anonymous shape in flying helmet and face
mask.

At some point during classes, I must have acquired, by a
swop, one-half of a small pair of binoculars. For currency at that
time, I was using prized splinters of a new kind of bomb. The spyglass was good enough, with one eye squeezed closed, to identify the
markings of German and British aircraft. My mother and I would
stand in the garden near the Anderson shelter and inadvisedly take
turns in observing the wheeling, diving, soaring Spitfires,
Hurricanes, Heinkels or Dorniers. Our Spits and Hurries came
mostly from Biggin Hill aerodrome about five miles away. Douglas
Bader, would have been up there most times, "mixing it" with an
opponent with murderous concentration. The kind that had helped
him walk again after losing both legs in a 1936 flying school accident.

Often, a "bird" was winged and then it fluttered and spun to
earth on farmland sending up an oily, black cloud into the mid-
summer air. A parachute might follow. Farmers, with their sharp-
ened pitchforks, were ready for this kind of action. And very fierce

and determined they looked as they strode toward a hapless figure struggling out of a parachute harness. Often badly burned. Friend or foe? It didn't matter much. They were almost always destined for a hospital. My mother and I must have lived a charmed life, but we saw something of the battle and the battlers who would repel the aerial invaders, change the minds of German generals and stop the seaborne invasion in its tracks. It really was The Battle of Britain, and who wouldn't be proud to have seen half of it and the ones who fought it with a gladiatorial spirit of old, high above the farms of Kent and Sussex.

Probably, around mid-August 1940, my mother would have been sorting out my clothes and things necessary for my Atlantic voyage now due to commence on August 30th. She had already taken me to a men's outfitters and bought me my first pair of long trousers. They were not donned then for, right up to my arrival in America, I was wearing the schoolboy rig of short grey trousers, below-the-knee socks with school colours, green, black, green, encircling the bit that doubled over at the top and the black blazer with green edging and school badge sewn onto the breast pocket. Oh, there was a grey shirt too and a tie with black and green diagonal stripes—and a school cap that would soon be discarded!

I had been taken to London again and received my first-ever passport. This described me as being 5 feet 2 inches tall, fair hair and complexion, eyes blue and no other distinguishing marks. The person looking out from the small photograph is familiar. For the moment, I resided at 38 Malvern Road, Orpington, Kent. Post Office area codes had not been invented and our telephone number was a simply remembered, Orpington 2108 and local calls were two pence of any length with an allocation of a dozen free calls per month. At railway stations, one penny got a small bar of Nestlés milk chocolate out of a platform vending machine and one penny opened the doors of a ladies public convenience wherever it might be. Men went in free. Presumably because the conveniences were either less or nil. Words like technology had not come into general usage and only London dockers seemed to use the four-letter ones.

Left over from those days of equipping me for the great expedition are two, shirt-size, cotton covers with securing tapes—envelopes might be a way to describe them. They were an innovation of my mother, at her sewing machine one morning. She made them from rag-bag pieces of curtain to keep (a) my three shirts tidy and flat (b) three sets of underwear, from getting all mussed up with two pairs of shoes, cleaning brushes and a tin of Kiwi boot polish, dark brown. But, for the shoes and a pair of sandals, she'd made three pairs of shoe bags out of assorted coloured pieces. These, I noticed recently, are now becoming a little stressed at the seams. A grey suit, extra trousers, socks, pullover, sweater, pyjamas, gloves, scarf, the small pocket bible I still carry, a pasteboard rendering of

The American Option

Kipling's "*IF*" poem with illuminated capital letters at the commencement of each line and a very large shoe brush, that doubled as the family clothes brush, went into the brown, fabric steamer trunk with the wooden reinforcing hoops my mother had bought.

There wasn't much else that I can remember apart from the flash, new imitation leather gas mask box with its handy snap clip to secure the cover. Similar ones were now being sold in place of the original, less than fashionable cardboard boxes and string. Needs for individuality were being fostered among increasing drabness. I intended to leave the small spyglass at home for my mother to use. Militarily, it could come in handy, I decided, but privately, I didn't think she would be in any danger at all. Not at the rate the Germans were being shot out of the skies above our heads. Yet, how very little any of us really knew or understood.

"Understanding," explains John Lukacs, referring to the scarcity of news back in May, about the nation's dire predicament, "...is the result of knowledge. Most British men and women *understood* some things they did not yet wish to know or...they understood some things they did not wish to think about even as they were capable of thinking about them. A very British inclination," he concluded!

A further letter from my future "Aunt" Elinor had arrived by Clipper, the famed Pan-American flyingboat trans-Atlantic air mail service that would enable my mother to retain some contact with me. Aunt Elinor was assuring my mother that arrangements to meet me would be made at whichever North American port might be the ship's undisclosed destination sometime in September. By what means persons were advised of individual passenger ship movements in American ports at the time, is uncertain. The progress of the convoy itself, however, would have remained under, at best, nominal security until it had dispersed at point of destination. For how could buttoned lips be assured from the crews of around forty ships plus company shore staff and stevedores on an evening before sailing?

My father was in a convoy somewhere and it wasn't certain if he'd be home to see me off from Liverpool. There was little likelihood of my seeing him for many moons to come. I now think back and wonder how he ever survived the onslaughts of unrestricted U-boat warfare in that theatre of war. Photographs show he certainly became a casualty in terms of stress and a weight loss to skin and bones. Did he ever lose a ship? Curiously, I have yet to find out and so a visit to Kew's Public Record Office is on the cards as I write. For I never learned personal details about my father from himself. Perhaps, if I'd tried a bit harder? Before both parents had passed on at eighty? I'd had long enough!

Again, I cannot remember if I continued travelling to students' homes each day for classes during the last week at home. All that has entirely gone from the memory. It would, in any case, have depended on air activity. What *has* been retained, and vividly, is the last morning at home, after a 5 a.m. breakfast. Our local taxi owner-driver must have been cajoled to drive up the rutted, unsealed road to our front gate, fretting about the vehicle's suspension, and no doubt helped with my trunk. My mother and I were then deposited on the platform of Chelsfield Station to await the 6:30 a.m. train for Charing Cross. According to the saved rail ticket it was the Workman's Special, for factory workers going on the day shift and it was a subsidised fare of one shilling. The journey took about thirty-five minutes including stops, if there was no line damage. We then got a taxi across London to Kings Cross Station to catch the Liverpool train, a journey of about five hours and due at Lime Street Station at 1:45 p.m.

On the train we ate sandwiches and drank tea from a Thermos flask prepared by my mother the evening before. That had been a sombre occasion, the last bit of packing, washing, ironing, the self-doubts over my decision which I could not show, my mother's silences, the realisation of things I'd never thought deeply about, until then.

I'd been having a final bath and my mother had come in and sat on the side of the tub and told me what I could expect as my body changed into that of a man's. It didn't sound too nice. She would have noticed that odd things were already happening. My thinking was not so totally immersed in woodworking problems as it had once been. I felt ignorant of how to deal with it all. My father had made a stab at this sort of education when I'd visited the *Baltrover* one day before the war during its stay near Tower Bridge. He'd asked me what I considered to be the differences between a man and a woman. "Breasts," I'd told him, hoping this correct answer would not lead below the belt where I knew I was pretty hazy and preferred to remain so. At that point in time I found it impossibly embarrassing. My mother had remarked once: "Of course, you don't have to worry if you never find a girl and get married. Some people are not meant to. It is nature's way of ensuring that certain people never reproduce themselves." I would wonder, in later years, when I was having difficulties with girls, if she'd been referring obliquely to me.

But perhaps the most unsettling words uttered the night before had been my mother trying to reassure me that, even if I changed my mind at that late stage, I wasn't to feel bad. The fare, already paid, didn't matter. *Nothing* mattered, if I wasn't completely sure about going to America. It would be okay. "Everybody changes their minds sometimes," she explained. And it *had* been a close thing. I'd already begun to question why I remotely imagined I wanted to take the step of living with some other family no matter how friendly. There was also a vague feeling of being disloyal to my mother, selfish even. I wanted to tell her how I forgave her for all the whacks and telling-offs she'd given me from time to time—in my interests. But I felt that could be pushing things a bit. I think there'd been a bit of crying too before a hot cup of Ovaltine had sent me to bed and to sleep. I do not now believe that she slept at all.

Now, she was saying, between snacks and watching the sun-drenched countryside flashing past the windows and occasional specks of soot drifting through from the locomotive up front: "Just once more, Philip. Any time, before you go aboard the ship, your father has said you can change your mind and we can go back home on the next train. Is that clear?"

"It's all right mother, I'll be back after a little while. We've got the Hun on the run now and please thank Mrs Nash for the book she's given me for the trip." The book would later trigger my interest in flying. The train pulled in to Lime Street Station in a cloud of steam and smoke that tried to escape through the huge glassed-in, convex roof above the various platforms. All of the stonework had been blackened over the years. Outside, the general impression was of buildings similarly stained with the smoke from millions of coal-heated homes and coal-driven ships.

A taxi took us to the main river landing stage just in front of the monolithic twin towers of the Royal Liver Building (pronounced L-y-ver), home of Royal Liver Assurance Ltd. and graced by gilded "Liver" birds. The fabled bird and its alleged habitat in the "pool" inlet of the River Mersey may have prompted some monastic scribe to pen a word like Liverpool. Who else? Like some primordial bird of prey of no known species and absent from every dictionary I've laid my hands on, they surmount each tower. The giant replicas, of moulded, hammered copper with a wingspan of twenty-four feet may also represent the traditional eagle of St John the Evangelist, Patron Saint of Liverpool. But this is Britain, where myths are buried beneath myths.

Deep underground, a complex of operations and map rooms provided Admiral Max Horton the facilities to fight Germany's Grand Admiral Karl Dönitz and his Atlantic "wolf packs" of U-boats. And he had those two guardian eagles, remember? I didn't know that then. I had never seen the great port city before. I would see it again in July 1944 not long before I enrolled in the Merchant Navy as a cadet.

For now, though, the air-raid sirens began their undulating wail over the whole city as we were deposited by the gates of the landing stage and administration blocks. Then, it was into a nearby air-raid shelter with my luggage and people, caught in the streets going about their business, crammed in with us in the semi-darkness alleviated by the open doorway and ventilation slots in the brick-work. Longer-range German bombers were now giving their atten-tion to Liverpool and the docks area took priority. It would soon become a highly visible target as fire fed on warehouses and narrow streets of the poor.

Option Taken

I don't know for how long we stayed in the shelter but before the sirens signalled a briefly comforting, single-tone, "all-clear," someone had emerged from emigration and passport control and was searching the shelter for would-be ship passengers. My mother quickly gathered me up and we made for the doorway by which everyone had entered in such haste. She held the handle of one end of my brown trunk and I, the other. She showed our two National Registration Cards to the "tin-hatted" air-raid warden. (I can't recall if there were ever two doorways to street air-raid shelters, i.e. entrance *and* exit. It's a point though!)

"It's my son," my mother began, "He's going to America, the ship is the *Baltrover*..."

"Ah, there you are young feller me lad. Been wondering where you got to. Come on then...er, Madam." He looked at my mother. "Maybe you'd best stay in here awhile, just for safety like. Pretty quiet now but you never know..."

"Yes, you stay here mother," I echoed the man's advice. "They probably won't let you past the gate anyway." It was the last bit of "looking after" I could do for my father in fulfillment of his instructions.

So it was in that rushed, rather public, regimented atmosphere that my mother kissed me goodbye stonily, her heart almost certainly about to break in two, but showing nothing, for my sake. I am quite sure that if her mask had once slipped then I would have crumbled. I would have used the veto she'd given me and crashed all her efforts without loss of face. Then we would have somehow got to smokey Lime Street Station, got a train and been home in our bungalow around midnight the same day. But with my mother, I had no chance of being a quitter. "It's the Morgan streak," my father would joke when they were having a tussle over some issue. It was a reference to my maternal grandfather's indomitable will and steely determination.

About then, a man came and hefted my trunk onto his shoulder and went off with it toward the tall iron gates of the Liverpool Passenger Landing Stage. It was where all the mighty liners of the day, with their three or four giant funnels, were once to be found and painted in the variegated peacetime colours their owners preferred. I followed and was able to look back at my mother about twice, standing in the doorway of the shelter, waving me on.

I cannot remember my thoughts after that. I went into a building, the door closed and I must presume that the officials inside found all my documentation in order. I could not see my trunk anywhere. I had my new gas mask case over my shoulder and I am sure I would have been wearing my school uniform. Uniforms were all the rage then. No one checked for my gas mask. It was at home, for recycling. The case was full of shrapnel souvenirs and the single spent cannon shell. I joined a queue of people which was edging forward

Landing Stage and River, Liverpool
"...crammed in with us in the semi-darkness..."

toward the bottom end of the landing stage on gangways. The stage itself was floating so that it always remained the same vertical height from a big ship's entrance ports. The gangways would move up or down with the tide. It must have been low water for the gangways were steep.

I moved, with the crowd, which included a number of small children with their mothers and a few about my age. I began to feel miserable then. I'd still not reached a point of no return. I could have invented a tantrum or a fit and been returned, back to emigration. No. No quitting, no baby me. I let the crowd carry me forward until we reached the black-painted bulwarks of a small steamer with a tall funnel spitting cinders and a lot of steam hissing from a pipe that led to near its top. There was a short gangway and the crowd and I stepped onto the tarred deck. It would have been about 4 p.m. this 30th day of August, 1940.

"What are we doing?" I asked someone.

"Oh, this is the tender that will take us out to the ship. See? She's at anchor, over there."

I succeeded in looking through the crush of people in the direction of the man's outstretched arm. And "over there" she certainly was, still not painted in wartime grey, her so familiar black hull topped by glistening white upperworks, four lifeboats on either side, her one funnel painted in the colours of the United Baltic

Option Taken

Corporation, bottom a buff shade; the top black. The navigating bridge, wheelhouse and two cabs each side, were all varnished teak. My father prided himself on keeping his ship sparkling and clearly, his supervision, terminated so recently, remained in evidence. There had been an annual bonus for a dent-free year. Ten pounds if the ship had avoided contact with a stone quay and no indents made by bumping barges tied up to her at night without authorisation. Bargee language had been extremely lower class, I remembered, when my father had remonstrated with them.

Eventually, the tender pulled away from the landing stage with first, a short, wheezy splutter ending on a high note from its siren high on the front of the funnel. Then, as the steam and water, which had collected in the diaphragm, cleared itself sufficiently, a longer and deeper note issued forth to join the other Mersey sounds.

The black hull of the ship was growing discernibly larger as the distance between us steadily decreased. The ship was anchored in mid-stream, almost opposite Birkenhead, a Mersey bastion of ship-building and repair in those days of near full employment getting torpedoed, mined or bombed ships back to sea again. Often with no change of crew.

I could see earlier arrivals lining the rails of the promenade and boat decks. Some waved; some on the tender waved back I noticed. The small ferry must have already made some trips out to deliver passengers and luggage. Emigration Hall acquaintanceships would blossom into shipboard friendships–and beyond. Some of the boxes and packing cases stacked up near the stern, seemed huge by comparison with my brown trunk, which I failed to spot. People appeared to be going to America for a long time, I considered. Now we were alongside and parts of the bulwarks on the deck nearest the water had been swung inboard. A gangway was being pushed across from the tender's upper deck and, when secured, we heard some shouted instructions.

The crowd, with me in it, made for the ladder up to the gangway and, almost as one, we soon found ourselves standing around and mingling with others on the afterdeck of the *Baltrover*, a ship that had swopped her River Thames berth for the River Mersey, closer to the Atlantic Ocean. It would be her new "trading" area for the duration of the war or until a U-boat, a bomb or a mine decided otherwise. Just then, however, I was incapable of visualising such a happening although I knew all about what torpedoes and mines did to ships. I'd had my father's two Great War sinkings to picture and the models I'd made of the two ships.

Someone was calling out my name: "That you Philip...here, over here." I saw a hand waving, the owner garbed in the white uni-form of a ship's stewardess. Martha! She pushed through the milling crowd and grabbed my shoulder. "Now, *there* you are, found you, we were expecting you much earlier, what held you up...oh, the red tape

I suppose, come on, this way to your cabin."

I told her the air raid had probably had something to do with being late. "I hope I haven't held the captain up," I said, feeling it may have been the right thing to say in the circumstances. I was hugely relieved to see the Martha of old, of peacetime days. "And, is Mary still aboard," I asked.

"Don't be silly," said Martha, hurrying me along one of the internal alleyways of the passenger accommodation below decks. "That was not the last load the tender brought out. I still have another 26 cabins to fill on my deck. A train hold-up, maybe. Yes, Mary's here, we're all here...well, except your father and Captain Walley."

"Where...who..." I began.

"Oh, Captain Walley was snapped up by the navy because of his Reserves rank, Commodore of convoys somewhere I believe. Captain Wells is here now. Mr Huggins is chief officer, came after your dad left, "Dusty" Miller is still purser and...oh, that's right, Jimmy, wireless operator is in one of the other ships...the *Baltannic*, or somewhere. Now, here we are, at last. Number 296. Another boy's in with you, two berth cabin."

Martha opened the door with a key on a large ring of keys hanging from her waist. Opening the door, she began fussing with the bunks. "I'll fill the water bottle," she said. "How did you get here? With your mother? How is she?" she asked, recalling a time when they'd once met.

"Yes, she's all right—I think. I left her in an air-raid shelter near the main gates." My last view of her returned. I felt sick. She looked hard at me.

"Cheer up Philip, we'll soon be riding the waves again like you did with us before, remember? Your tonsils haven't grown again, have they?" She laughed and patted my head. "We must go and find your trunk...brown you said, with your name on?"

"Yes, wouldn't give us any labels, something to do with dangerous information or something," I replied, picturing my mother sewing Cash's cotton name tape on every article of clothing and finishing up with painting my initials P.M.C. on both ends of the trunk above the handles.

"I'll give you some labels later from the Purser's old supply. Souvenirs."

"Oh, *thank you* Martha."

Martha would have been in her forties at that time. Mary was the younger and handled boat deck passengers and their special needs. In pre-war years, Mary had been stewardess in "steerage," that least comfortable area of the ship near the stern where the steam-driven steering gear in older ships would have been situated. A lot of noise and the worst part of the giant see-saw, the ship herself, was reserved for third Class fares. In reality, in the 1930's, the occupants were mainly those being driven from their Polish or German homes in fear and loathing of the new German order.

It is probable the United Baltic Corporation of those days exacted no monetary payment for their four day passage to freedom across the North Sea, bringing what they could in pathetic bundles tied up in the curtains of their living rooms. Pathé Newsreel cameras were often to be seen on Mark Brown's wharf, adjoining Tower Bridge, filming the latest gangway-full of refugees stepping ashore in blessed safety and freedom—sometimes in transit to America. Now, I was following, yet not escaping, as they had done, from the unique and horrifying predicaments we would learn about only at war's end and long after that, even unto the present.

5 Evacuee–Separation

Research for this book tells me that sometime in the 24 hours of August 30th, the Dutch passenger liner, *Volendam*, bound for New York, had been torpedoed and sunk with evacuees on board.

I can imagine now how her young passengers, probably with their parents, would have been engaged in very similar activities to our own on the day preceding the disaster. For example, my mother had made last minute visits to the Orpington shops for an extra pair of socks, a tube of toothpaste and the "Old Uncle Tom Cobbleigh 'n All" musical jug. I would be temporary custodian of that gift to my new Aunt Elinor and Uncle Roy.

Had the news of the sinking been broadcast when it happened, as the media now does in two inch headlines, or even leaked it as a rumour, as governments always do, it is likely but by no means certain that no more packing would have been done. For the *Volendam* would not be the last ship to go down carrying child evacuees. Six weeks hence, on September 17th, the Ellerman liner, *City of Benares*, would be torpedoed and sunk in the North Atlantic with seventy-three children in her passenger list. Some survived, picked up among the flotsam by naval escorts many hours later. More of that in a subsequent chapter. Churchill had initially disapproved of overseas evacuation. He demurred, prevaricated and deprecated and foresaw a possible stampede, like rats leaving a sinking ship. Evacuation to the British dominions seemed to him like passing the nation's young on for adoption. He could not visualise many returning to the mother country.

Parents did not share this view of things at all and the War Cabinet had little option but to endorse the general scheme for children under five and to bear the cost. With me being over-age for government sponsorship at twelve plus, my family bore the costs. These, I sincerely hope and believe, would have included contributions to my dear "Aunt" Elinor and "Uncle" Roy during the period of my stay with the family. As for providing shipping space, and ineligible for a government-paid passage in the faster ships allocated to the scheme, my parents had done what they could by getting me aboard my father's former ship. In any case, I would not have swopped the old 13-knot *Baltrover* for any other vessel afloat—even given a choice!

The so-called "faster ships" chosen were, however, with few exceptions, still convoyed. The only passenger ships regularly sailing independently were RMS (Royal Mail Ship) *Queen Mary* and the newly launched RMS *Queen Elizabeth* of about 81,000 and 83,000 tons respectively having design speeds of between 28 and 30 knots. *Queen Mary*, pre-war, had vied with her American and French rivals, *United States* and *Normandie* for the coveted Blue Riband Atlantic speed record. *Queen Elizabeth*, completed in 1940, virtually did her acceptance speed trials on her secretive maiden voyage. She came out of the mist off Sandy Hook, New York, looking like a couple of Broadway "Flatiron" buildings end-to-end to aghast New Yorkers! Both great ships, by out-running U-boats of the period, inevitably reserved their people capacity for troops and VIP's. In the latter category, there could have been a sprinkling of the more fortunate evacuee.

The programme was still well underway in August 1940 despite the one sinking. The distances to Canada, South Africa, Australia and New Zealand, called for accommodation in large, fast ships. Dutch and Polish ships were used as preference because those countries were out of the war and effectively neutral and might have a somewhat longer life than British ships. But the fallacy of even that became apparent when certain U-boat commanders took pot shots at them to increase their scores of "kills" and "possibles." Germany had promised safe conduct for American ships while the USA was still neutral, but Churchill would not be compromised by such a deal. What would Germany want in return for such a favour, he rightly queried? Historic "Lend Lease," to be signed and sealed by Churchill and Roosevelt on the approaching 31st December, could not be jeopardised by agreements with Hitler. No doubt the two Queens were used exclusively and safely. Throughout the war the two largest ships in the world came to no harm. Only one of the *Mary's* escorts, the destroyer, HMS *Curacao*, tried to cut across the larger ship's bows, miscalculated and was cut in two.

I said it was *likely* that no more of my packing would have been done the night before my mother and I had entrained for Liverpool's smoky, blackened Lime Street Station, the dockside air-raid shelter and now the ship. Yes, she might have used her veto, unpacked and sent me off to school next day, or rather, to some student's parent's house, wherever. There would have followed endless discussion with me, friends and neighbours such as:

"Wasn't it lucky your boy didn't go to America. 'E might 'ave been drowned, like the others on that terrible *Volendam*." Or might the same people have opined later, as they, my mother and I were being herded into railway cattle wagons, then deported to slave labour camps in Germany: "What a terrible decision you made Mrs Cheek, not getting your son away on that ship to freedom when you had the chance, paid the fare an' all...dear, dear, poor little mite, 'ere, luv, give 'im some of this bread-n-drippin' I've got 'ere in me 'andbag..."

That would have been a fair comment in the stylized speech

effected by a number of people in our south London road so that I am being reasonably correct in its portrayal. But, like as not, I imagine we would all have been quite silent about our desperate lot. Speechless with horror and disbelief as German guards gloatingly perfected their sadism and cruelty in an ancient, vanquished and desolate kingdom.

No. Knowing my mother better in later years as one does with one's mother, I rather think that if she'd known about the *Volendam* via some source, perhaps Mr Pettifer himself ringing up, she would have thought hard then secretly taken the responsibility from me making a switch and staying home. I would not have known a thing. We would have got on that Liverpool train just as planned and I, ...well I would be exactly where I then was, standing in cabin 296 waiting for Martha to return with my travelling companion and be introduced. Later in this book, the reader will learn something of the alternatives that might have affected our small family if our "Brylcreem Boys" had not fought themselves nearly to a standstill.

"This is Master Philip Jacobsen," Martha was saying as she turned from the main alleyway into the short one that went to the

Philip Jacobsen
"...I noted that we were of similar height..."

ships side, and my cabin. She was applying the still-used prefix when minors were referred to or addressed. "And this is Master Philip Cheek," Martha said, coping well with her surprising find—two Philips!

I noted that we were of similar height while he had darker hair than mine. We were dressed almost the same for boys of our age. Grey, short trousers, three-quarter length socks and, in my case, my school blazer. He had a kind of tweed sports coat, grey shirt with attached soft collar and tie. Everyone, at least in our sector of society, seemed to wear ties when going anywhere outside the home. Usually, if one wanted an open necked shirt, one just left the tie off with a couple of buttons undone. There seemed to be no "sports" shirts with short sleeves as we now have. Stiff collars, worn by business men, came separate, fixed by a stud front and back. An advantage was that the shirts came with two collars so increasing the duration of use. (A week or two?) Wipeable plastic collars appeared, followed by packets of paper collars—cleanable with a piece of India rubber of the kind given us at school.

One might see manual workers wearing such shirts, collar-less, with a neckerchief of sorts, engaged in dusty tasks around coal mines, quarries, in the docks or as knots of men working along railway tracks. Similar shirts with dated stripes, would appear on a beach, in summer. Even suit waistcoats would be sweatily retained by contemporary sun-seekers; the long shirt sleeves tightly rolled above the elbow. A totally fashionless sight for men who now look out from family photo albums. The snaps evoke recollection of the snail-pace evolvement of male dress style somehow sanctioned by the womenfolk—until the famed American "Arrow" shirts, with collars, and their plastic stiffeners attached, took off, helped by American service men when they appeared later in the war.

"Hello Philip," I said to my cabin-mate.

"Hello Philip," he replied, a strained face relaxing in a tight little smile. He took my outstretched hand in the manner of grown-ups meeting and winced slightly at the firm grip my father had always said I should use in this form of greeting. "A man is often judged by his grip," he would say, and then we would do a great deal of experimentation accompanied by squeals of pain and laughter and my mother calling out: "That's enough, that's *enough* I say!"

"Oh, you two," exclaimed Martha, "we'll have to call you Philip One and Philip Two. Your brown trunk, Philip One," she said, looking at me, "has been found and one of the sailors is bringing it along. What's yours like Philip Two," again looking hard at my cabin-mate to confirm him in our new identities.

"Umm, sort of black, I think with brass corners."

And so it went on and finally we two boys got ourselves sorted out with me opting for the top bunk and P.2 expressing his preference for the bottom bunk. I had always liked the cosiness of top

The American Option

bunks and, visiting the different ships my father had been in, I had always seemed to be climbing small ladders into top bunks. There, I could draw the bunk curtains around and exclude the normal world from my vision. All bunks on passenger ships and cargo ships had curtains, a grandeur reminiscent of the age of fourposter beds in Elizabethan times right up to the Edwardian era.

It was not that ships cabins had not advanced in line, technologically, with shoreside bedchambers. They had, but it was just that ships, and those who sailed them, somehow belonged to a different planet with strange laws all their own. And that was certainly true of curtained bunks, invented, in the practical sense of course, to block glare from the main cabin light when one's cabin-mate was moving about and trying to keep upright. All these things had to be thought out in the design of a ship. It just goes to show how much the greatly maligned naval architect has to think about in addition to stability, outward appearance, number of funnels, etc. To a landsman and travel agent, funnels represented power and prestige. The *Baltrover* had one funnel and would be assigned to a ten knot convoy—maybe three knots below her maximum speed. A tasty morsel for a U-boat wolf pack if the escort screen, on the convoy's perimeter, was penetrated allowing a determined U-boat commander to get inside. Like our people, they were pretty determined too.

I had no idea when the ship would sail. Martha didn't know. No one looking like crew, seemed to know. They either said right out that they hadn't a clue or they might say airily: "Ah! I heard it's tomorrow sometime." Oh well, I decided, I would write a short letter to my mother anyway and hope the pilot, possibly already up there in the captain's cabin waiting to safely guide the ship to deep water across the Liverpool bar, would post it when he reached the pilot boat station on his return. It had always been a favoured way of my father's in getting a last message ashore to my mother outward bound on a long voyage: "My dear Gwen," he might have said, (although the actual words would have been more heartfelt), I am sending this with the pilot to cheer you up and as a last reminder that I..."

I unlocked my trunk, fished out a pocket diary and my fountain pen, tore out two unused pages from January and sat on the trunk. I was about to begin when a gong sounded somewhere in the ship. Looking up I spotted P.2 glancing at a wristlet watch I'd not noticed before.

"What time is it?" I asked.

"Nearly seven," he said.

"Didn't Martha say dinner was at seven when she brought that tea and sandwiches?"

"Can't remember now," replied P.2 "I was writing a postcard."

The gong was banged again, closer, at the end of the short alleyway outside. A steward—the dinner gong. It reverberated

Separation

Mr Huggins, Chief Officer
"...he's got a fat face so you needn't worry about me..."

throughout the lower passenger decks and almost ordered us two lads
to feel ravenously hungry. Then Martha came to show us the way to
the main dining saloon and I wanted to say that I knew the way
already.

Surprisingly, quite a number of people of both sexes were
trooping down the wide staircase and being guided to tables,
showing boarding cards. Martha had ours and we approached a circular table with five chairs underneath a large, polished brass porthole. We sat and soon an officer came and joined us. I noticed the
uniform showed the same rank as my father had once held, three
rings of gold braid on either cuff surmounted by a circle. Chief

officer, said the uniform, and second-in-command of any merchant ship.

"Hello boys, Jack Huggins, which one of you is Philip?"

"We both are," I said, giggling, "but I'm the one Dad told you about I think. Mr Pettifer said you were going to be a guardian or something. Is that right?"

"Absolutely right," answered the large man now seated opposite. He had a friendly face with blue eyes, big hands and rather large ears, I thought at the time. He looked about my father's age who, as I've already mentioned, was as old as the year. "Yes, we're going to keep an eye on you, and your friend, all the way across this time so eat up the good food while you can and oh, don't forget your books. Your dad expressly said that."

"Left them at home, didn't we P.2?" We looked at each other and laughed.

"What's this P.2 all about?" said Mr Huggins. "Sounds like a convoy number or something."

"We're both Philips you see and Martha invented the code...er, P.1 and P.2. I sort of got in first."

"All right then, no books eh? Well, you can study one of my navigation books and start learning your future business P.1. Come up to the bridge as often as you like and do your chartwork!"

Our first meal on board came and was devoured. Mr Huggins got up and left, taking P.2's postcard with him. I became impatient to return to our cabin and get my letter written. It would demonstrate that my mother and I would never lose touch. There were always letters and I'd already come to know the value of those. There was a stack of letters at home which my father had written to me from all over the world. They, and my replies, would form the basis of my letter-writing habit which, one day, far off, would stand me in good stead when, on one occasion, I needed money rather badly and took up writing for a newspaper and shipping journals.

Mr Huggins, like everyone else, did not know when we would be sailing. Philip 2 amused himself after dinner in the passenger lounge and library below the bridge. I made for the cabin, closed the door, sat on the trunk and wrote on the pages removed from the diary:

August 30th 1940–s.s. Baltrover.

Dear Mother,
I hope you are not worrying about me, and I hope you did not worry about me in the air-raid shelter just after you left me. I was very surprised at the amount of people I had to pass before I could get through. I was taken out to the ship in a tender, as she was in mid-river. I arrived on board and saw all the people I knew including Mr Huggins. He is awfully nice, he's got a fat face so you needn't worry about me while I'm at sea.

I had quite a nice dinner, it consisted of soup and some chicken I didn't want any more because I had a bit of a headache its gone off now though. I hope you will go and sleep in Mrs Hutchs tonight and stay as well at Mrs Fords for a week. I expect when you get this note that I will be when I sail, so cheerio for now.
Love from Philip XXXXXXX

P.2 returned, Martha came with two cups of cocoa, and took my letter to Mr Huggins, wherever he may have been, so that he could add it to the few private letters taken ashore by the pilot. I was confident he would find an envelope and address it, maybe to the company's head office for forwarding. All these years later I wonder how it was done. I felt immeasurable relief at the prospect of getting those pages from a pocket diary ashore. We climbed into our bunks, drew the curtains, switched off the bunk reading lights and went to sleep with our private thoughts.

Ashore, on mainland Britain, thoughts were being concentrated with increasing urgency on the need to once again get children away from cities in the south and from those front line areas most likely to be the scenes of appalling, bloody carnage in the business of repelling German ground troops. The categories would be the same

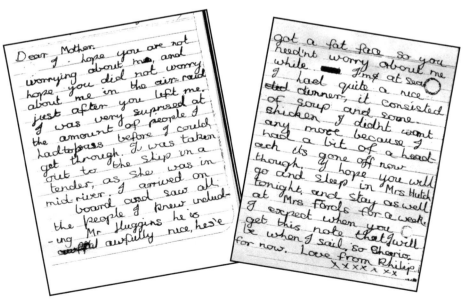

"...wrote on the pages removed from the diary..."

as those who had offered themselves for the government's initial voluntary evacuation programme the previous year, but who had mostly drifted back to their homes during the "Bore War." The scenes would be repeated with pregnant women, mothers with children under five, school children, the blind and infirm, riding the trains, buses and carts in infinite discomfort. (There were fewer private cars around now that the war was taking hold and the trains even more crowded as the military were moved to the more strategic and threatened south of the country.)

Many of the train carriages were requisitioned from local, short distance lines having twelve-seat, individual compartments. Children became distressed, worsened by family farewells on railway platforms, calls of nature grew too strong, seat upholstery soaked up urine and one train had to stop after only fifty miles and disembark the passengers. Many of these failed to reach planned reception areas and billets.

Brothers or sisters, who'd resolved to stick together, became separated. Normal long-distance rail carriages had side corridors which enabled people to get out of the cosy, individual, twelve-seat compartments, and move along to intermediate toilets—or a restaurant car. Twelve-hour journeys were common and if food had not been taken with them, nothing was provided. Usually they ate or drank nothing until around midnight, in some cases, and when billeting officers had found a family willing to take them.

In Angus Calder's *The People's War*, the author writes:
"Local householders had assembled to pick their evacuees when the trains or buses arrived and scenes reminiscent of a cross between an early Roman slave market and Selfridge's bargain basement (a London store) ensued. Potato farmers selected husky lads; girls of ten or twelve, who could lend a hand in the house, were naturally much in demand; nicely dressed children were whisked away by local bigwigs. Those who became 'second pick' were often resentful, and there was likely to be a residue of unwholesome looking waifs whom nobody wanted, but whom somebody would have to take when the billeting officer began to mutter about compulsory powers."

The schools, having done it all once of course, were more organised second time round in the marshalling and re-grouping of their charges but, when it came to the transportation, reception and billeting, the misery and trauma for both evacuees and foster-parents was similar to that of September 1939. In all, around 3,750,000 people had been moved between June 1939 and the outbreak of war. Half perhaps, had dribbled away back home. This time, 1,250,000 would go to relative safety. The figure would include 141,000 unaccompanied children.

Evacuation, per se meant the billeting of millions from towns onto country householders. There would be little time to give thought to the match or mis-match of the cultural backgrounds of child and foster-parent. Many would be the memories of fond unions formed. Many were the horror stories of unruly, desperate, unclean children from poor or slum origins. These frequently arrived having been literally sewn into the vestiges of garments their parents provided. Most, were unable to make the adjustment from city streets to rural town or village considered sufficiently distant from German terror bombing.

From Angus Calder: *"The official or government-sponsored evacuees, came disproportionately from the poorest strata of urban society, i.e. the better-off would have made their own arrangements. Evacuation areas were mostly areas of high population density with severe overcrowding. Poorer classes maintained a higher birthrate. A social survey of several provincial towns in the thirties gave twelve to fifteen per cent of families below the poverty line. The statistic accounted for twenty-two to thirty per cent of children! Parents having one or two children were less likely to send them away and swifter to bring them back than six-children families; the smaller the family, the more it clung together. Then there was housing, with disproportionately more room to spare among well-to-do foster parents. A survey estimated only four out of ten children from working-class Clydebank went to working-class homes.*

"Rural Britain became electrified with tragi-comic confrontations. Elderly gentlemen found their retirement invaded by half a dozen urchins from the slums of London or Liverpool. Neat spinsters who'd agreed to take a schoolchild might be gifted instead with a sluttish mother who arrived smoking a cigarette over her baby's head and disappeared with her offspring as soon as the public houses opened. With incomprehensible obtuseness, Catholic families from Liverpool, with its rich underworld of Irish immigrants, were dispatched to rural Wales, where a narrow Calvinism held sway and where there were certainly no Roman Catholic churches. One priest felt it necessary to insist parents take their children home. Any danger from bombing was a trifle contrasted with the spiritual dangers children ran by remaining.

"A thirteen-year-old Jewish boy, from the friendships of Stepney, London's poor East End, was billeted in green Buckinghamshire with his young sister. They had refused to be separated so no home was found for them until close to midnight. Rose whispered for days, said he. Everything was so clean in the room. We were even given face cloths and toothbrushes. We'd never cleaned our teeth before. And hot water came from a tap. And there was a toilet upstairs. And carpets. And something called an eiderdown. And clean sheets. This was all very odd, he exclaimed. And rather scary. But some children went to farms with no running water or flush toilets in farm labourer's cottages. Fields provided sanitary facilities and water was drawn from a well. Emotionally unsettled by all this, countless children wet their beds.

"Mr Oliver Lyttelton, who would become a member of Churchill's government, had volunteered to put up ten evacuees in his spacious country house—and received thirty one. 'I got a shock,' he writes. 'I had little dreamt that English children could be so completely ignorant of the simplest rules of hygiene, and that they would regard the floors and carpets as suitable places upon which to relieve themselves.' But, if sophisticated public men were sur-

prised, the average middle-class house-holder was stupefied. Schools used for reception of evacuees had to be fumigated. Some children appeared to have been unbathed for months. Many mothers and children were bed-wetters and were not in the habit of doing anything else. The appalling apathy of the mothers was terrible to see."

The fact that children from poor homes had never worn pyjamas was taken as a sign of the near criminal negligence of the parents—who often merely could not afford such strictly inessential additions to the wardrobe. Certainly a number of the children, and their habits, would have struck hardened social workers as pretty deplorable. But the social worker would have known about the poverty which had produced them. This was a lesson which the more intelligent and sensitive middle-class billetors, recovering from the shock, began to learn for the first time. And much of the information emerged from random reports submitted to Women's Institutes in England and Wales.

Life in new classrooms with new teachers would likewise be accompanied by either a happy phasing-in or extreme nervous stress for both pupil and staff. Evacuation had to be a classless exercise leaving no room for selection. But, as Angus Calder tells us:

"Evacuation dramatised disunities and showed how far out of touch was Chamberlain's government with conditions and opinions of those it purported to represent. It exposed the inadequacy of social services and offered experimental proof that the poor were really hideously poor. It thrust a better standard of living in front of small townschildren—and a far worse one against the noses of middle-class householders."

J.B. Priestly, novelist, in his radio programme *The English Journey*, once discussed the 2,750,000 British unemployed which in 1932 represented a 1 in 4 average. The British Empire was still *virgo intacta* and he maintains that, *"The poor were not as badly off as an unskilled labourer in 1913. The wages were better and they did well from the plight of the poor in colonial countries. The street corner and the public library had become the habitat of the hopeless. The dole and other public assistance was means-tested."*

It is, perhaps, an invitation to try and picture the British poor *without* the so-called wealth of a perpetually sunny empire overseas.

For the unemployed of pre-war Britain or for those on low wages, decent clothes were a luxury! Cheap Jack clothing clubs sold shoes with cardboard soles and cheap cotton blankets. Second-hand garments from street markets could be infested with bugs. Strangely, later in the war when full employment and rising earnings alleviated abject poverty, (for Great War heroes) the Board of Trade, responsible for rationed clothing, was faced with an immense, unsatisfied demand for childrens' shoes despite increased production of footwear. The habit had caught on?

Yet while the British evacuation *"Exposed diversity and the*

Separation

social conditions of a people that had stumbled into war, it became the first of numerous social developments stemming from the militerisation of civilians, i.e. the Civil defense. And during the first weeks of war the country experienced the most bizarre phenomenon. In the buses, trains and public houses of Britain, strangers were speaking to one another." (Angus Calder)

To expand the question "what miseries, what trauma?" Ruth Inglis, in *The Children's War (1989)*, succinctly lists the origins of each: In London's east end, 90% of the houses had no baths. The curious prevalence of head lice is claimed as a legacy of parents who emerged from the Great War only to head in to the Great Depression. Up to World War II, Britain had one of the highest infant mortality rates. In some cases children arrived at reception areas shoeless and without underwear. And that, for brevity's sake, was the scenario of British evacuation of the British on home ground. I would refer the reader to books used in research for this volume for an in-depth analysis of the internal measures for extending the life of our children.

On the continent of Europe unspeakable measures were being taken to keep alive certain categories of children and exterminate others. Speculation on what I and my namesake, asleep in the bottom bunk, might have escaped, how we would enjoy the first months of proverbial peace and security of life in America, how I would cycle home with a litre carton of chocolate-mint-chip ice cream in the handlebar basket to accompany our Sunday dinner dessert, will occupy me pleasantly in a coming chapter.

I'm not certain, at this distance in time, but I like to think it was me who climbed first from the bunks. I stood on the small square of carpet covering the pitch-caulked planks of the deck and looked out of the porthole to where the landing stage and the giant Liver Building ought to have been but were no longer there. Instead, my gaze settled upon an empty sea. The Irish Sea. Or it was empty, until I looked sideways and then I saw two ships, then three and as I craned my neck there seemed to be a whole fleet of ships. The convoy!

There was hardly any movement and this is what had confused me as I'd lain, for the few moments after waking, still behind my curtains, and ruminated on the previous day's events; whether my mother had got home safely; whether she could work my improved lighting system for our Anderson shelter. *Her* Anderson shelter now! I was no longer a part of anything back there. Perhaps I never would be again. The ship had crept away silently from Britain sometime in the dark hours, I imagined. There'd been none of the sounds that came from a ship about to sail on a long voyage; no short or long blasts on her siren, no... Ah! my letter...that would have gone ashore with the pilot...a noise behind me. Turning, I saw the curtains move on P.2's bunk, a face appeared. Funny how I couldn't remember how Philip had looked when he was awake.

The American Option

"G'morning," I said, "how d'yer sleep?"

"Oh, ah...yes...not bad really," came from the pyjama-clad figure. That was something anyway, I thought. Everyone wore pyjamas in our house, even in the Anderson shelter, and that took a bit of planning sometimes but we insisted we would maintain an illusion of normality, as though we'd done that kind of thing all our lives, and not live piggishly now. And actually, it had been quite fun during the spring and summer months. Now what? My mother would now have no one to share our cosy shelter and would boil the kettle over the upturned flower pot with the lit candle inside glittering through the hole in the bottom, just to make one cup of tea. No, it's no use, I remonstrated, I should not have come away, it was all wrong, wrong, wrong. Tears welled up in my eyes.

But Allan Dorday, now living in New Zealand, at age six, had cried himself to sleep night after night after being virtually snatched from school with the whole class one day by order of the government and packed off to a variety of rural billets without word to his family. I, at age twelve, was also verging on tears as I stared out to sea, with only one difference. I'd evacuated myself, without compunction and was beginning to bitterly question the decision I'd made. I'd deserted my family at probably the hour of their desperate need. P.2 came and stood by me at the porthole.

"Cor, look at that," he uttered.

"What," I asked. "What's happening?"

"Big explosion over there!" By then, his head and shoulders were all but preventing me seeing whatever was happening in our quite suddenly insecure world.

6 Social Experiment

I tried to edge Philip a little to one side of the porthole so that I could glimpse what he had obviously noticed. The noise of an explosion had eventually covered the distance with a kind of double thud, but by the time I got my nose up to the glass, no smoke from an explosion was visible.

There were some white eruptions of water in the distance and later, after breakfast, on the bridge with Mr Huggins, we learned that the "waterspouts" were from depth charges dropped astern from one of the tiny escort corvettes. Contact with a U-boat had evidently been made early on in the voyage so, what might be our fate? The question, so far as my memory goes, never crossed either of our minds for we were totally innocent of enemy violence at that stage and, if we were to witness any at all, it would doubtless come as a fresh and frightening experience which we were intellectually ill-equipped to measure by any previous yardstick.

Naturally, there was a good deal of chatter among other passengers about this first naval action in our small world of around twenty-five merchant ships. The horizon, when we got up on deck, was one unbroken circle of sea and sky beyond the convoy and which, at that time and position, would have been steaming in a north-westerly direction toward the northernmost tip of Ireland. Before that land mass had been left astern we would have proceeded either north-north-west toward Iceland before turning south-west for Newfoundland and the Belle Isle Straits. (If Montréal was to be our destination.) Alternatively, the convoy could join a Great Circle track via the Portuguese Azores islands for American eastern seaboard ports. The kinder weather not U-boats would influence that one. However, our Captain Wells would have his sealed orders and it would be they, and confirmation from the convoy commodore, which would provide the latest intelligence on enemy dispositions which, in turn, would determine the route and make choices academic.

There were ships of every imaginable design and purpose and, in my short experience with ship types and the models I'd made of some of them, my imagination had been well honed. Close by, on our starboard side, was a big tanker, high out of the water, its funnel right aft, obviously sailing west in ballast. Eastbound, she would be deeply laden, perhaps with benzine–aviation fuel. A floating bomb. Ahead, another passenger ship, bigger than *Baltrover* was pitching majestically like a nodding old lady, wisps of diesel fumes emitting from her two funnels, her foremast signal halyards "ablaze" with coloured bunting.

The American Option

Mr Huggins had referred to it as the "commodore" ship having aboard the naval officer in charge of the whole convoy. He, it was who would direct all defensive tactics and manoeuvers, if there were to be any, against attack from submarines, surface raiders or aircraft. The difficult task for him would be to try and co-ordinate his strategies with the merchant captains of some twenty-five yawing, rolling, pitching merchant ships—commanded by very independently minded men indeed—now in thrall to the Royal Navy!

A significant number of convoy commodores were Merchant Navy captains who held RNR rank and had been drafted into the job. It freed up the regular naval officers for appointments to pure naval vessels. Notwithstanding a former background as merchant captains and their familiarity with the sort of men who were pacing the bridges of the gaggle of geese astern and on either side, chafing at the interference of "naval types," it often proved a superhuman task to gain automatic response to signals sent out from "mother goose." With nil radio contact, groups of single letter flags of the International Code of Signals, would be run up aboard the commodore ship and had to be acknowledged with an answering pennant and identical groups bent on, then hoisted aboard every ship. In this way, and if the nearest ship to the commodore had read his signals correctly, the ship next closest would rely on his neighbour's hoist and yank identical flags from their flag lockers. And so on throughout the convoy. The signal could be a time given to commence zig-zagging; to upset the periscope sightings of U-boat commanders. Upsettingly frequently flags would be misread by one or more ships and the zig-zag courses, unsynchronised, would end up with ships in a terrible tangle and even colliding. The damaged ship(s), perhaps unmanageable, would be left to await the arrival of a distant tug. If they weren't finished off in the meantime. And two ugly ducklings (pardon, geese!) being towed home at, say, four knots, did not suggest a lengthening life span for ship or crew.

At night, signals were exchanged by an "Aldis" signalling lamp, perhaps using a blue shade to reduce brightness, a sure giveaway to a sharp-eyed enemy. The chance of collision was even increased if the Morse Code was inexpertly employed; the message garbled. Ships kept station fairly easily in clear weather. In fog or at night the method used was to try and keep in sight a dim, shaded blue stern light of the ship in front and a kind of buoy or float towed behind a ship, splashing and visible, something like her log line, used to determine speed via the small propeller or rotator spinning at the end. Station-keeping, in tidy lines of "geese" with engine revolutions—down four, up two—bawled down through an engine-room speaking tube (before telephones became universal in merchant ships) were an officer-of-the-watch's reason for staying awake and living. Matchsticks could be injurious.

Special clocks were supplied to merchant ships termed "zig-zag clocks." When each zig and zag from a set course was to commence, the clock minute hand would make an electrical contact with a series of adjustable metal clips at the clock's circumference. Intervals in minutes between pre-set clips would determine the time of course changes and duration of each leg. A nerve-shattering alarm bell would alert the officer of the watch and the helmsman. On board the commodore ship the hope would always be that the convoy would zig-zag as one unit.

I knew nothing of all this. I'd been nudged away one last time from the porthole by P.2 and then we'd got washed and dressed—neither of us shaved then—and headed in the direction of the cooking smells and the dining saloon where Mr Huggins was finishing his breakfast and he would explain what Philip and I had just seen. The evolutions of merchant ships in a wartime convoy would be absorbed by me and demonstrated later in the war. In two years time, to be precise.

There is little I can recall now of our day-to-day activities aboard the *Baltrover* in her east to west wartime passage from Liverpool to...somewhere in America. I don't remember being told our port destination even and, for some reason, I appear never to have enquired the intermediate stops before I would reach the only place I'd heard of...Verona, near Montclair, New Jersey. It would have been enough for me anyway. I must have been supremely confident and trusting on sighting the dear old ship again, equating her with my father and who my mother and I relied upon and depended implicitly for all our needs; who would still somehow be in charge of us, even out of his sight.

I cannot remember having to give up my passage ticket. Where would that have been? About my person? Maybe lying on the top layer of shrapnel in my new, flash, gas mask case? But it probably sat secure within my first-ever passport. Did I have to present a letter to anyone on board? Probably. And written in my mother's careful hand using her familiar straight pen-nib in its holder, so identifying me. One of those TO WHOM IT MAY CONCERN letters? I do not know. Perhaps Martha had relieved me of all necessary documents and passed them to the ship's purser. Yes, that must be it. Had there been any formalities at all they would have been speedily handled by the officers and ship's staff whom I'd known for some time. I cannot recall meeting Captain Wells. He had been recently promoted, I believe, from one of the company's other cargo freighters and was said—and I do remember this—not to be very communicative. But then, ship's captains seemed never to be communicative with anyone below their rank in those far off days when stiff, unbending protocol reigned. And being chatty to passengers could be a difficult business at any time. In war, buttoned lips meant safer ships.

I think now, having commanded some 26 ships myself of various shapes and sizes, that it must have been a terrifying leap in the dark

The American Option

when one was finally promoted to captain's rank before the Second World War and just after—maybe into dead men's shoes. One almost *had* to await either the demise of one's superior or his untimely dismissal before getting a crack at independent command, as it was nicely termed. And on board the *Baltrover*, nice, chummy, chubby, kind Mr Huggins, second-in-command, might soon, himself, be landed in a sudden vacancy of war. His own ship. But I cannot see him ever becoming aloof, unapproachable or curmudgeonaly—if he survived the war that is. Today's captains have less to be aloof about in terms of a diminished authoritative role increasingly shared between people called managing agents, their operations managers and even lesser ranks among the land people. Responsibility, however, is not so avidly grabbed—when the chips are down. That much I have learned since I took up with the sea as a livelihood almost 60 years ago. Independent command is virtually dead. Alive and troublesomely well, is human error, child of indecision and over-stressed smaller crews, that puts huge oil tankers ashore and wipes the local ecology for indeterminate periods of time. There are some who think that jailing captains is the only deterrent and remedy.

As I've said, memory plays tricks at this distance in time with any one special event that may have occurred during the *Baltrover's* fifteen-day crossing of the Atlantic in September, 1940. The event of a torpedo slamming into the hull would have been the chief one to occupy the minds of my elders as the days passed. For us two boys, it seems our days were spent in all the customary peace-time distractions of life aboard ship. We played deck games such as quoits, deck golf, tennis (by throwing rubber rings across a net) and cricket. Unlike baseball, which I would soon learn, cricket on board ship could be played within the width and length of a promenade deck. Runs could easily be made in that scope. Fielding was simple and netting caught a stray ball before it sped over the side. A softer-than-usual ball was used, specially made by sailors with a kind of cro-cheted string cover around a softwood core packed round with layers of paper. Standard cricket bats were used. My father had always been captain of the ship's cricket team and sometimes there would be an "away" game at a country club when the ship's annual refit came around. My father was a fast bowler and his batting average was not bad either.

Either day or night, distant thuds would be heard which we boys assumed to be a repetition of what we'd already observed on day one. There always seemed to be the same ships in lines either side, ahead and astern. There were three or four naval signallers on board to handle the communications with the commodore ship.

Between two and six army gunners were allotted to each merchant ship in those days, to both maintain and fire the main and secondary armament. There was not a lot of that early in the war. *Baltrover* would have been provided with one four-inch calibre gun

Experiment

on a strengthened steel platform at the stern. This positioning limited a ship to defense rather than attack, a status quo deleted when Germany tore up the rules of the game in The Great War. The Cunard White Star Line's RMS *Lusitania*, suspected of carrying war material in violation of a Geneva convention protecting passenger ships, is thought to have been the pretext. The liner was torpedoed in the Irish Sea. The death of American passengers fueled the outrage that speeded America's entry into the war on Great Britain's side. Thereafter, Germany tacitly permitted unrestricted sinkings by its submarines with the one exception of hospital ships, painted white and clearly marked with red crosses on the sides. In the current war there seemed no similar rule for ships carrying children as evacuees.

To be fair, in war as well as in love, a select few of British and German swashbuckling naval types had, in 1916, employed innocence as a weapon. Germany sent out fast, innocuous merchant ships with naval guns behind drop-down bulwarks—with naval crews. A notable exception was Count Felix von Luckner's full-rigged sailing ship, *Seeadler*. Britain sent out her equally famous Q-ships, humble coastal sailing vessels and simulated, down-at-heel deep sea tramp ships—with naval guns under fake canvas deck houses—and naval reserve crews. When challenged by a surfaced U-boat, a "panic party" would take to the lifeboat, rowing in undisciplined fashion, leaving the hidden gun's crew to finish off the U-boat when it had drifted up nice and close to inspect its prize. In one rare instance, attacked and attacker managed to sink one another. Whatever the merits of this novel warfare it removed the non-combatant cloak of protection from merchant shipping forever. The story of the Q-ships and Germany's commerce raiders is a gripping one.

On our ship, Lewis and Oerlikon guns *may* have been fitted at strategic locations but generally, merchant ships of the Second World War began to be adequately armed only later, about 1942. By then, we would see American "Liberty" ships in all maritime theatres of war armed to the teeth, bristling with light armament and a heavy job mounted in the bows. Merchant ships were no longer symbolically defensive!

So we boys would have some fun with the navy signallers and the navy signallers would join with us in some innocent teasing with the few girls on board. I have never really thought back on them until now, in the writing of this story. Or all the others on board—Captain Wells, Mr Huggins, "Sparks" the wireless operator (looking a mite shy at Philip's camera lens). And Martha and Mary—did any survive the savage, at first unequal Battle of the Atlantic?[2] Well, few will be around now, but Philip Jacobsen, P.2,

2 *Attack & Sink, The Battle of the Atlantic, Summer 1941*
—by Bernard Edwards, Brick Tower Press, 2005.

should be, somewhere in the world. A bearded academic? A dispensing pharmacist in a shopping mall drug store? A movie cameraman or a clever surgeon at The University of California or, yes, now that I study the spare passport photo (see page 55) he gave me, he did have the look of a "some day" bank governor? Perhaps he may yet let me know which he became.

About this time in the war also departed for America a schoolgirl, Shirley Catlin, daughter of Vera Brittain, novelist and George Catlin, professor of politics, Cornell University. As Baroness Shirley Williams she now leads the Liberal Democrats in the House of Lords. Her soon-to-be-published memoirs, may provide asides on British women in war and politics. One other former schoolgirl comes to mind: Dame Elizabeth Taylor, actress and supporter of AIDS research; and founder of The Ben Gurion Fund for Children of the Negev. Reaching California in 1939 then high school, she would emerge in the film, *National Velvet* and be twice feted an Oscar-winner for subsequent work. The list of Britain's lifeblood in a 1940's America, adapting with perhaps mixed hopes of return in certain cases, underscored by up to 7,000 sea and land miles from Britain, was a significant though mainly privately-funded show.

The Childrens' Overseas Reception Board, CORB, funded a total of 3,500 children. America (836), Canada (1,532), Australia (576), South Africa (353) and New Zealand (203). The English Speaking Union played an important liaison role with American foster parents. More children would have gone but for predictable shipping losses. Nonetheless, a further 14,000 children took the long haul, privately funded, of whom over 5,000 found homes in America. Like me, with the generosity of a shipping line. Among those who did not opt for an overseas billet were the two princesses, Elizabeth and Margaret. Elizabeth, the present British Queen, joined the ATS, (Auxiliary Territorial Service) and, in khaki battle dress, could be seen wearing her "tin hat" inside sandbagged anti-aircraft gun emplacements operating gun-sights with the crew. Her younger sister did things in the International Girl Guides which became involved in a postwar rehabilitation of both Eastern and Western Europe's children, the destitute and its infirm.

Apart from Churchill's dislike of appearing to pass on children for adoption overseas, evacuees did adjust and parents did not forget them. The British Broadcasting Corporation beamed out from London, personal voice messages from one or the other parent on a regular basis, similar to arrangements made for the armed forces. At a pre-set time, usually in the Children's Hour programme at 5 p.m., one could tune into the BBC and listen to mum or dad saying a few encouraging words right into the living room of one's foster parents.

Among the concerns of parents was the possibility of their child picking up a different accent with resulting loss of their British identity. Might this, conjecture ran, prejudice in some way, their attempts to enter a university back home? For on October 12th, 1941 legislation produced a government Act guaranteeing, if sought, the postwar repatriation of all evacuees sent under the auspices of CORB. No claim could be entertained from those sent privately and my twelve-pound fare sealed my status, but not necessarily my fate. My subsequent emergence from American soil would later be effected by somewhat irregular methods!

As for the parents who had done the sending, there can be no criticism of their action. Frequently there would have been much agonising over decisions. My mother had clearly agonised during the train journey to Liverpool and in the taxi to the Landing Stage and in the air-raid shelter. I, secretly, had agonised right up to stepping onto the boarding gangway thrown across the watery gap between tender and ship. After I'd passed that point, no avenue of escape remained, under any pretext—except sudden illness or death.

Ruth Inglis, in *The Children's War*, again gives us an evaluation of overseas evacuation describing: *"...how parents suffered acutely from Separation Anxiety Syndrome. Mothers particularly, went into a temporary decline after the final parting at docksides while the evacuated child, often experienced an inability to bestow allegiance on one or other culture when he or she reached it. Eventually, evacuees tended to become groups apart and to whom strange things had already happened with others anticipated. It would become the essence of magic experienced each day and could be bewildering or humiliating. Some elements of schizophrenia were also revealed.*

In short, evacuation overseas and to safer areas on British soil would become a gigantic social experiment of far-reaching influence. It did become an unparalleled foundation stone for future child welfare policies in the postwar world. Its legacy, cobbled together so clumsily and desperately in war more than half a century ago, lingers on to the extent that former evacuees are hardly aware of the momentous changes they, as a group, set in motion."

Child benefit payments to mothers were just one of many spin-offs grievously lacking in the stressful times of the depression years and indeed, right up to September 3rd 1939, when the newer war once again would be the prime mover and shaker in tackling social issues.

As the *Baltrover* pulled away further from Britain and further into the Western Hemisphere enemy air activity would increase dramatically in the south east of the country. Research for this book now jogs a fading memory of those times and it is clear that while I was still at home, abstractly aware of what was being decided over my head, the air-fighting on August 8th had reached a quite bloody crescendo for the RAF, with 31 enemy downed.

On August 13th, Germany's date for activating Sea Lion and invasion, it lost 45 planes and of course all their pilots, for the RAF's 13. By all accounts, Göring's vaunted Eagle Day sally to finally destroy the RAF's fighter arm, had been a very messy business indeed. And most allied pilots somehow got back to their airfields using the trains, commandeered private cars, motor cycles and "push-bikes" or just hitch-

The American Option

hiking, to report dutifully to their station commanders for debriefing.

So the battle of and for Britain raged over a land whose hedgerows of flowering may tree, hawthorn and gorse, sectored the whole into the patchwork quilt seen from above, over fields, haystacks, village pubs, church spires, hop kilns and the farm cottages of Kent, Sussex and Hampshire. August 15th saw an apparent maximum German effort with 75 enemy down for the loss of 34 allied fighter planes. So, the tolls were rising. Then, quixotically, a frustrated Germany dropped empty parachutes and radio transmitters over Scotland and middle England—with no human tracks leading from the drops!

While my mother, in and around Orpington, was dashing hither and thither on August 24th, servicing gas masks, building up my modest assets for sea travel and my immediate future in America with scratch visits to the shops, Hitler, down in Bavaria, possibly consulting astrologers, concentrated on tactics new.

That night, certain German pilots lost their way. Instead of on airfields and factories, as directed by Göring, they unloaded their heavies over central London "by mistake." Churchill, thus prompted, ordered a raid on Berlin, a token raid, because of the extreme range for bombing aircraft at that time. The first German civilians were killed. Hitler was incensed. His astrologers had fouled up. His anger was echoed appropriately by Joseph Goebbels, Hermann Göring and the Irish-American, William Joyce aka "Lord Haw Haw." Göring then ordered the first major attack on a British city. He chose Merseyside, 150 bombers, four nights running, until August 31st. In Liverpool's commercial district 160 fires were started. My mother never mentioned if she'd managed to get a train south, back to London before the onslaught and I always assumed that she did. The ship, with me, Philip and around 150 others aboard, had obviously slipped out to sea, probably as the first bombers appeared, and forestalled becoming a chance target and sunk in mid-river. Philip-2 and I had heard nothing.

The new tactics mentioned would almost baffle our radar system by employing feint attacks and combining constant patrols over the English Channel. The strategy worked for a time. It wore down the RAF whose fighter planes were bombed on the ground. Continued losses by this method almost outstripped factory replacements at one point in the fourteen day period to September 7th. Then, enemy fighter losses peaked and the Luftwaffe switched to bombing London. But it was a critical phase and in that sense, it is acknowledged our battle in the air was all but lost.

One week out, on September 7th, perhaps while Philip, I and new friends in mid-Atlantic were playing hide-and-seek around the lifeboats, 625 German aircraft broke through all defenses and set London ablaze. The determined attack signalled the onset of the "London Blitz," but it would take the pressure off our battered airfields. Orpington, the small village railway station of Chelsfield and my mother were eight miles distant on a bee line from London Bridge Station and about fifty miles from the closest surrendered French airfields. I could visualise, from where I might have been sitting, in the library of the ship, that about this time, the second country-wide evacuation of city school children, pregnant women, mothers with under fives, the infirm, the blind which had begun in June, might still be filling the railway stations and sharing their priorities with troop movements.

On that first night 430 civilians died and 1,600 were seriously injured with many thousands made homeless. On the same day British reconnaissance aircraft spotted a large concentration of invasion barges in French rivers and harbours. Chiefs of Staffs issued the code word CROMWELL, a stand-to alert. It remained in force for twelve days during which the army stood ready on beaches and in country lanes to repel a Nazi horde whose recent historical record for bestiality and perversion would only become general currency at the 1945 Nuremberg Trials of some of the chief perpetrators. Those, that is, who had not obtained suicide pills from visitors or jailers.

Aboard ship, in mid-ocean all the passengers were isolated and insulated from events in Europe and the stepping up of the war. In our capsule we had no personal radio contact with the shore and if we'd possessed cellphones then, they would have been confiscated. (Although I still had my gas mask case full of souvenir bomb shrapnel.) For many of us I suppose it was a case of being out of sight and out of mind. By the time we would reach our destination, wherever that was, Britain–and London in particular–would have been at least two weeks into the savagery of Germany's calculated bombing of non-military targets. Göring had astutely gone for the soft option. We would see, in 1945, how such choices had affected Germany's cities. I would see piteous sights. It was far worse than London, Coventry, Swansea, Southampton, Plymouth, Liverpool, Hull or Glasgow had experienced–or, in fact, anything that ordinary British people could have imagined without the help of movie newsreels.

Following the September 7th onslaught on London, Hitler believed Britain must sue for peace. Code SEA LION...invasion, was postponed again from the latest date on September 15th, to September 21st and the RAF bombed all the visible invasion barges and support craft. Despite losses, the Luftwaffe continued to wrestle with Hurricanes and Spitfires long into September.

The days and nights rolled on with nothing untoward happening to the convoy. I do not think that I was overly concerned about my mother at this time. I would have been quite confident that everything associated with my family would be as I had left things...my friends being tutored at a variety of parents' homes, nights in our Anderson shelter, roused by the sound of the milkman's horse at five o'clock–unless we'd been aroused by something else, my

The American Option

mother getting ready for her day's war work, pinning on the ARP badge to a change of blouse or jacket, brushing her long, uncut auburn hair, the plaits done up behind, then applying a curling tongs, pre-heated in the flames of the cooking stove's gas jets, to the fringe over her forehead, putting my two sandwiches and an apple in a bag, train delays, getting a penny bar of Nestlé's milk chocolate from the slot of the railway station's vending machine—I was usually given sixpence for pocket money each day—"beachcombing" on the way home for more interesting shrapnel shapes, tea with a slice of my mother's fantastically light cream and jam sponge, supper, fastidious care with butter and sugar, filling hot water bottles for the shelter bunks, filling kettles of water for emergency use and finally, tossing about finding the best position on unyielding bed springs to tempt sleep. Yes, that I believed, would still be the routine, with just me missing.

But my mother would never overtly let on that she missed either me or my father. The give-away was always one of the several ash trays around the home. There would always be one left unemptied of butts and ash which would give her a feeling, maybe, that he'd only nipped out to the nearest shop for another packet of Players. Now, on board, I tried to concentrate on what was up ahead, without success. I had no reference plots. I believe, today, that my mind would have been, at that time, devoid of all but the vaguest expectations. I could anticipate our entering a port. Beyond that, nothing. In my private space capsule I was heading at about ten knots for a yet-to-be-discovered, unseen planet in the universe. And one morning I landed.

7   Pilgrims to Boston

North Atlantic–September 13th 1940

The manner of the *Baltrover's* approach to the North American continent and whatever port (for there was no official notification to passengers), was slow and gradual and not a bit like the space ship of our boyish imagination.

Oh yes, P.2 and I had both read H.G. Wells and Jules Verne. We could indulge our fantasies and doubtless had done over the previous thirteen days, fed by real stories of the naval ratings and gunners, who'd turned out to be our super pals.

Martha had come into the cabin about 6 a.m. "Wakee wakee...land-ho...rise an' shine for the Baltic Line," she sang out. No sound came from the bottom bunk. I pulled my curtains to one side and clambered down to the deck via the wooden ladder.

"What's happening?" I said, rubbing my eyes and moving over to the porthole.

"We're nearly there," she replied. "Halifax! Here's a cup of tea for each of you." She put the tray down on Philip's box which was flatter than mine.

"Where's Halifax?" I asked. I was vaguely aware I'd noticed the word on a map, somewhere higher up than America, on the Canadian coast.

"Don't worry, you won't be disembarking here. It's a dispersal point for the main convoy we came over with. Only the navy and
army get off here and a new lot come on."

"Where to then, Martha?"

"Weeeell... I *have* heard it could be Boston, this voyage. Don't take my word for it though."

"All this secrecy," I complained. "How many days more, to Boston then?" I could see that P.2 was emerging from the bottom bunk. I handed him the cup of tea.

"What now?" he enquired. "There's no more rolling." He went over to the porthole. "No land, no ships anymore."

"About a couple of days more, I should say," said Martha, answering my query." We'll be picking up the pilot soon. Best get dressed. Mr Huggins said for you to go up on the bridge before breakfast."

Somewhat excited by then, Philip and I collided with each other in our hurry to use the small compact wash-basin and pour in

The American Option

the hot water that Martha always brought in the brass kettle. Cabins on our deck had only a cold water tap. Cabin stewards brought passengers their hot water in the brass kettles with their large spouts which, today, one occasionally spots in antique shops. One proprietor explained to me years later that they were nineteenth-century indoor watering cans for plants. His glittering specimen had a price tag of forty-five pounds!

On the bridge, Mr Huggins was waiting in the chartroom, just behind the wheelhouse, and normally inaccessible to any but the captain and his navigating officers. Thus hidden from the view of habitually curious sailors and stewards, its location was designed to frustrate shipboard rumourmongers bent, maybe, upon gaining a snippet of information in peace or war to further magnify below decks. Early in the century the captain was sole possessor of a key to the door of this sanctum inside which, in tiers of drawers and boxes lay all the mysteries of navigation and maybe even clues to the riddles in the captain's personality.

"Good morning you two," greeted our chubby guardian, resplendent in his number-two uniform, reserved for meeting pilots and other port dignitaries interested in the cargo the ship carried. His bright, number-one uniform would be donned for socialising with passengers or going ashore. His number-three, with its smell of salt spray and Brasso metal polish, was what we'd seen him wearing on the bridge and in whatever dirty weather the Atlantic threw up. My father used the same utilitarian fashion rotation. As for the one item that capped everything, the peaked cap, he would say: "An officer is not an officer without his cap on," and the rule was generally observed aboard purely cargo-carrying merchant ships until the 1960's. About then it seemed, a creeping liberalising of shipboard authority, as reflected by a properly worn uniform (business suit), became a partial consequence of modern ship-management policy—and the loss of the old-style, stern and concerned ship-visiting superintendent who somehow inspired apprehension, attentiveness and appearance. Naval peaked caps adorned with distinctive company badges remain an inferior substitute for plastic hard hat protection of the steel erector. Woven with gilded copper wire, badge art manages always to have an anchor somewhere included to denote the head gear's connection with the sea, an illustrious calling and a once smart image.

At school, headmasters and their prefects appeared to take similar pride. If the round cloth cap with the school badge above the peak, being a gloried school emblem, was stuffed in one's trouser pocket when going public, the punishment meted out by one's betters (so called, we would say), could be frightening and impacting. The later pseudo-macho baseball cap might have been more proudly worn, but then one did not go around usurping the hattery of a baseball player or anyone else. Baseball headwear had specific and practical uses associated with the game. I would soon know about that. For the same reason, one supposes, one did not impersonate a policeman by wearing a replica helmet. That, I'd been warned, could bring a prison sentence.

Captain Wells, wearing his cap with its gilt, oak leaf-encrusted peak exclusively denoting captains rank, passed by on his way into the wheelhouse. He wore this headgear set roughly at the Beatty angle which is a reference to Admiral Beatty, a Great War icon of rakish uniform fashion whose cap would always be tilted left-ward and down. He gave us boys a rare smile and a wave. "We made it you see?" he said over his shoulder. Some of his restrained affability was showing through now that his charge had arrived unscathed, thus far, at least.

Mr Huggins was saying: "Better come in here, boys, then I can tell you some of what you're bursting to know." He smiled broadly. "First of all," pointing to the current working chart laid out on the chart table, "this is us, now." He rested the closed-up points of a pair of brass chart dividers on an indentation in the coastline. "Halifax," he said, "Nova Scotia. Ever heard of the place?"

"Noooo," we chorused.

"Yes, well this is where we part company with a lot of our friends in the convoy we came over with. Some will go into the har-bour ahead, some will branch off and end up in Montréal and some, like us, will go south, to Boston in the state of Massachusetts, er, America."

"And that's where *we* go?"

"That's where we go," said Mr Huggins.

"Are we supposed to be safe now, then? I mean, no more convoy and signalling? Because I want to say goodbye to 'Jock' and 'Terry,' two of the signallers."

"Well, in that case, you'd better get going. They're leaving us here to join a return convoy in a few days. 'No,' confirmed the chief officer, no coastal convoys. We'll be in neutral waters in a few hours. Then, you've got people meeting you. I don't know who though."

We went down to the saloon for breakfast and on our way, we just had time to see the naval signallers and one of the gunners sit-ting on a hatch.

"Hey," we called, "goodbye...thanks for all the lemonade and chocolate and things."

"Goodbye P.1 and 2," they grinned, "Yes, you can pay us later," explained Jock, the tall one.

"You bet, Jock," I said, stoutly, "And watch yourselves with the girls on your next ship!" A rolled newspaper banged us on the head. We shook hands all round and, of course, we never met again. We each said we'd write from wherever we ended up, but I cannot remember having done so. They, along with Martha, Mr Huggins and "Sparks," the wireless operator, out of a whole shipload of people, they alone are recalled. Yet many, many people would have spoken to us over the previous thirteen days. And we'd enjoyed plenty of boat drills and making sure the lifejacket tapes were securely fastened about the slender waists of girls. Perhaps, at twelve and three months, I still retained different priorities. I was not, at that time particularly bothered with self analysis and the journal, which my mother started me on, never saw England again.

All the passengers lined the rails and bulwarks on the *Baltrover's* promenade deck as the pilot cutter, with our army and navy pals and passengers we'd made friends with, drew away toward the port of Halifax some three miles off. We two boys thought we'd get a better view of the proceedings from the boat deck and were thrilled to have our waves answered, almost privately, from that vantage point.

When the pilot cutter became just a black dot and the ship, each link of its anchor cable squeezed over the lip of the spurling pipe with successive thuds, finally weighed anchor and gathered way on its southern course, we turned away, sadly. Those men had kept everyone laughing and joking all the way from Liverpool with their breezy, good-natured service humour. We'd had army jokes and navy jokes and our wireless operator and other ship's staff had donated their Merchant Navy brands. Chief officer, Mr Huggins, unofficial staff captain, had ruled our small village of around 200 souls like the benevolent mayor of Toytown in the favourite childrens' hour programme of that name—which we might never listen to again. Suddenly, it all became just too awful to think about. A new and less friendly phase of the voyage was about to begin. Had begun.

We both descended rather miserably, it must be said, to our cabin. We heard six bells being struck on the bridge bell before noises in the accommodation blotted out the chimes. It was 11 a.m. In that mood, we moped about until the first sitting for lunch gonged out and we slipped in and occupied our table, deserted now except for Mr Huggins whenever he could join us. Ghosts of those now landed in Canada still sat in their places. On our way, we'd noticed a few ships of an England-bound convoy had already formed up as the remaining landmarks and shore line of the port faded astern. Canadian sea gulls swooped and quarrelled over the galley refuse in our wake. I wish I'd thought to send a letter home from Halifax. I'd had time to scribble at least a few lines. Regrets, regrets. My father had always told me not to build any. How did one avoid building regrets about anything? But, I saw his point, right then.

With many of our friends gone and, since we'd now reached North America, the short two day voyage to Boston proved something of an anti-climax. I began to feel apprehensive; unsettled. Perhaps Philip too. Although he generally said little about his feelings. On-board blackout precautions remained in place. Stewards entered cabins ensuring portholes were closed and "dogged down" the heavy circular steel plates called "deadlights." They served a double purpose–if a porthole glass cracked or shattered ingress of water would be minimised, a sinking slowed. And lighting up or smoking a cigarette on deck was a punishable offense.

Climbing the stairways to the main-deck again and, as if to accompany my somber mood, we heard the intimidating groan of the ship's siren. One prolonged blast at intervals not exceeding two minutes, says the sailor's bible on such matters. Fog! Opening the door onto the deck we were enveloped in swirling, wet mist. The surrounding sea was blotted out and Philip's mouth worked soundlessly as another blast echoed around the lifeboats swung out on their davits for speedy evacuation. Moving to the rail it was possible to make out the water fizzing and hissing along the steel plates before merging into the maelstrom generated by the ship's propellers then disappear dimly astern in an ever-widening wake. We didn't seem to be going very fast.

Philip said he would read a book in the library. I made for the wireless room at the end of the boat deck where I could discuss induction coils for an improved crystal set with the "Sparks." The siren groaned on through the afternoon every two minutes so that its intrusive regularity became noticeable only when it eventually stopped. Then, usual shipboard noises returned and one would need to be reminded not to shout in conversation.

Next day, the sun was bright and warm, the sea rippled, shyly exhibiting a few white specks. If I'd been able to gauge the strength of the wind in those days, it would have been about a Beaufort Scale 2. As it was, one got the feeling that here was an American Indian Summer. The ship was then in the latitude of Maine–September 14th. We'd been slowed by the fog but, Mr Huggins' estimated time of arrival at the Boston pilot gave 8 a.m. next morning, the 15th. The ship seemed to have a charmed life. Yes, there had been emergencies crossing the Atlantic, thuds in the night, two non-practice calls to lifeboat stations, the gunners firing off live rounds, a bit of noise and Martha had ordered us to sleep in our life-jackets after that.

With hindsight, we ought not to have relaxed, for U-boats would soon be sinking neutrals in American waters–and some American owned and crewed ships flew the ensign of Liberia, a de facto American "colony" on the West African coast. Naval escorts, there were none. The main trans-Atlantic convoys took priority. Later in the war, American coastal convoys with escorts, were approved by the American Congress after a qualifying tonnage had been sent to the bottom. Some evidence of that body's more pragmatic stance in the face of hard-core isolationism and some choice erudition by Churchill, had secured for Britain on September 3rd, fifty surplus destroyers from the Great War. They would be paid for by granting America cer-

The American Option

tain long-term leases on British West Indies possessions when they would be transformed into American military bases.

The more reasonable arrangement, termed Lend Lease, a form of buy-now-pay-later deal to be signed by President Roosevelt on December 31st, assured us of more up-to-date war material. He would say then that America would, henceforth, be the arsenal of democracy. As for the mothballed, future Royal Navy convoy escorts of an earlier Great War well, the mouths of gift horses should not be looked into too deeply. The four-funnelled veterans would prove their weight in leased territory in America's back yard. For now though, the *Baltrover* stayed lucky and we picked up our harbour pilot on schedule.

That morning, Philip and I dressed a little more carefully than had been our custom during the days at sea. I went for a full Beckenham College dress rehearsal and looked fairly smart (I thought), in the school's colours of black and green. Philip opted for less flamboyance in a Harris tweed jacket. His greeters may have been briefed to look out for Philip wearing brown Harris tweed, perhaps overly confident they would recognise the cloth in a crush of disembarking bodies. I wasn't anticipating being picked out of the crowd. I could not think who might be looking for a black-coated school boy with a gas mask container full of substituted bomb shrapnel over his shoulder.

I can remember the ship being manoeuvred between the wharves and jetties of Boston Harbour, everyone were out of their cabins for early breakfasts and lining the rails. I can remember joining a queue and being moved along in it toward the place where the gangway would be rigged. The ship, in slow motion, closed the gap between it and a crowded quayside, the propeller wash stirring up the harbour rubbish including a dead American sea gull. I do not remember saying: "goodbye and thank you" to anyone, but I must have. Such automatic social graces would have been drilled into me long before by my mother. But it is worrying to imagine that I might not have and been swept up in the general mêlée. To Philip, however, I had certainly said goodbye, about the time he gave me his spare copy of a passport photograph, and wrote on the back: "With my best wishes."

I think it must have been at the point when the gangway was being hauled into position. I was somewhere near, looking down to where its foot would be secured and men were there with strong arms waiting to grasp hold of the roped stanchions. I saw my father then, looking up and waving and smiling. He had on a dark overcoat and the kind of felt, trilby hat he habitually wore when at home. It was difficult to take in, my father being here, in Boston! He was supposed to be at sea or in Canada about then. Where were the people I was to stay with? Then, near him, I saw another person wave and look straight at me, a woman wearing a hat and spectacles—not unlike my mother, but taller. Then a boy and girl about my age, waved shyly. I waved back. What was going on? The gangway was rigged at last and I got carried along like I'd been fifteen days before in Liverpool. Down I went, my gas mask case over my shoulder, my trunk trustfully forgotten.

At the bottom, the passengers were guided along by barricades to a point where officials were seated and, ultimately, with my father's hand gripping my shoulder, I was being introduced to grown-ups, "Uncle" Roy, "Aunt" Elinor, son and daughter, Harold and Audreta Sheldon. And that, dear reader, was that, until I remember riding in the back seat of a large Packard-8 racing toward I knew not what. My brown trunk? I imagine my father would have got aboard somehow, thanked Captain Wells, Mr Huggins, Martha and organised my single piece of luggage. For him, it would have been a nostalgic return aboard a ship he'd known for so long in peacetime and perhaps wonder if it would survive a return voyage to Liverpool. Well, we know it did—only to be sent to a shipbreaker's yard some years after the war's end. A very lucky ship indeed and survived by at least one picture, done in oils by the old Estonian Bosun when on the ship's pre-war, Baltic run. The picture was painted using only the colours available from the paint locker on board. Regretfully it passed out of family ownership some years after the war ended.

The longish drive south from Boston in the big Packard did not seem long when I look back. We were dispersed thus: myself, Audreta and Harold in the back, my father, and my new Aunt Elinor in front with Uncle Roy driving. My brown trunk was presumably in the luggage compartment called the "trunk" in American idiom. We stopped at one point for lunch at a Howard Johnson roadhouse, a place of wonder to me with more food set before us than I could deal with. Soon, my new big brother and sister introduced me to the twenty-five or so flavours of ice cream on the soda-fountain menu. Harold would recall, many years later, how his nose had somehow entered a double-filled cone of chocolate-mint-chip, nudged there by my father accidentally on purpose and so rocking the dignity of the sampling process. The exotic mix would become my choice forever more in honour of big brother Hal who, after retirement from IBM, died a few years ago. He was the brother my parents couldn't give me while Audreta became the perfect sister of my American experience.

The remainder of the journey took us through New Hampshire, Connecticut and New York before the car crunched up the driveway of a Tudor-style, brick, chalet home at 90 Park Avenue, Verona, New Jersey.

"Everyone out," commanded Audreta, who was nearly thirteen. She'd been in centre position for too long being teased and mussed about by brother Hal, then a mature sixteen. Not even our restrained finger-touching under the travelling rug had soothed her

The American Option

s.s. Baltrover, *London*
"...and perhaps wonder if it would survive a return voyage to Liverpool..."

impatience to change places at some fuel stop. But the car had had enough petrol! My brand new Uncle Roy would prove efficient in many other matters.

"Here we are then," said Aunt Elinor, brightly, "c'mon Stanley," she called to my father, seated on the wide bench seat in front. "You surely know your way around here after all these years. We have to get Philip's trunk out of the trunk," she laughed. Uncle Roy, who'd talked little while handling all the driving, must have been pretty tired although I understood they'd driven to Boston the day before and checked into an hotel so to be up early for the ship's arrival. He and Harold between them had hold of my worldly possessions and were halfway through the wooden, iron-studded front door. All these announcements and pronouncements following my arrival in my new home, are remembered.

What I could not know at the time, but which became a glow of hope as September 15th advanced by the wrist watches of Spitfire and Hurricane pilots, was the astonishing tally of German aircraft they were destroying. A kind of pigeon shoot, by some accounts. This was happening even as we, in *Baltrover*, were eating our hasty, final breakfast on board. As we later, in the Packard, were progressing through New England, the skies of old England in the south became the battlefield of a new Waterloo.

To the British people, gazing skyward from below, the dog-fights were wild and punishing. And the Royal Air Force gave no quarter and apparently none was asked. Enemy and allied planes alike fell in smoking, fiery, ruin into the sea; on the beaches; on the farmlands. Today, the remains of their machines, driven deep into marsh or sand on impact, continue to occasionally reappear, snagged by fishing nets, farm machinery, dug out, salvaged and human remains buried with military honours.

Göring's familiar dependence on the dreamland, his congenital vanity and the misnomer of the word invincibility to describe his air force, ultimately sealed Germany's fate in the Second World War. But what, in purely material terms, had September 15th meant for Germany and an invasion plan only postponed, not cancelled, to again be given a green light on September 16th and again on the 21st?

It does appear that Hitler had based his expectations on a slowed British aircraft production due to bombing, but replacing the RAF's fighter losses never posed a problem—a shortage of pilots always was. Between August 24th and September 7th, fourteen days, 103 pilots had been killed and 128 wounded. By then, experienced pilots were either dead or exhausted. Few from the training centres were battle-worthy. In the situation thus facing Britain, radar, with its graphic early warning system, would become decisive, making possible relatively late takes-offs from airfields to intercept intruders. On the 15th, therefore, it was as though the German pilots saw ghosts of Spitfires and Hurricanes rising up before them where few should have been flyable. And 52 confirmed enemy aircraft were shot down (185 claimed at the time) for the loss of 26 allied aircraft. "Allied," at that time, would have been, British, American, Polish, Czech, French, Dutch, Belgian and Empire pilots plus the ground crews of each nation. One could call it a damn good show!

Next day, September 16th, remains a blank, but some group photographs show the family and my father with me wearing, for probably the last time, the English schoolboy uniform of Beckenham College my mother had so proudly provided at no mean cost. The black school blazer with its green trimming and breast pocket coat of arms, looks fine. My three-quarter length socks look a bit uneven and wrinkled. I must have forgotten the elastic we boys would use, concealed under the tops. The school tie? I don't seem to have quite got the hang of the knot. So, there we all are, with Audreta holding her darling Binkie, the black spaniel, and my father, in his go-ashore suit, smiling and revealing a recent dental casualty.

I discovered the reason for my father's happy presence in Boston. His ship was in Montréal. He'd flown down to New York, rendezvoused with the Sheldons and accompanied them to Boston. How all this had coincided with the *Baltrover's* voyage I am now unlikely ever to know. I accepted his remarkable ability to overcome every obstacle where our small family was concerned, without ques-

My suddenly-acquired slightly elder sister plus Binkie.
"...Everyone out, commanded Audreta..."

Dear "Aunt" Elinor
(Courtesy: A.M. Pape-Sheldon)
"...We have to get Philip's trunk out of the trunk, she laughed..."

tion. And, sadly now, I did not enquire of him the circumstances in detail. All of his efforts on my behalf were rather badly taken for granted. Whatever my difficulties I knew things would always come right. They always seemed to have. He was my dad, wasn't he?

He stayed on a further day before returning to his ship. There would have been discussion over a choice of school, I imagine, and he would have been advised by the Family on that one while, perforce, having to leave the details to them. He had done all he could for a time.

With the Battle of Britain all but won, it is recorded that Göring planned to fly over London himself in a bomber, for a look-see, but that physically he was too fat to get through the aircraft's entrance hatch. In Verona, we'd all gone on an outing to somewhere I cannot recall now. My father would fly back to Montréal next day. I am photographed, having aged enormously in two days, wearing my first pair of long trousers my mother had bought and packed the

"...wearing, for probably the last time..."

day before we left for Liverpool just over two weeks earlier. She may have said, as she laid them carefully in my brown trunk: "I won't see you on your thirteenth birthday Philip, but all boys go into long trousers on that day. Get your father to take a photograph and send it to me." And I probably got an advance kiss of commemoration on my head and my hair patted back into place. At that period in my life I shirked demonstrations of affection toward my mother. Kissing was definitely out and I reserved my hugs for when it was nearly too late; when she was old and very ill. Thank God she was able to still respond, if barely. And this record of events ought to have been written forty years ago. But there I am in Aunt Elinor's snapshot after our return, wearing those long trousers. Paula is in it, the girl next door or rather across the road, soon to symbolise repressed, teen passions. She endowed the brown paper bag of groceries hugged to her breasts and emphasised by a white sweater, with new meaning and promise. There was still 8 months to go before my thirteenth birthday. "War 'n wimmin" advanced things remarkably.

The 17th marked my father's departure and a visit to a department store in the nearby city of Newark. There, I was kitted-out in what my Aunt Elinor, with great foresight and wisdom, evidently considered a more appropriate fashion for an American school than my Beckenham College, school uniform. I would soon see what she meant and now, looking back, I can understand how I would have been the object of some intense, perhaps embarrassing interest though not unkindly curiosity. Either or both could well have delayed my assimilation into whichever school might then have been the Family's preferred choice and, not least, a school's acceptance of me. A sort of blind date for each of us, one might say.

Allowing for a small time difference of about two hours ahead of American Eastern Standard Time, while I was trying on shirts, long pants and jackets in the Newark department store, naval records now recount, in tragic detail, the terrible scenes unfolding in the Atlantic, about three days steaming due east of Halifax. There, the Ellerman liner, *City of Benares*, in convoy to Halifax—as had been the *Baltrover* four days earlier—was among the vessels torpedoed and sunk. Seventy three evacuees had taken passage in her. One wonders how might we, then in the security and home environment of 90 Park Avenue, have felt if news of the sinking had been a normal peacetime feature of the 6 p.m., CBS news (Columbia Broadcasting System); perhaps with Walter Winchell reading it and sponsored by the famed and beneficial Jurgen's Lotion.

But we did not know and his sponsor has outlived him, the product still on store shelves, prompting one to marvel at the longevity of beauty preparations.

8   Montclair Academy

It could have been the next day, September 18th, that I was ushered into the registrar's office of Montclair Academy at the top of Bloomfield Avenue. Perhaps it was the initial visit, to be assessed, signed in and allocated to a class. I may even have been introduced to the headmaster and owner of the school at that point, Dr Walter Head. Or I may have enjoyed a week's grace before commencing one of the more interesting experiences of my life. Well, at the time it would have been full of interest. Looking back, it proved momentous.

Assuming that I'd been given a week to aclimatise to my new surroundings and my new clothes and my wonderfully equipped bedroom, study, sanctum, and the meals and the household routines and Audreta's piano lessons, and her occasional attempts not to smile because of her teeth braces, and the next-door neighbours and Hal's roughhousing–I imagine I would have been reasonably prepared to have my knowledge tested by various schoolmasters.

I discovered I was an eighth grader in the Upper School. This order of merit was about right for my age group and it is the mathematics master I remember well on that first day. I parked myself in a chair whose right (or was it left?), arm curved around one's front forming a flat surface for writing. This democratic individuality was a nice change from being one of a class of sufferers in row upon row of forms. And there wasn't an inkwell in sight that I recall. Ballpoints were ten years into the future. Karl Billhardt would have done his level best to judge the extent of my expertise with, for example, algebra, fractions and long-division. I believe I would have acquitted myself acceptably in the last two. To this day, however, I regard algebra with distaste and suspicion. It does not appear to play any part in keeping the world spinning on its axis which, when all is said and done, is the single most important thing in life. I do not remember feeling sorry for Karl Billhardt at that time. I do now.

Within the first school week, I would have sampled all the subjects with which my assessment had suggested I was familiar. They were not numerous. I'd been coming on quite well with engineering and architectural drawing. The Academy didn't teach that. I'd had no French or Latin and Welsh didn't count, even if I'd ever been good at that ancient and mysterious tongue. A history track record was invalid. I would now begin again with American history. I cannot remember having taken science or chemistry at Beckenham Technical College but somehow, I knew about crystal wireless sets and model steam engines, and land irrigation mock-ups, having built them. In the use of English and English literature I found I could hold my head up high having won a few prizes for essay-writing. Among the diplomas and citations, one sponsor of an essay, Cadbury's Chocolate Company, must have liked what I'd written about their esteemed product. Its carton of chocolate bars had kept my family going for a week.

By the week's end I had met Claude Monson (Latin), Charles Jaillet (French, Spanish, counselling), William Miller (science and chemistry), William Avery Barras (English department head), Howard Parker (English literature) and, Karl Billhardt has already been mentioned. I do not remember being taught math by John Vail, but paths would cross when I made the photographic staff of the school's year book. John Vail became faculty adviser to the student-produced *Octopus* whose 1942 edition would see a few of my pictures staring back at me. Ed Van Brunt, coach of all sports, would come later. Apart from Charles Jaillet, I would not have made much impression other than that I was a new boy dropped in from a different planet. But their names, personalities and teaching styles are remembered.

About this time too, someone felt it could be a good idea while my memory of events were still fresh, to give a talk to the school about how I came to be there. Suspicion falls on William Miller since he was assistant headmaster and presided over the boarders and it was they who, as a special after-dinner treat, would be a captive test audience to hear my maiden speech. Maybe, if I did well, I would be invited to repeat the performance to a day-time, whole school gathering in the study hall. But it didn't come to that.

Walden House was the venue for my debut as a public speaker. Both boarders and some of the faculty lived and dined there. The occasion was not unblemished. I ate nervously. Despite the notes, neatly typed by my Uncle Roy's secretary in New York, I read too quickly, glanced up at my rapt, curious audience as I'd been told to do, lost my place on the page, apologised, found the place, reached words that said "The End," sat down to boisterous clapping, fist thumps on the table and clattering plates—and felt sick.

The content of the talk, now unearthed, was generally the same as already narrated earlier in these pages. Some details are at variance. There were 40 ships in our convoy not the 25 referred to on page 66; two days out from Liverpool the first ship was torpedoed, naval escorts depth-charged the U-boat; it came to the surface then sank. It seems the weather was not good and precluded indulging in many of the deck games until near the voyage end when cricket claimed the attention of the male passengers led by the officers. I told my audience, demonstrating great patience I imagine, that "I am very happy in my new home and everyone is so very kind, but if I had my way I would have stayed home with my mother." Therein lies a small clue to the regrets I'd begun to feel on that first morning after sailing. But I'd made my choices; taken up my option. Why waste time hindsighting, a luxury denied most who lived through a war. I ended the dinner ordeal with: "My impression of your country is that everyone is so sympathetic to our cause, which I consider is a just cause, but I certainly hope you will remain in peace."

In reality, of course, Winston Churchill's hopes were in a somewhat different context while in the American hinterland, war would remain a distant aberration providing newspapermen with abundant copy. Great Britain's ordeal at that time would assail American senses, stiffen resolve, chip away at a former isolationist viewpoint and resulted in a steady stream of home-knitted "comforts" for Merchant Navy men and general forces. Food parcels and a formidable army of women in shipyards, who'd forsaken saucepans in favour of welding torches, just followed on naturally. Via such activities, war slowly encroached upon the American conscience and perhaps prepared it for the wider conflict with Japan.

Following the talk, written up in the school's newspaper, *The Montclair News*, M. Jaillet, in his official, extra-curricular role as students' counselor must have thought I was worthy of some interest and got me going well with his mother tongue. The counselling bit was beneficial too. In that guise, I was invited to his home, over a period, introduced to his wife and partook of French-style cooking. I particularly remember the potatoes. Baked, as round as golf balls and about the same size. I decided there would have been a special tool to make spherical potatoes. He professed difficulty remembering my guardian's name, Sheldon, and would jokingly jog the memory with: "Bomb... Ah!... Shell-(bomb)-don." One of his hobbies was the collecting of picture advertisements from magazines which he considered to have artistic merit. He had filled several leather-bound volumes with examples of the adman's art. (Recently, I thought to emulate his objective and informative pastime with, to date, three volumes!)

In a later English school, as a boarder then, Charles Jaillet's counterpart would be my sort of live-aboard housemaster filling a quaintly beneficial role in the English educational system. A housemaster's "day job," as compared to his after-school activity, could be one's math, Latin, sport's coach or any other master. As a confidant to lonely boys, who might receive beatings from a prefect concerned that some misdemeanour signalled a sure drift downward into moral turpitude, the housemaster could be an antidote. A beaten and thus chastened miscreant would be invited into the housemaster's cosy study, usually on a rotation basis, although if a wave of rebellion had been discerned by sneaks, there might be two or three of us sitting together feeling homicidal. Seated in comfortable chairs like at home, we would consume tea, crumpets and jam around the coal fire and have our vigour and spirits restored, murderous inclinations

The American Option

dampened and a sense of security maintained until released to our parents at term's end. A curious and sometimes contradictory system indeed! But none of that would compare to being taken into the home of one's teacher—and fed! As an out-of-school activity it is now better understood and appreciated with the benefit of time.

Now though, still in America, an outing to the 1939 New York World's Fair one weekend may have been designed as a partial antidote to the strangeness of my surroundings and the people I was meeting. I never felt that I was being paraded as a newcomer in the family but friends and neighbours, their sons and daughters were expressing polite interest in my sudden appearance among them. I would discover that Americans do have that indefinable quality of genuine interest in and helpfulness to strangers. Doubtless a legacy of their own times as early settlers and immigrants in an often forbidding land.

The Family had been once to the Fair, over in Flushing, Queens, across the East River, an arm of the great Hudson River divided by the island of Manhattan. With the second visit, probably to further ease any residual effects of my resettlement, Harold and Audreta were getting a second bite at the cherry and wished to demonstrate sibling unity by forking out dimes for large ice-cream cones. It was moving, acceptable and I was profuse with thanks despite the advice of my father who, at an early briefing at home to forewarn me on American manners, had said: "They're a bit different to us here in England Philip. Americans don't say please-and-thank-you's in the same way we do. You'll get used to it."

Well, of course, I already had in a sense—from the films I'd seen. George Raft, James Cagney, Joan Crawford, Mickey Rooney, Buster Keaton, Barbara Stanwick, Clark Gable...they'd all been my tutors. Insipid thanks was rarely in their scripts.

There had already been one forgettable experience to confound me and possibly acutely embarrass all within hearing although not I it seems. It had happened on the very day of my arrival. At some point, dutifully omitting the redundant "thank you" for some generous gesture given by aunt or uncle, my father urged: "Now, say 'thank you' to Aunt Elinor."

"But you said I shouldn't say thank you in America."

Knowing my father, a plausible explanation of a screwed-up briefing would have been instant. I think.

The parklands of Flushing, Queens, were studded with the Fair's grand events and inside the buildings one could gaze on the magical properties of a magnetic hot plate with an egg quietly frying on its cold surface (forerunner of the microwave?), or other electronic wizardry that would become commonplace and in an auditorium, hear the dulcet tones of Vaughn Monroe. Outside, one could test one's nerve in a simulated parachute drop, or visit the astounding planetarium or head for the edge of the universe in advance of a latter-day Star Wars screenplay. Then I discovered the American frankfurter in a bun for the first time. Hot dog, *that* was a day and half!

I think I could emphasise just a little that for me, a bare three weeks from having left my own bedroom in my parents' bungalow in Chelsfield, Kent, there was really very little in my new home that I could relate to my former surroundings and daily life. If I was in the kitchen of 90 Park Avenue, I would see a refrigerator opened for the first time ever. Our first fridge would be dated 1954. Out of the "ice-box" as it was still called, before the evening meal, always came ice cubes... (a) for Uncle Roy's bourbon-on-the-rocks or (b) to be crushed up in a sturdy glass container with an ice pick plunger acti- vated by hand through a metal screw cover. I managed to destroy this kitchen appliance in the first week of being assigned, on a regular basis, to this essential mealtimes task. Harold cleaned up the floor of broken glass and blood. I made noises of regret and Audreta handled the Elastoplast. I never returned to that duty.

"The crushed ice," Audreta informed me on the first occasion I saw this demonstrated, "is to go over the bunny-food."

"What's that?"

"Don't you know? It's stuff like lettuce and radishes and young onions and...here, try some of this." She plucked a Ritz cracker from a packet, took a knife and smeared on a yellowish sub- stance.

"What is it?" I asked, sniffing the generous offering.

"Go on," she urged, reminiscent of Eve pushing Adam to take a bite of the apple. "It's peanut butter."

Putting peanuts, which I knew existed, and butter, which I knew was wholesome, altogether, I chanced a bite and had a new world revealed.

On successive school days, it appeared that Audreta, after breakfast, was our lunch time, sandwich-maker. My transportation into American life then really began with the peanut butter and marmalade sandwiches and bologna and gherkin sandwiches which she expertly packed in grease-proof paper to sustain me, Harold and herself in our school lunch breaks. Shortly after the issuing of this bounty our ways would separate for the day. With Audreta and Harold in the back seat, Aunt Elinor would drive Uncle Roy to Montclair Railway Station for his New York City train, then she would drop off her other two pas- sengers at Montclair's College High School. The school was co-educa- tional.

For my school, I would walk to the trolley stop nearest to Park Avenue, in Verona, and ride to the top of the hill on Bloomfield Avenue. There was then a suitably inspiring walk past the bronze, Montclair Academy name plate on the stone entrance pillars, up a series of steps, five more into the arched, medieval-styled portico and so into the second Academy building on the site, erected in 1910. Boys only.

The American Option

It had begun life in a large wooden, clapboard private home with around seventy students in 1887, becoming The Montclair Military Academy in 1891 to prepare graduates for the armed services, but chiefly, explains an official history, to expand student attendance and revenues. Military drills and small arms training were impressionable adjuncts to academic pursuits while a resident colonel of the armies taught science, history and military tactics. A form of uniform was worn until the military identity was dropped from the curriculum after the Great War.

I wonder if my parents had previously sent the Family a photograph of me wearing the black, green-edged blazer creating perceptions that suggested they apply to the English-style Academy for a place when I arrived? Could I, perhaps, have assimilated even faster in the co-ed, College High School, with Audreta and Harold and other mysterious females? In the end, the Academy did me proud. Castellated at roof-top level, it had the aged appearance of an English country mansion, and just as durable. Sadly, it became a victim of the wrecker's ball in 1964 being replaced with, some say, a more functional design. I expect that is true. And there is a William Avery Barras Library!

Montclair Academy—1940
(From the book: Within These Halls *by Robert D.B. Carlisle)*
"...had the appearance of an English country mansion..."

Montclair

In the home, the living room radio (now translated from "wireless"), was a large affair standing three feet from the floor and filled the high, cathedral roof and the pseudo minstrel gallery at one end, with grand modulated sounds hard to beat even today. At the other end, the natural stone fireplace could throw out heat from the four foot logs resting on fire irons. The internal stone chimney extended up and disappeared into the shadows of the roof. In a corner, stood a piano at which Audreta would practice. The sound I remember best is the still popular *On Blueberry Hill*. But *Elmer's Tune and Tangerine* were also in her repertoire and for that recollection I know she will be pleased!

Merging into a dining room routine so unlike what I was used to, is also a significant memory. At home my mother and I were two. When my father was on leave we were three. Only at the traditional English tea time would more be seated at the oak, draw-leaf table and then, we would have a merry, talkative interlude demolishing all the favoured tomato and ham sandwiches and the home-made pastries eased down with countless cups of tea. All the best china and cutlery was in use. My mother was an informed conversationalist and my father a practiced raconteur with a store of tales to tell. Such gatherings of family, friends and table-talk ranging the whole world have yet to be equalled.

90 Park Avenue, Verona, Montclair, New Jersey, USA
"In a corner stood a piano..."

The American Option

Now, I was seated at evening meal times at the long polished table in the dining room adjoining the kitchen, with my new brother and sister, aunt and uncle and we had all undertaken some duty in the preparation of the meal. For a start, Uncle Roy would do the cooking most evenings, a role he took seriously. Arriving home from his Manhattan office, he would pour a bourbon onto ice cubes and so fortified, stand in the kitchen until it was time to serve up. Aunt Elinor would have prepared all the vegetables, Harold was master of the ice crusher in my place and stacked it over the bunny-food, Audreta and I set the table. A weak link there, I remember for, on being seated, the head-of-the-household's dedication and Amens recited, the meat carved, dishes passed around, then the vegetables, then the sauces and so on, someone was bound to ask for the salt, the butter knife, the gravy spoon etc. Then an accusing cry: "Who laid the table?" from Harold or, "Who laid the table?" from Audreta–looking hard at me, and followed, perhaps, with: "Well, *you* go and get it then!"

To save valuable time and the chef's patience, my aunt would leave her place at the bottom end of the table and search for the missing items in the sideboard drawers. Napkins and napkin rings sometimes became bones of contention: "That's not my napkin!" "S'not mine eether!" "An' it's not eether...it's eyether!" etc., etc. With meals increasingly eaten by the young using one hand on the way to somewhere, the family dinner table has largely lost its place in the family learning cycle. Pity.

Washing up and drying was handled fairly even-temperedly between us three youngsters. Aunt and Uncle would retire to the lounge, switch on the radio and somehow romantically share the out-size, stuffed armchair opposite. A news commentator might later try to compete with my uncle's sonorous breathing. We three kids would disperse into our rooms and tackle homework, returning later to sit on the large sofa and drink Coca-Cola from ice-filled glasses. But we each had small radios in our rooms and more often than not, would end the evening listening to some favourite big band sounds, drama or a comedy series. Let's see...Jimmy Dorsey, Glenn Miller. Vocalists: Vaughn Monroe, Ann Shelton, Frank Sinatra, Jo Stafford. Then the *Hit Parade...Tchaikovsky's Piano Concerto in C-flat major*, at the top three weeks running over Christmas 1941! Radio shows: *The Shadow*, ("The weed of crime bears bitter fruit, The Shadow knows!" followed by extended, maniacal laughter), Superman. Comedians: stingy Jack Benny, his wife, Mary Livingstone and their side-kick, Rochester.

And so went the weekdays. A very different life to the one I had left behind so short a time before but to which my thoughts returned in quieter moments or were arrested by the sudden appearance of an envelope with an English stamp, my mother's writing and a sticker with the censor's printed number. Inside, the text, minus a few blotted out words or lines of some minor indiscretion, would be avidly read; passed around; the envelope itself scrutinised; Harold's stamp collecting magnifier hovering over the stamps. My mother, however, was particularly wary of the censor, as she was in most things. The instances of censor attentions were rare. Women, I would learn, are really quite wary creatures. As I got older I would have included wariness among the differences between men and women in addition to breasts.

Served, therefore, by the Clipper airmail service not only I, but all my American family, became personally involved in another European war. At the time, in September or October 1940, they were a bit over one year to becoming militarily involved. Meanwhile, at 90 Park Avenue in respectable Verona, New Jersey, USA, tales of Germany's aerial blitzkrieg against the ordinary people of London, and the then unequal Atlantic contest against a fearful underwater enemy, filtered through to five people enjoying an amazing normality of daily and nightly life. For, via my mother's written accounts of a northern sky red, not from sunset but a city on fire end-to-end, we would learn how she'd stood on the toilet seat to reach the window and viewed the scene from hell eight miles distant.

Via my father, in a more direct sense, during his visits to check me out, the family would learn of oil tankers and men incinerated in an instant or more slowly drowned; of hospital ships sent to the bottom due to a U-boat commander's confusion and, out of my hearing of course, how he feared he might get "the hammer" by a simple law of averages.

Some of the aura of death among the innocents would invade the family in the house opposite. Paula Dean lived there. About Audreta's age, therefore a bit older than I, her father was a *New York Times* reporter and journalist and we would glean a few of the less printable facts regarding the main players in Berlin.

I think I may have taken to Paula as the year drew to a close and we all got more wound up in the campaigning to elect a new president, Republican, Wendell Willkie—or retain the incumbent, democrat Franklin Delano Roosevelt. Photographs show us, with my father, during a visit, wearing the outsize lapel pins and badges of the favoured candidate. At school, we would compete in amassing and somewhere pinning, the widest selection of "winner" slogans. A large round one in support of Willkie, cheekily stated: "I WANNA BE A CAPTAIN TOO." Fortunately, it may now be said with hindsight, FDR was re-elected for an historic third term. And Paula Dean went on to becoming more and more attractive and showed me many, many more differences which, for one reason or another, still exist between the sexes.

About this time too, amid the growing pains of my sexual awakening, came the American hamburger which, by filling my stomach with roll, minced beef, gherkin and tomato sauce, managed, by a consuming of energy by digestion, to corral an unruly stampede

November 1940
Campaigning for a new president.
"...a large round one in support of Willkie..."

into unfamiliar territory. Harold was a master of this technique in assuaging the needs of the inner man. The family, perhaps returning late from a trip somewhere, would sanction Harold, at nearly 17, to drive the big Packard to a nearby "White Castle" hamburger drive-by. He would return with a brown paper bag filled with square meals in round buns and be first with the catchup bottle. Sleep would be dreamless. catchup seems an adequate anti-aphrodisiac agent when used in large quantities.

Returning to vestiges of wartime correspondence, regrettably, only one letter survives. One from my Aunt Elinor to my father, back aboard his ship soon after I'd arrived in Verona and a picture postcard to me from my mother. The picture is of Churchill, striding out from Number 10, Downing Street. It seems my parents were disinclined, in talk, to dwell upon or return to that part of our lives. My mother, however, retainer of sentimental relics, would in any case have needed to circumvent my father, opposer of "clutter." We would one day, all of us, call ourselves supremely lucky, not fortunate, to have come through as two families. "Providence ought not to be tempted by too much analysis and dissection," might have been their guiding thought.

So it is left to me to retrace what I am able from those years of war; from scraps of remembered conversations; old passports; train tickets; a clothes brush; a bible; a shoe bag with a Cash's name tape still firmly sewn on. And record how we coped, how the swift flowing daily events changed us and prepared us for the sixty plus years of uneasy peace which have followed. But still peace of a kind and rationing of food and clothing would come to its dreary, extended end by 1954, nine years after Germany's unconditional surrender to the great commanders in the field. Their names rang like today's celebrities. Among them the more remembered Generals Eisenhower, Montgomery, Patton, Marshall, Bradley...in the air, Air Marshalls Tedder, Park, (New Zealand), "Bomber" Harris and on the sea, Admirals Cunningham and Ramsey–for the European war. America would fight on in the Pacific under General MacArthur and Admirals King and Nimitz... But we go too fast!

At school, I slipped into the routines and rituals of American high school life very quickly it seems. I really cannot recall any one instance where new boy status was emphasised by either the demeanour of the masters or in the closer contact with other pupils. I appear to have merely put on an old and comfortable pair of shoes. In this particular case, a pair of the ubiquitous "saddle" shoes, an item which had evidently surfaced following Aunt Elinor's shopping spree in the Newark store soon after I'd arrived. These comfortable white buckskin, rubber-soled shoes, with a saddle of brown leather stitched across the instep, were worn by boys and girls alike. The girls, in their short white socks, became the "bobbysoxers" of the era. I accumulated a drawer-full of multi-ringed, gaudy-coloured socks like everyone else. Uniform school clothing was out, individuality was in. But still, we dressed conservatively with sports jackets and neck-ties and each week, the Arrow shirts would come back, laundered. Blue jeans were still reserved for holiday or work wear, never for school.

Visits to the school in more recent years establish an interesting fact. Parents and students appear to separately respect older dress codes combining the comfort and neatness we knew. Perhaps I notice the greater prevalence of baseball caps on campus but there again, uniformity has taken a back seat. Everyone is a captain of something I've never heard of!

In America, as the month of November advances, so do domestic preparations for the great turkey-fest in celebration of a God-given land, its bounty and the life-sustaining know-how of those North American Indians first encountered. Certainly, the *Mayflower's* pilgrims of 1620 had knelt, at the hour of their deliverance from an ocean which would similarly bear others from England in more recent history. Soon, I would be introduced to the event which occurs on the third Thursday of November[3] in every year and Uncle Roy, looking professional in a tall chef's hat, took command of the oven while aunt handled the vegetables and we, the dining room. A good deal of tasting would go on but finally there would be produced at the table, with due ceremony, a large, golden, roasted turkey well stuffed with chestnuts and further garnished with cranberry sauce on our plates. Prayers for the occasion would be said with Amen being the barely awaited signal to hand round the dishes. Now that was a sight to behold and a smell that momentarily halted all chatter! Appropriately, it would be mine and my parent's day of Thanksgiving too, for different reasons.

Among the many new vegetables I remember trying on that first Thanksgiving Day dinner in 1940 were, corn-on-the-cob, artichokes (each individual leaf removed to be dipped in melted butter on the way to the mouth!), baked pumpkin, large baked potatoes (the skins then eaten separately—with more butter!), yams (a specie of sweet potato, no doubt the original American Indian offering to the tall-hatted first arrivals) and, oh yes...that chestnut stuffing!

I cannot remember anyone drinking table wines. We three youngsters were Coca-Cola and root beer addicts by that time. A dessert untried up to that point in my life had been lemon meringue pie topped with ice cream. It will do me for the remainder of my days and I give thanks to that first Thanksgiving dinner!

Whether or not someone had made mention of my own deliverance from whatever was going on back at 38 Malvern Road, Orpington, Kent, I have now no way of knowing. Unless Audreta, living in Denver, Colorado, can search her memory of those years and say: "Oh, sure, we did all that and Hal chased you upstairs and whacked you with a rolled-up *Life* magazine that Daddy hadn't yet read and we all of us got into trouble 'cos of you!" A fair reconstruc-

---

[3] Lincoln declared a Thanksgiving observance in 1864, establishing a precedent that was followed by Andrew Johnson in 1865 and by every subsequent president. After a few deviations (December 7, 1865, November 18, 1869), the holiday came to rest on the last Thursday in November. However, Thanksgiving remained a custom unsanctified by law until 1941! In 1939 Franklin D. Roosevelt departed from tradition by declaring November 23, the next to the last Thursday that year, as Thanksgiving. Considerable controversy (mostly following political lines) arose around this outrage to custom, so that some Americans celebrated Thanksgiving on the 23rd and others on the 30th (including Plymouth, MA). In 1940, the country was once again divided over "Franksgiving" as the Thanksgiving declared for November 21 was called. Thanksgiving was declared for the earlier Thursday again in 1941, but Roosevelt admitted that the earlier date, which had not proven useful to the commercial interests, was a mistake. On November 26, 1941, he signed a bill that established the fourth Thursday in November as the national Thanksgiving holiday, which it has been ever since.

Thankgiving Cookery by James W. Baker with Elizabeth Brabb, page 18, 1998

tion since Hal and I were always skylarking, while Audreta was practicing the piano or stretched on her tummy in the conservatory doing
her math homework.

Now, I begin to wonder what everyone really thought of me,
a sudden family addition from virtually nowhere. Slipping into a
family environment like the manor born. It is barely remembered
now but, within weeks and certainly months, I'd become a comfortable extension of my own family to America. Whilst there must have
been some days spent just feeling around for some commonality that
I could relate to, the period must indeed, have been quite short and
I am certain—as I can be certain of anything—that Audreta and
Harold, by unquestioningly accepting me as their number three,
were chiefly responsible in helping me to adjust on the purely
domestic front. In saying that, I can acknowledge the preliminary
chats that Aunt Elinor would have had with her two after she and
Uncle Roy had made known to them both my existence and
impending inclusion into the household. It proved to be a totally
painless exercise and I marvel at it now.

In dramatic illustration, readers may draw comparisons with
the miseries and trauma even then being the lot of many of my contemporary evacuees, in the loneliness of unfriendly, sometimes hostile billets of rural Britain. I have already drawn word pictures of
predicaments unique to the times. And I am surprised never to have
made similar comparisons myself before beginning this book. It
throws up in sharp relief that the toss of a coin and the choice of
options had come up heads for me. Chance, however, had kept the
Baltrover afloat for fifteen days. Most of the *City of Benares* evacuees
would celebrate no American Thanksgiving dinner—ever. I didn't
think all that out in 1940, 1941 or 1942, but it is not too late to
think about it now. And I would have silently made my own uneasy
comparisons aware that the melted butter, in which we dipped our
artichoke leaves at Thanksgiving, would have lasted my mother a
week and provided her with one of her favourite meals. Brown
"Hovis" loaf, thinly sliced—and butter.

One day, the pure wheatmeal Hovis loaf was a loaf no more and
ceased being seen on bakery and cake-shop shelves. The day of the great
British standard loaf had arrived. Coloured neither brown nor white it
would remain the staff of life for the English, Scottish, Welsh and Irish,
though there might have been a little more oatmeal in it north of the
border where the independently-minded Scottish folk lived.

Never let it be said that the standard loaf was deficient in the
secret nutrients that went into it. Both it, potatoes but lots less of
everything else, turned *all* of the British, not just some, into a nour-
ished nation for perhaps the first time since the Great War. Food
rationing did it. The compulsory sharing thing. In peace, economists
and health experts would have gone wild with unalloyed joy.
Obesity? What was that?

"Uncle" Roy, Audreta, Binkie, Me
"...proved to be a totally painless exercise..."

9 90 Park Avenue

With the *City of Benares* at rest on the Atlantic floor, parents no doubt reflected that by that time, Germany may have become aware of the existence in certain ships of the nation's young.

The selected ships did not have the word: EVACUEES painted in white on either side of their hulls. Or even the code: KIDS. And the words: WOMEN AND CHILDREN may have reacted on certain submarine commanders, both German and Japanese, like a matador's red cape to a slavering bull. And hospital ships? Well, sorry...no children allowed. Once word got out that hospital ships carried evacuees they could claim less of the paper immunity they currently enjoyed. So the majority of parents decided to keep their children somewhere in Britain. Who would blame them? Despite left open doors, a North American sanctuary seemed no longer a viable option.

Other British dominions left their doors ajar and, depending on available convoy escorts, plus an appropriate ship and shipping space, a few evacuees continued to trickle through to South Africa, Australia and New Zealand. But, for all intents and purposes, the CORB programme's ideal, that of saving the "crown jewels," was put indefinitely on hold. Saved, had been about 5,000 mixed emeralds, diamonds and rubies. In the main, British children would stay in the British Isles.

As November passed and a thankful Thanksgiving Day once more was twelve months ahead, in London the bombing was terrible. In 1924, the minutes of a sub-committee on Air-Raid Precautions had estimated the weight of bombs dropped in the first twenty-four hours might exceed that of the whole Great War period. Reference to the second evacuation from cities has been made in an earlier chapter. It was now peaking at a near desperate pace.

Harold had donated his bicycle about that time and I was riding to school with my books in a handlebar basket with many different things on my mind. There was the infernal Latin homework one morning that I hadn't a clue about. Paula had loaned me a *Cosmopolitan* magazine with explicit advice to mothers with teenagers. The bike would provide me with independent mobility, after Harold had shown me its braking system unique to American bikes of the period. One simply peddled backwards. The bike and rider, then stopped. Some of the Academy twelfth graders drove old jalopies to school. I had my own wheels.

The American Option

Back at home, I had possessed two bikes. One, my first ever on which I'd learned to ride, had only recently been upgraded to a "big boy's" bike, one with 21-inch wheels. I'd bought it with my own saved pocket money. A total of four pounds and ten shillings. It was a gleaming and amazing piece of machinery, an example of the bicycle-maker's craft. It had direct action brakes via chromium-plated levers on each handlebar—in fact just about every metal part was chromium plated, especially the wheel rims. The famed Sturmey Archer, sophisticated three-speed gearing was fitted inside the rear wheel hub with its control lever on the left handlebar. The drive chain was encased in a metal cover, removable for oiling. There was a thumb-operated handlebar bell, a rearview mirror on the right handlebar, a saddle bag containing tools fixed behind the saddle and, as would be proved, a valuable extra in the form of a carrier secured by struts over the rear wheel mudguards.

My bike gave to the family some unaccustomed mobility too. My mother did not ride, but I'd passed temporary ownership to my father with clear instructions on oiling and polishing and who now rode it, he'd said in one letter, to the shops for food rations or into the country lanes to pick blackberries. (That was where the rear carrier came in, you see.) My six-foot-one father was not very good at queueing at food shops but he would do his share when home on leave. Unlike women, he had little patience with chatter and graphic stories of how a bomb had missed or failed to explode. Everyone had their own hair raising bomb story. He would park the bike at the curbside, lift a carton of blackberries from the rear carrier, stride in to the butcher's shop as though he was delivering something—which he was—and next day, up to our house would ride Ralph, on his delivery bike with its smaller front wheel which provided for a deeper carrying basket above. Ralph, who with his brother Frank and their parents, would become post-war family friends, was the apprentice butcher-cum-delivery boy for our part of the week's meat ration, plus a few extra sausages or a tin of corned beef thrown in. He had a wide-ranging delivery round. People could not stock up with a whole week's ration since the majority had no refrigerators, only wire mesh "safes."

In the exceptionally long, hot summer of 1940, it had been a struggle to keep the butter ration from melting even in a bucket of cold water. The morning's milk might last long enough for "tea at four." Milk powder had not been invented. New-laid eggs, if one could come by them in addition to the ration of two or three a week, could be "put down" (preserved) in a bucket of isinglass, a preparation of nearly pure gelatin made from the viscera of fish (according to the American, *Funk and Wagnall's New Standard Dictionary of the English Language*–1944). Packets of sugar and tea, measured in ounces per week, would be carefully torn open right down to the bottom and granules trapped in corners extracted.

Park Avenue

Fruit in season, was bottled for the winter using air-tight clip-tops. Preserving sugar could be obtained as an extra to the regular ration, in lieu of branded jams, for those who made the time and effort to go out to farms, pick the fruit then turn to and make their own preserves. The occupation was classified as a "war effort." A great deal of fruit was allowed to be eaten on site! Diarrhoea may have been a consequence for some. With labour gone from farms into the armed forces, farmers were desperate to harvest crops. The "Land Army" girls tried valiantly to fill the gaps but much produce was given away as the season drew to a close. The "pick-your-own" pickers kept fit in an otherwise unfamiliar outdoor occupation. At one time we seemed to live on strawberry jam and the standard loaf.

The blackberries my parents picked in September/October, rich in Vitamin-C, plus gooseberries, black and red currents and raspberries, became an important supplement in the absence of lemons, oranges, bananas, pineapples and any fruit that had once been brought to the islands by ships. Those fruits would have few export markets until the late forties. Children would be born and grow to six or seven years old and would have learned of the existence of these absent items perhaps from primary school geography books or encyclopaedias. They would have to be schooled in the tasting.

Beckenham Technical College fell to incendiary bombs and the woodworking shop, with my uncompleted book rack, must have raised the height of the flames just that much more. With that hub of learning gone the students and teachers had no base and would be absorbed into other schools already occupying some of the larger country houses commandeered as an expedient of war. Martial law took on a whole new meaning.

So, as before, in 1939, the over-fives, pregnant mothers, those with children under five, the disabled, the blind were urged–never compelled–to allow the cities fewer mouths to feed, fewer to be injured and ultimately fewer dead to deal with. The Government moved one and a half million in a week. Two million were moved privately and the result became possibly the largest mass movement since biblical times.

We have already discussed the social price and methods of landing these people and then anchoring them among the rural, more rustic folk of the land. I can't be sure if I would have liked that option better or less. I don't recall it being a point of discussion. And all my aunts, uncles and cousins bar one family, lived in Wales. By then I saw myself as being as English as St George, the country's patron saint and, wherever I ended up, a dragon would be overpowered and slain with the English flag, the red cross of St George, nicely draped over the bloodied, still smoking carcass. My relatives could easily take care of the Welsh red dragon as depicted in their national flag. It would be entirely regrettable if the conglomeration of multi-coloured crosses in our Union Jack, drawing together our diverse

The American Option

United Kingdom, were to be substituted with an ominous, sinister, black swastika on a stark, red background. The Emblem of a nation-state gone mad with the crudity of an irredeemable bloodlust devoid, even, of the artistry of black magic evolutions. In November, 1940, as the American electioneering bandwagon rolled and came to a victory stop for Roosevelt, there were signs that he was of the same mind. The prospect of a swastika flag flying next to Old Glory over the Capitol's steps on American national days of the future if Britain went under, and "Uncle Sam"was forced to do business with Hitler's Europe, simply could not be countenanced. America's interests must come first.

One of *my* interests, among the many I was rapidly acquiring, now that Beckenham College and its related activities had gone into "background" mode rather than the "here and now," had been American football. One weekend, Harold and Audreta took me along with them to a match between Princeton and Rutgers at the Newark Stadium. This was a great event testing the sheer physical abilities of the men from both these major American Universities. The aura of boisterous, good natured excitement seemed to permeate throughout the stadium's rows and rows of cement seating resembling a Roman Amphitheatre. Hot dog, hamburger and ice-cream sellers were within arms length. If one was down in the front of the tiered terraces, the teenage cheerleader girls in short-skirted uniforms, were also within an arm's length as they simultaneously sang and shouted slogans and gyrated for about three or four minutes every fifteen. This appeared to have the effect of either maintaining player morale or reviving a flagging one. If a game was desultory, they provided substitute, visual entertainment. It was a colourful scene.

On the field itself, the heroes performed on a "gridiron" of white-painted five yard lines, frustratingly interrupted by fouls or mysterious technicalities. From our vantage point, the knot of armour-suited players, whose side might best be identified by the colour of helmets, meandered tortuously line by line toward a touchdown on either goal's hundred yard line, their progress relayed by loudspeakers in staccato, explicit Americanese.

Often, it seemed to me, a doctor, protected only by a white coat, and carrying a bag, would hasten onto the field. The unremitting shoving, elbowing, pelvis-crushing collisions would cease momentarily, the oval, rugby-type ball would be recovered by the referee and a player, helped or stretchered off. As soon as this was noted, a reserve player would pounce up from a bench seat, transformed from the comatose to the belligerent, don his helmet, which had lain on the ground and move, toward the area of temporary tranquility with a gorilla's gait, masticating, as he trotted, the rubber mouth guard into a more comfortable position.

Once the reserve player had assumed his field position, the game would restart with even more fervour and commitment. A

"Gridiron" football, Montclair Academy, 1940

great game, American football, having a mix of pure theatre and the melodrama of a Spanish bull ring. But, more importantly, an entertainment for *the whole* family, not just supporters and who, it seemed to me at the time, drank nothing much stronger than root beer. But my memory may have failed me there.

Back at school on the Monday, the game and the players would be taken to pieces in snatches of replay wherever there were more than two students together. The lunch room, down steps beneath the academic building, was the obvious venue for informed discussion.

Twice a day, school classes would stop for mid-morning and lunch breaks and we would troop down from various floors to the peace and restoration zone. Here, a bag of peanuts cost a nickel (five cents), a bottle of Coca-Cola, the same, and a jam-filled donut, a dime (ten cents). Standing or sitting in small groups about every subject on Earth would be under discussion and reporting staff of *The Montclair News*, the school's newspaper, might be noticed scribbling copy. To this day, the aroma from a freshly opened packet of peanuts transports me back to a subterranean cellar where age, disparate background and academic grades united rather than divided us.

I was given a quarter (twenty-five cents) each day for such expenses. I saved on tram (trolley) fares by riding the bike to school and I could come out in the black with a nickel. Other expenditures incurred which I could not readily control or limit by similar, careful husbandry, as with my quarter, were clothes, food, school fees and probably text books. I believe financial installments would have been forthcoming from my father. Leaving it to the end of the war would not have been prudent the way things were going in the Atlantic.

The American Option

Why had my father elected to dodge death in this way for the entire duration of my stay in Montclair? Would a simple answer have been: to retain a tenuous, irregular contact with myself, risking making my mother a war widow and me an orphan? Yet, less active war zones would not necessarily guarantee a long life. Merchant ships were going to the bottom in areas remote from the warring nations. But, unlike many fathers we read about, mine was exceedingly interested in my existence; obviously chuffed to have had a share in my production. Conversely, I was permanently aware of that and so, had a pretty good feeling of being just me.

I do not know how he came through it and so many did not. Destined to be lucky? Perhaps. Yet, I once heard him explain to some of our friends how, in violation of orders laid down at convoy conferences by naval officers, he always had, in the steam-driven ships of his day, all of his ship's boilers ready for immediate extra speed. Blanket instructions were to save coal in a slow, 8-knot convoy by shutting down unrequired boilers. To reactivate from shut-down to full-steam pressure would take hours in some cases, when minutes only would help a ship to slide away from a surfaced submarine in the dark, or to get clear of violently manoeuvring ships after the commodore had flashed the signal: SURFACE RAIDER–SCATTER! The presence of a latter-day *Graf Spee* [4] on the loose dictated a rapid dispersal of the convoy toward any point of the compass favoured by individual merchant captains, virtually on a throw of the dice.

The pocket battleship could only chase one ship if the manoeuvre had been timely. Chief engineers on every other ship would have been hell-bent on getting up additional steam pressure from the boilers they'd obediently left cold. Hypothetically, my father in one would have been already a good fifty miles away, with his chief engineer's steam pressure gauges on the point of shattering their protective glass. Snatches of his conversation over years makes me suspect that in maybe more than one instance his and others' salvation came at the expense of a few tons of coal. It had not worked of course, in the two sinkings of 1917. Then he'd been an apprentice–not in independent command.

For both motivation and his philosophies, we could return to Chapter One and my father's experiences with certain naval officers and their decision-making early in, and throughout the entire war. If initiative was called for my father used it, to save his various ships, their priceless cargoes and barely replaceable crews–naval, merchant mariners and army DEMS gunners (Defensively Equipped Merchant Ships). Tossing code books around then fiddling with flag hoists or signal lamps at night seemed not the way to go.

---

4 *Beware Raiders, German Surface Raiders in the Second World War*
-by Bernard Edwards, Pen & Sword Books, Ltd. 2001

Park Avenue

He might have said to his accusers, if any, that the few tons of extra coal he'd used in an Atlantic crossing by keeping all boilers flashed up, might be restored to the stockpiles after the minister for power, or whatever was his title then, negotiated with striking coal miners in Scotland, Yorkshire and Wales for an improvement in their sub-standard work environment. There remained four hundred years of coal reserves under the soil of Great Britain. It required digging out by men and machines in a better managed industry. That was all. Patriotism need play no part. The government and people had, however, far less to be forgiving about as striking dockers, at intervals throughout the war, delayed the movement of materials to heavy industry and the food shops. Their's had been a reserved occupation. Fit men of military age could opt for work in the nation's docklands. By the same token, they could lose that special immunity and get shot at in the Libyan desert, on Crete or on the Anzio or Salerno landing beaches. They had a choice denied to some others.

One morning, at school, in study hall, one of my new confederates tapped me on the shoulder. I half turned. John Vail (mathematics), at the commencement of the free study period, had parroted his customary welcome with: "Good morning. Now, sit down and shut up." The furled Stars and Stripes on the raised dais where Mr Vail was then seated and safely pre-occupied with a book, signalled law and order. Former President Lincoln's *Gettysburg Address* to the soldiers on their field of battle, had already been recited by some unfortunate to whom Dr Head, after morning prayers, had singled out with a blackboard pointer. In row nine from the front, our situation seemed secure.

"So what's your background?" hissed my shoulder tapper, a boy with fairish hair, wearing a grey, check sports coat and, whenever we subsequently talked, a challenging smile.

"I'm from England."

"I *know* that. What did you do over there, I mean?"

"Umm, engineering drawing, building crystal sets, mock-up irrigation systems and, er ships."

"Wow! Did you have your own company then...have you got any samples?"

"Er, I've got some bomb pieces."

"No kidding...what, on you...let's see."

From my pocket, I pulled two lumps of shrapnel wrapped in a handkerchief. With a careful look toward the absorbed study master, I set the sharp, jagged pieces on my accomplice's desk with a backward movement.

"Wow," he exclaimed again.

"What's your name?" I asked him.

"Totten," he whispered. "Art Totten."

Arthur Cranston Totten Jr. and I enjoyed a good eighth grade study-hall friendship. He was a great joker, always kidding me in a kindly way about what he imagined my background to really be. He probably ended up being drafted into one of the services. Perhaps he passed through some part of Britain, in uniform, maybe via the U.S. Army Air Forces like actor, later colonel, James Stewart. Might he have got himself into the "Battle of the Bulge," Hitler's 1944 surprise attempt to regain the port of Antwerp and repulsed at great American sacrifice? Maybe. The war lasted long enough. He could even have stumbled on people like me. Our friendship would end finally with a message written small alongside his graduation photo in the *Octopus*, the Academy's year book. It seemed to mirror, typically, his interest in things British and, by twelfth grade, at 17, he would have studied American history. He would have been a proud graduate of the school, primed for some college of which I am ignorant. I'd estimated that, with a bit of luck with my grades, I too would be a twelfth grader by 1945, writing classy messages and scrawling my latest signature style for the year books of awe-struck juniors. A minor celebrity at last. But time has faded the green ink he habitually used in his fountain pen and made his signature less legible.

In my home city there was less to be celebratory about unless, as in the devastation of New York's twin towers' collapse, one person buried alive was dug out, still alive. Then a cheer would go up in the city's East End borough of Stepney; in Coventry (November 14th), Liverpool, Southampton even seaside holiday spots. A lone German raider foolish enough to attack Buckingham Palace, aroused fierce solidarity right across social classes. The Queen explained: "I'm glad we've been bombed. It makes me feel I can look the East End in the face." Their unique pile would be hit twice more.

As I went to school and fought my small battles of assimilation, Londoners were grimly acclimatising to the Blitz. They had been led to expect massive assaults by day, not night bombing. Available shelters were thus pressed into constant use for sleeping, eating, excreting. The steely courage of detachments sent to dig twenty feet, then defuse unexploded bombs (UXB's), is best just imagined! One in ten bombs were duds.

Retaliation initially rested on anti-aircraft gunners. Night fighters became effective only late in the Blitz. Meanwhile, they merely complicated the aim of gunners and were withdrawn in favour of massive gun barrages. This kept everyone awake but the noise was inspiring and morale soared along with the shells. Ear plugs, cracked ceilings, cracked toilet bowls and barking dogs were indulgently accepted.

A few not too boring figures: During the twelve months that would follow, up to November 13th 1941 that is, an average of 160 bombers per night dropped 200 tons of high explosive (H.E.) and 182 canisters of incendiaries on London. But during the full moon of October 15th 1941, 410 planes dropped 538 tons of H.E. killing 400 and seriously injuring 900. Yet one effect on the people was to spread the habit of adaptation. This became addictive and so, the immensity of the Greater London area, with its peacetime population of around nine million, meant that three or four hundred bombers wasted their efforts several times on buildings already hit and destroyed.

Churchill, in a speech that could have been titled "Statistics," claimed: "Statisticians may amuse themselves by calculating that after making allowance for the working of the law of diminishing returns through the same house being struck twice or three times over, it would take ten years at the present rate, for half the houses of London to be demolished. After that, of course, progress would be much slower!"

London had a problem other cities did not have. Sheffield, for example had erected a dummy town in the hills. The capital's sprawl extended twelve miles on each point of the compass. The unique curves of the River Thames, reflected in moonlight, was impossible to disguise. Wherever pilots of German aircraft opened their bomb bay doors they could be sure of hitting something of cultural or sentimental importance. I include this observation of Angus Calder because it links properly and fairly, I feel, the later proxy actions by Bomber Command's Sir Arthur Harris in Churchill's name, to give like-for-like over Germany when the allies gained air superiority.

War is about reprisals. Destroying the mainly cultural and cathedral cities of Coventry, in England and later Dresden, in Germany were morale-busting operations. After Coventry, Britons still had a lot of mileage in the courage stakes, and carried on. Dresden 1945, became a German civilian's nemesis, finally destroying, in the fire storms, myths of invincibility, of hope and a will to fight longer for a cause already lost. Whoever's decision it was to target Dresden would observe in seven months a parallel strategy to halt the bloody prolongation of the Pacific war. President Truman executed The Manhattan Project's atom bomb. Churchill, too often castigated as a warmonger had, in two world wars, always had his mind on shortening war, not prolonging it. By the end of 1944, World War II, Hitler's baby, had simply gone on for long enough.

It seems that either I hadn't done too well in the end-of-term tests, or my original tester had overvalued me, or my various grade teachers had all got together in a collegiate mass and pronounced that in their opinion, I was somehow missing out on some vital school culture necessary to my already steady academic advancement. In any event, after Christmas, I found myself transmigrated from eighth grade and making new friends in seventh grade. Whether this was so that I could graduate back into eighth grade with all the traditional pomp and splendour of these occasions, then be called up to my peers and be handed a rolled diploma tied with red ribbon, I cannot be certain. Privately, I would have preferred to wait until I reached twelfth grade, like Art Totten and then become the minor celebrity I've already described. Doubtless the good sense of the new arrangements would have been explained to me. Perhaps I wished to erase it from my mind. I was old enough to recognise a personal failure. The sensation was not strange nor the method I developed for recovery: just start all over again. And there was no French or Latin in seventh grade as I recall. Furthermore, I was able to learn American history from its roots and could already recite Lincoln's Gettysburg Address in advance of some others.

My first Christmas in America was both memorable and sombre. Perhaps a special effort was being made to establish, with Audreta and Harold, a routine that was familiar to them, a family of four, two males two females. None would visualise how my family might handle the annual festival. For a start, I was now nearly four months into being as much of a fifth family member as it was possible (for me) to be. Yet I remained an extension, in a quite different world, of my parents and friends, mostly bonded, if that is the right word, with my mother. I had been fathered but was a product, culturally speaking, of my mother's family tree. For, with my father absent for long months in the early years, I'd been reared by her and learned at second hand about his side of the family in Cardiff, Glamorganshire. I knew my paternal, widowed grandmother well there and two of my uncles and young cousins but, for understandable reasons, it was to my two maternal grandparents I was drawn, because my mother would seek to alleviate some of her feelings of isolation by more frequent visits to them in Newport, Monmouthshire. And my grandfather Morgan had tales to tell about the sea!

Our Christmases were, shall we say, treeless. Where was the stimulation to emulate other families with their magnificently decorated fir trees or festoon our house with paper streamers and lanterns? Or fill the table for the two of us with one turkey and two Christmas crackers by the side of each plate? Christmas is a time for families and we were not. We would have a "Christmas" when my father returned, be it December or June. And since I had conveniently believed in Father Christmas until relatively old, Christmas presents were never a problem for my mother. A pair of my mother's silk stockings tacked to the wooden mantlepiece over the living room fireplace, from which Santa would have crawled, was always crammed full into leg shapes undreamt of by the manufacturer. A new harmonica and fountain pen were always in there somewhere.

No, it wasn't material things that set the Christmases of two families apart with an ocean in between. It would have been the general hubbub, the comings and goings, even some turbulence of a larger family, friends, callers and the demands of three teenagers. Well, Audreta would soon become one of those and by the following Christmas, 1941, I would be thirteen as well. Yes, perhaps there was one difference I've omitted. I used to write my requests and my hopes direct to Santa Claus and post it over the fireplace before being sent to bed. I would now be given a sheet of paper, list my needs on it and hand it to Aunt Elinor. Audreta and Harold did the same. I do not remember being in the least abashed with the length of my list. It wasn't as though Santa was going to have to carry the stuff. We had the big Packard. Also the selection was thoughtfully designed to give to my dear Aunt Elinor and Uncle Roy the widest possible choice—in case certain items were unobtainable?

What, however, had not been asked for by any of the three of us, was a pair of skis each. My father's contribution for Christmas 1940. I cannot remember if he joined us then, as he often would at unscheduled times. It was a great and happy Christmas though, with Cody and Harold Nash, Roberta and Arthur Harris plus their two, Janet and Reed calling in to share the coffee, cake and ice cream, Christmas pudding and rum butter—and around the Christmas tree, on Christmas Day morning, from about eight until eleven, we all sat and opened up the named, gift-wrapped boxes piled beneath with the predictable Oooo's and Ahhhh's of either surprise or relief.

Somewhere in all that would have been long letters from my parents to me and to the Family and from them to mine, via the Clipper service. With Roosevelt again president, about the only telephone links would have been between the Oval Office and Churchill, at Number 10, Downing Street, London and where, by that time, he had taken up formal residence. One item I had not asked for in my Christmas list had been a harmonica and maybe some handkerchiefs. Those would remain my mother's entire prerogative and responsibility. And what had *her* Christmas Eve and Day been like? If I still had her letter I know it would be like so many of her later ones, which I do have, filled with a remarkable variety of doings, promptings, love, positive thinking and always a small reminder to give God a place in my daily life. Which I do.

10   Sex, Terror and Touring

With Christmas over I could have looked back upon four months of a transformed life. But then, of course, I would not have mulled over my past in the sense of evaluating it, as one does later in life. My past had been too brief to bother with, my future, infinite.

However, as a relatively mild and unemotional separation from home, engineered wholly by my mother, followed by an incident-free voyage, then an uncomplicated absorption into new life styles, began to take on the normal order of things; rather than the exception, I did notch up a significant scholastic achievement. Howard Parker (English literature), had discovered the extent of my familiarity with engineering draughting. Back in November, he'd roped me in (lassoed, might be a better action for an Irish-American), during the production of the end-of-year, school stage drama. This event was produced jointly with The Kimberley High School for girls at 201 Valley Road, Montclair. The cast of players was also shared by Kimberley filling the female parts in scripts. "I'm behind, so I am, with getting the placards and posters done," Parker had complained in his lilting Irish.

It led to my discovery of the attics in the old building. They'd been converted into art studios and the large trestle tables were there, ready for use! I'd got to work with an abundance of materials, coloured cardboard, poster paint, brushes–and undisturbed isolation. I like to think the lettering and artwork, advertising *The Hottentot*, was professionally done. And so, one morning, in the New Year of 1941, I entered seventh grade with a small non-academic credit all of my own. I would always, it seemed, make my way through life extant of curriculums. In consequence, measuring success or failure with the usual yardsticks, became difficult. Failures, never made me downcast for long. Optimism took root instead and is now incurable.

Among the memory relics of my first morning in the halls of the Lower School and notably the most senior grade there, number seven, is the pleasant face of John Moore. He approached me at some point, possibly to direct me to a spare seat behind one of a row of desks, a detestable symbol of pupil hierarchy. Once seated, one could not move oneself around the room as in the chairs of adult eighth grade. One was marked down according to the geography of the classroom, as being the dud in the front row or the dud at the back, or wherever a dud was put for teacher-pupil eye contact. Life was going into reverse, I thought. I may even have said it.

"Never mind," someone would have replied, "Miss Johnson is super, and we'll all be graduating to the Upper School in June."

"I've just come from there," I lamented miserably. "Oh, well!" I grumbled philosophically, if that was indeed being philosophical. "What's on today then?"

"Geography this morning," someone else replied.

"Oh, well," I said, (the philosopher again), "I know a bit about that at least."

However, the 10:30 break did much to assuage the sharp chagrin of my academic demotion to a class whose age group was one year younger than myself. A small interval of time is more apparent when one is young. It is likely that I would have first made the acquaintance of Bill Brown in the lunchroom, but on that first day I would have been fraternising with my pals in eighth grade over a Coke and jam donut. In that curious way I bridged the gap and suddenly had around thirty colleagues instead of just fifteen. That, and Bill's developing friendship toward me, somehow got me over a dive in schoolboy self-esteem and we ascended the slippery slope, more or less together, to the sunlit uplands of the Lower School's graduation day.

I say, more or less together because, employing the analogy of a ship when weighing both anchors, Bill, the port anchor in the end-of-month Roll of The Enlightened, was bang up into the hawsepipe while I, as the starboard anchor, was bumping along the sea bottom. But I didn't seem to mind. Any sign of brilliance on my part might have frightened me. And anyway, Paula said she thought I might be a late starter and kept feeding me *Cosmopolitan* magazines to increase my awareness of sex, motherhood and fatherhood embellished with weird "facts" in the columns of agony aunts. And Harold could always be depended upon to help with the graphics by passing on *Esquire* magazines having within, colourful inserts depicting the totally unreal perfection of the female form by artists Varga or Petty. There was a problem, of course. For some time I believed all women, if they could be instantly disrobed, would reveal similar arrangements of flesh and bone as presented by Varga or Petty in their idealised art. To humour the fallacy, Aunt Elinor evidently allowed me to pin one up in my room at 90 Park Avenue. A rare photo I took, shows one artistically displayed on one wall. In my new seventh grade class it was my belief, desire even, that Miss Johnson, if she were to be suddenly stripped of the lackluster, totally ineffectual camouflage of the severe, grey check business suiting, which she effected, would stand revealed as a cloned Varga or Petty girl.

There had been several falls of snow over the Christmas period sufficient to cloak Verona golf course and the slopes behind with an adequate depth for Audreta and I to try out the skis my father had bought us. I managed to stay upright for a photograph

standing, with sticks in action mode, alongside Audreta. At some
point I fell incorrectly and the days of inaction with a twisted knee
saw most of the season's snow out. Somehow, we got on toboggans
on the same slopes and a pair of ice skates granted from the
Christmas list, got me going on a nearby ice rink. For school tennis,
Aunt Elinor took me along to Jacobsen's Sports shop and we came
away with my first ever tennis racket complete with compressor and
four wing nuts. Harold gave me his old wrist watch. I was all set to
face the grown-up world.

As the weather grew milder and the baseball season drew
near, I put on one of Bill's catcher mitts for the first time and we'd
practice, one throwing, one catching, wherever there was someone's
large expanse of green in South Mountain Avenue or almost anywhere else. I had to explain to him that cricket players, with the
exception of the knee pads worn by the two batsmen and wicket
keeper, had no other protection, bar the wicket-keeper's gloves.
Fielders caught fast balls with bare hands and broke fingers doing it.
He may have thought that was a bit pagan. Yet today, with the game
apparently speeded up, even helmets and face guards are worn, while
tea-time breaks in the Pavilion may be considered effete by space-age
bowlers and batsmen. And baseball umpires get stoned or shot.
Sport?

About this time, in mid-school term I suppose it would have
been, Bill must have invited me to his home, to meet his parents and
to show me over his work room. The old house had a tower topped
by a turret at one corner, like one of those fairy-tale castles. Bill's
haven was at the top and it was there that I beheld squadrons of
mixed, model aircraft of many contemporary types, including British
and German. They were parked on most level surfaces and hung from
roof timbers on cotton.

For one having so recently gazed up at real ones buzzing
around our house and using the published identification charts supplied to the population, it was a startling sight. Bill's smallest model
could have been an inch long. Larger ones were flyable using petrol
engines. Being a user myself, of drawing and draughting instruments
and needing to be watchful over detail, it was obvious that Bill had
spent many hours in faithful reproduction of each model. He
explained how he simulated Duralumin-covered fuselages and wings
right down to the tiny rivets.

"How do you....?" I began, with what must have seemed a
disbelieving look.

Bill gestured toward a typewriter. "Periods," he said, by way
of explanation.

"Periods?" I repeated, dumbly.

"Oh, that's right, you call them "full-stops" in England don't
you?"

"What's that got to do with building aeroplanes then?" I

William (Bill) Ferdinand Brown II
(Courtesy: W.F. Brown)

Bill's Place–63 South Mountain Avenue, Montclair, N.J.
"...like one of those fairytale castles."
(Courtesy: W.F. Brown)

said, thus reminded of differences in American and English terminology. But, by then, he'd realised he'd lost me. Patiently, he stopped his adjustment of a Great War, Fokker Triplane completing an Immelmann turn on its cotton suspension, and came over. From a work table he produced a sheet of tissue paper on which there were rows of embossed dots made by the typewriter's full-stop (period) key.

"See? You just cut strips off, paste onto the model where seams would be on the Duralumin...like this...." Bill did a small test piece for my benefit.... "then apply the dope!"

Now who else, I asked myself then, *and* now, would have thought of that?

In a box of assorted, fascinating objects that might have been labelled "surplus to requirements," Bill pulled out several Brownie and other makes of camera. "Would you like one? That's if you haven't got one," he said.

So I acquired my first camera with a see-through viewfinder as compared with the little prism affair which the photographer had to snap this way and that to get horizontal or vertical shots. (Remember?). I christened the camera The Bill Brownie Special. I can't remember the actual make, but its status was up with the Leicas.

The tower room was, as I first described it, a work room also because, pinned to drawing boards, were sheets of white paper covered with designs of aircraft one saw only in science fiction comic strips. Only Bill's "ships" were not comic, they had the look of being aerodynamically airworthy! Serious stuff, I decided. He's heading toward becoming an aircraft designer or aeronautical engineer or both.

That impression would be strengthened when his mother suggested she take us into New York to see a film called *I Wanted Wings*. Veronica Lake, she who fostered the long blonde hair look hiding one eye, was the female lead. We can forget the male lead although he, no doubt, was prominent in the flying scenes. It was also my first visit to New York City's theatre-land, Times Square. And it would, surprisingly, even accidentally, as he now explains, be where his eventual vocation would find expression, not at Cape Canaveral's rocket launch pads or with California's Boeing Aircraft Corporation Inc. Before that, a great deal of water would pass under lots of bridges. His and mine.

For now, though, life-size versions of Bill's model aeroplanes were doing fearful, sickening damage over Britain, but mostly among the streets of suburbia, theatre-land and dock-land in London. Some ancient London streets dating from Roman times, were too narrow for fire-engines to get into. Then, hoses were often too short to reach fire hydrants, so those parts of the old city around Christopher Wren's St Paul's Cathedral and many of his distinctive city churches, were left to burn, leaving their bell towers standing. Today, they feature as curiosities in communal landscaping together with a number of modern architectural devices of a shape and material deplored by Prince Charles and other traditionalists.

St Paul's, with its surrounding area cleared by courtesy of Herr Hitler, itself victim of a direct hit, remained grandly visible without much competition until about the sixties, when certain revisionist developers appeared to have been given carte blanche with notional schemes to make ugly what once had been scenes of disorderly appeal. In the re-built London, many of the former views of one of the great edifices of the world, disappeared to the sounds of jack-hammers, wreckers' balls, and the sprouting of land survey theodolites.

Meanwhile, the huge basement areas of bombed buildings, as the sites were cleared, were adapted. Former basement walls were coated with bituminous paint then turned into water reservoirs, to fight future fires. Mysteriously (some said), a mauve coloured, flowering weed, named *Rosebay Willowherb* not seen in the City since the Great Fire of London in 1666, found nourishment in the dust of shattered brickwork and for years, until all the construction cranes moved away, the wild flowers of London flourished each Spring and Summer in pretty memorium over the subterranean wastes of the capital.

And how had Germany fared? At this time her cities had suffered little by comparison. But that would change. The Luftwaffe had bomber superiority on both range and endurance. Not much question about that, but it paid the price in the limited range of its fighter escort which could not remain over the target for long. From our side, Wellington, Blenheim and Halifax bombers were unsuited for reaching parts of Germany, Austria, Rumania, Italy, to attack oil refineries, say, at Ploesti or the great Mohne and Eder dams that supplied power for Rhur industry. Sir Arthur Harris, chief of Bomber Command, would have to wait for a modified Avro Manchester Bomber to become larger, get four engines and be called the Lancaster. That formidable aeroplane along with the B-17 Flying Fortress of America's Eighth Air Force, would return terror to where it had first originated, been planned then perpetrated with the smug satisfaction of Germany's leaders and the German axis powers. Before then, however, Londoners and the populations of provincial cities would bear what Nazi pilots let loose on them, with not always a grin.

On March 19th 1941, perhaps when Bill and I were taking advantage of a windy day on the green swards of South Mountain Avenue, to fly our balsa wood model Piper Cubs, London had its worst raid yet, with 750 civilians dead. From April 16th to the 19th the moon may have been about full because, 1,000 died each night. By May 10th, the first anniversary of Churchill becoming Prime Minister, the London Blitz was eight months old. It would be the night of the final onslaught. There was a "Bomber's Moon" when

The American Option

Spring tides would produce a low ebb in the Thames and water would be short. That night, 1,436 were killed and 1,792 seriously injured. 2,200 fires burned for eleven days and nights.

Then, Göring shifted his focus to Europe, to prepare for the great attack on Russia. London had received 19,000 tons of H.E. In the wider Britain some 43,000 civilians were killed outright and 1,700 died later from injuries. London had qualified for about half of these figures. As a campaign to systematically terrorise a population, it would know no equal until, in 1943, the allies returned the favour with interest–having been taught how it should be done by experts.

When I visited Hamburg in 1948 most structures above two floors had gone. Taller ones remaining were church towers, bunkers and the monolithic statue of Bismarck on the hill above St Pauli staring stonily down over the ghostly, macabre panorama of rubble. People walked the cleared city streets that divided up the whole into a chessboard, a square here and there occupied by some structural remains like a sidelined chessman. Firestorms created by several 1,000 bomber raids between 1942 and 1944, had swept the city through from end to end. Hamburg pre-dated Manhattan's "Ground Zero" by more that half a century. One German design of air-raid bunker several floors high like a small tower block had, curiously, faired better than anything under the ground. Most of London, at least, was still standing and recognisable. Terror is terrible; retribution, regrettable–when the effects are viewed after peace has been made.

Surprisingly, this kind of war from the air: *"...led to no great increase in neurotic illness in Britain; no increase in insanity. The number of suicides fell and drunkeness halved between 1939 and 1942. Certain types of mentally sick people actually felt better. Emergency schemes represented a kind of revolution in the State's attitude to the welfare of less fortunate citizens. It came about simply because the need was so pitifully obvious.*

The effects of the German aerial blitzkrieg on children, direct or indirect remain, however, incalculable. Patients, whose nerves had cracked through the noise of incessant anti-aircraft barrages close to them, sat up in their hospital beds and wimpered like puppies. One little girl was completely dumb through terror. Another, became stiff as a ramrod when sirens sounded. Her face turned scarlet; she opened her mouth to scream, but no sound came. Yet the physical condition of Britain's children improved during the war. Their psychological and intellectual development was another matter!"
(Angus Calder–*The People's War*)

America's Lend Lease programme contributed 1/15th of all food arriving by sea in 1941 although, in the first months of that year, the national diet available turned out to have been the poorest of the war. Lend Lease was so appreciated, Mass Observation (M.O.) found, that some people hoped America might stay neutral since it was presumed there would be less aid for Britain if her ally in name became one in deed.

Sex, Terror

Bill, I and the citizens of Verona, Montclair, New Jersey and the other forty-seven states in the union, with the possible exception of those in The District of Columbia, were happily unaware of all these complex effects of war on domestic Britain. Sixty plus years have allowed us to collect and digest them—and to possibly retain the warnings, strewn around for others to pick up at random, of an earlier, prolonged terror campaign that had really begun in the thirties! We now face terror enhanced by the electronic age. Neither Bill nor I nor any American boy or girl of the period, could have been seduced by foreknowledge or the most evil comic strip characters, into a suspicion of current perils within our western society. *"The Shadow"* character, in the popular 40's radio series of that name, could amend his weekly warning to listeners about the weed of crime bearing bitter fruit. The fruit can be sweet after all, when the degenerates of nation-states become latter-day scarlet pimpernels—turned around.

My own criminal activities had their first flowering in Washington, D.C., the nation's capital, no less. One of those long weekends in the American calendar was coming due and Uncle Roy came up with a grand idea.

"Why don't we," he announced, with an enthusiasm which must have been bubbling all night, "all go to Washington, D.C. next weekend?" (D.C.–District of Columbia)

"You mean like James Stewart did in the movie *Mr Deed Goes to Washington?*" someone ventured.

"I'm not sure if it was him or some other guy," said my Uncle Roy, "and I think it was *Mr Deed Goes To Town*, but anyway, we shall certainly go there."

"When?" Harold put on a studious look, as though an appointment might clash.

"I can add another State to the one's I've already been to," calculated Audreta. "Philip's been to four already."

I think I must have thought it was a very good idea all round. I was developing a wander lust. The sole of one foot was already itching in a spot that was out of reach. A sure sign of impending travel.

"We can start this Saturday," Uncle Roy said, "stay over that night and Sunday night and return on Monday afternoon...nearly three days."

"Wow!" went Audreta.

"Okay, great," said a visibly relieved Harold, "I can get ahead with class chemistry experiments down in my lab." That was a reference to Harold's superbly-equipped laboratory which he'd been permitted to set up in the basement. Buying Harold presents never posed a problem. One just gave him a test tube or a flame-proof, glass retort. At sixteen and a half, he was set to become a chemical engineer. My Aunt Elinor looked at us all benignly through her rimless spectacles.

The day came. Harold had washed the Packard and touched up the white-wall tyres. The distinctive, fluted bonnet and chrome radiator grill with the sharp lines of a ship's bow, glittered as Harold delivered the impressive auto, to the front of the house, his special privilege in the sibling order of pecking.

"Do you have to see anyone in Washington, Daddy?" queried Audreta.

"No, sweetheart, the President will be relaxing somewhere with Elinor. He won't be needing to see a New York Life Assurance consultant *this* weekend, I imagine."

"I do wish the First Lady would spell her name a bit differently to mine," said my aunt, pulling a face.

"You could always write her a letter," suggested Harold, cheekily. His mother flicked his head with her hand, mussing up his carefully combed hair.

"C'mon then, let's go," Audreta commanded. And we all went to Washington.

I'd made sure to pack Bill's camera. My debut as a lenseman was close. Details of the drive south from Montclair, through Maryland, then via the few arterial highways of the day, remain few now, but two things are recalled: We were trapped in a long line of vehicles on some road or other and the midday heat was such that we three kids were getting out of the car, walking forward, then back, sitting about and no doubt drinking whatever liquids were within reach. I do not remember seeing things like "Coolboxes" or "Eskis" if only because it was an age before the versatile plastic, as we now know it, was developed. But my aunt would have thought of all that and packed lunch in some form. Bologna and gherkin; possibly Audreta's peanut butter and marmalade sandwiches? Perhaps.

My next memory is of the marble front door steps of Baltimore's suburban streets, scrupulously scrubbed each morning by householders determined to have the whitest marble slabs in the road and jealous of their perceived records. The mind picture looking ahead through the windscreen and then back, through the rear window, is of a white dotted line of front steps and polished brass door knobs. Maybe, as soap advertisements took off, the whitest washing on backyard clothes lines would provide equivalent domestic rivalry.

At some point during the car journey or it may have been while still at the house, Uncle Roy handed us all itineraries, neatly typed by his office secretary. They listed times and places of interest we would visit each day and what we could expect to see. The action and detail were those of a military mind turned civilian re-enforced by the Washington landmarks he'd picked out.

"Kiddos," remarked my aunt, addressing us three at dinner that evening while consulting our tour plans, "you have a very special man for a dad, I can't think of any other father who would take this much care over a family weekend."

Almost to the month, forty years on, while working in

Harold Stuart Sheldon–1943
(*Courtesy:* A.M. Pape-Sheldon)

Rotterdam, Holland, my parents visited from England. They stayed in the small hotel with me at 21 s'Gravendijkval and I remembered the Washington visit. I'd drawn up a three day itinerary of what I proposed to show them and, with one or two less important exceptions, we kept pace with the ground-plan. My Uncle Roy's industry and legacy had paid off, once again.

And in Washington, each morning and afternoon, we faithfully tracked each item listed and trod the steps of the nation's Capitol building, the Lincoln and Jefferson memorials, the Smithsonian Institute, to see Charles Lindbergh's Spirit of St Louis, the 555 foot Washington Monument, George Washington's Potomac River home at Mount Vernon and the Arlington National Cemetery. We admired the mock cherry trees in full bloom lining the grassy street verges. A profusion of pink, plus multi-floral displays complemented the 1791 French landscaping, a godsend to picture postcard manufacturers–and the American capital city manages to predate the more clinical lines of a 1927 Canberra, A.C.T., (Australian Capital Territory), by more than a century.

I clicked away with Bill's camera at anything and everything and fed it with more Verichrome roll film. The elevator ride up

Washington D.C., December 1947
"...an image of floodlit splendour..."

"...showed the capitol dome in bright sunlight..."—1941

inside the Washington Monument was utilised at the top with the zeal of the true photo-journalist. In my first ever photo album, the 1x2-inch snapshots remain fixed today, the negatives preserved. Mute evidence of how, in 1941, an American family of almost five spent their time in Washington D.C.

It could have been during our final evening meal that the seeds of my criminal life were sown and bore an unusual fruit. The coup, for it was nothing less, followed an interest-packed afternoon that had included a stroll down Pennsylvania Avenue. We'd all waved toward The White House, just in case President Roosevelt and Elinor had returned early for some pressing matter of international importance. Uncle Roy had selected a seafood restaurant for dinner and we all took our places in one of the cubicles. For two days, we three juniors had been collecting an array of souvenir material, booklets on this and leaflets on that. Tea-spoons, drinks coasters, napkins, almost anything that identified an establishment, were fair game to us at our age. And there'd been on sale, at the base shop in the Washington Monument, replicas of the obelisk itself, fashioned from compressed, withdrawn dollar greenbacks. I bought one, intrigued by the probable value of the paper money used.

In the seafood restaurant I was equally intrigued by the swizzle sticks, made of some cost-saving, base metal, used to stir our drinks. On the backs were stamped: "STOLEN IN WASHINGTON D.C." This, we decided unanimously, was a most sensible and enlightened eatery and no further invitation had been necessary for us to carry off our trophies. When I eventually returned to England, I would show a unique souvenir to friends as being evidence of a very practical American philosophy toward hardened criminals.

I would see Washington once more six years later when the ship in which I was serving was in Baltimore. I went by bus on my own and I was then using a quarter plate, roll film, Kodak folding camera. In rainy weather, I stood the opened-up camera on the steps of the Capitol. Autumn leaves were blowing across the lens but a guessed time exposure of some seconds, produced an image of floodlit splendour unmatched by more modern cameras.

But in 1941, shots taken with the "Bill Brownie Special," showed the Capitol dome in bright sunlight. In a few short months, America's declaration of war, first against Japan then Germany, would be made from within. Harold, is in the picture, walking toward the steps in a smart sports jacket. He would graduate from College High School, Montclair, to Williams College, Massachusetts, to read chemical engineering. Caught in the military "draft," he sent me a passport-size photograph. The military uniform made him look strangely youthful.

11   The Jewish Solution

In London, St Paul's Cathedral, having a dome of similar appearance and proportion to America's Capitol building, was illuminated at night by the fires of the burning "square mile," as the City of London, within its medieval walls, has long been dubbed by modern business folk.

The scene remains one of the more spectacular wartime photographs and seemed, at the time, to provide a seriously needed symbol of the country's invincibility. But it was just a photograph. It served its purpose as photographs must always do; like the star spangled banner, nailed to a pole, being manhandled aloft on Iwo Jima, MacArthur wading ashore after his return to the Philippines, the sailor kissing a girl in Times Square on VJ-day, August 14th, 1945, Churchill, cigar between teeth and two fingers making euphemistic victory signs toward Germany, King George VI and Queen Elizabeth, picking a way over fresh wreckage from a night's bombing of London's East End, Patton, steel helmeted in fawn-coloured cavalry twill breeches, pearl-handled Colts slung on each hip, Montgomery, khaki jersey, shapeless work trousers, wearing his multi-badged beret at El Alamein, addressing his "desert rats" from the rear of a truck. Okay, some were orchestrated, some were not. All were important in counterbalancing tales of bestiality, scientific torture, perverted medicine and murder of the unwanted that by this period of the war, were seeping through from European underground sources to an incredulous public at large.

The British people, were reasonably safe with the sea all round them and the immediate threat of invasion removed. I, in America, was even more safe. An invasion of America was not in the cards. Perhaps my comfortable destiny—school, weekend trips, sports, hot dogs, ice cream, and a graduation coming up—should not be used to contrast the barbarism endured by the children of Europe. I do it to show in relief, as it were how, with American power hypothetically subverted by a hostile one, its capacity to retaliate somehow neutralised, the vulnerability of the nation's children would then become a central, perhaps the *central issue.*

As with British children, would a proportion of them be included in State evacuation programmes? More importantly, what might be their ultimate destinations? Where could America's "crown jewels" be sent? What manner of hostile power could possibly exist that might compel America's politicians to scratch their heads then come up with solutions? Academic questions? An absurd hypothesis just to pad a chapter? If you insist. But one of the objects of this book was to create parallels utilising the awfulness endured by populations over half a century ago. Terrors that then were regarded as neither possible nor credible by those who'd already witnessed, twenty years before, an incredible Great War. The war which deployed all of the equally incredible inventions whose development had spanned a mere six generations—from the realisation that steam from a kettle meant power and radio waves had no boundaries.

So I would say to the futurists: "Get to work, begin to imagine. It can never be too soon. But it could become too late. As earlier pages have shown, I was one of the comparatively fortunate of my generation. Let us gaze, within this chapter, upon the misfortunes of optionless orphans of, say, Germany's Third Reich, of Poland, Greece, Yugoslavia, France, Rumania, Norway—of Europe's Jews. For most of the facts I shall be indebted to Dorothy McCordle's 1949, *Children of Europe*. It is the perfect work from which to make comparisons!

If the events of 1940 marked the end of an entire age of an antiquated Britain, its modes of behaviour and thinking, so too, had the 1933 events in Germany brought to a mischievous and violent halt the way of life of most Germans. Insidious inroads would be made into a nation's heritage. In the context of motor tyres there would be an ethics re-mould affecting some 80,000,000 citizens in the image of National Socialism. And it would be that cult's methods in gaining a unified Germany under a flag of novel design, that would perpetuate State evil and linger in the recollections of freed peoples in 1945 and beyond. For Hitler's promised "Thousand Year Reich" will *endure*, though not in greatness, as he had visualised.

Instead, the world's people will quietly remember a Germany of the twentieth century and the untold miseries it sponsored—for one thousand plus years. Not least will they remember the Nazi corruption of the nation's youth and the twisting of their heritage into unrecognisable shapes until successive post-war leaders straightened out the mind-sets. The preliminaries to the mind-cleansing and how Germans view their short Nazi legacy has so far taken nearly sixty years at the time of writing. That leaves, at a quick count, nine hundred and forty years to go without parole. But maybe there will be a parole. As they say, it all rather depends....

Winston Churchill became a European before the British were seduced into joining a later, so-called Common Market of Europe. His unifying concepts were, ideally, to militarily stifle future European conflagrations among leaders by the fragmentation and dispersal of antagonistic sovereignties. After all, he'd been variously and personally involved in two German attempts to subjugate her neighbours and was plainly fed up with the intrigues perpetrated by a number of Queen Victoria's extended family—dissenting Kings and Queens, Princes and Princesses of Europe and Russia.

The American Option

In Germany, after Hitler engineered his election as Chancellor, the Jewish and Gipsy populations were targeted first as possessing of genes least desirable in the German programme of Aryan race purification and harmonisation considered essential to the nurturing of a "Thousand Year Reich." To that end, the subversion of Hitler's own citizenry began early under the "disciplines" exacted by the Brown Shirt irregulars of the really-gay, Ernst Roem's exclusive re-moulders. How these were employed; how the much vaunted Hitler Youth movement came about; how it aided the weaning of a new nation-state partly founded on the perversion of its unformed minds, is best left to the authors already mentioned, and others to describe in perfected detail. This book is confined to an overview, to pointing–and warning. It can still all happen to *us*. Been there, done that one might almost say.

In Germany crude passions were unleashed as compassion in people was slowly deadened. Perhaps the re-militarising of a Teutonic, European race historically receptive to triumphant war and the wearing of intimidating, decorative uniform clothing, assisted the transformation. The unsatisfactory terms of the post-Great War Treaty of Versailles would have provided additional input.

Curiously, the first victims of Nazi oppression were the children of Germany while those of annexed territories were to be Germanised in the plan to foster and create an idealised prototype Nazi from the more receptive specimen. Cloning would be simple. A restructured educational system would be the narcotic and the mind-controlling poison from daily classroom "fixes" would be channeled into making fanatical little devotees eager to blackmail or expose their unpoisoned parents. As we know, it all worked to substantiate Hitler's claim: *"He who possesses the youth possesses the future."*

Leaders and citizens of endangered nations were aware of what was happening to the children of Germany. They could therefore foresee something of what would be done to their own children if invasion and occupation came to them. Germanisation! It would be of a kind adorned not by music, literature, art, or pure science, but wasted by the baseness of hate and cruelty. And a simplified honour could be invoked from the inscription on the ceremonial daggers presented to inductees into the Hitler Youth movement - "Blood With Honour."

In what high purpose such honour would be needed is now anyone's guess. Today, these adornments of pagan idolatry, mindlessly worn by twelve-year-olds, may be obtained from owners of shops who trade, and somehow profit, from a redistribution of former emblems of the Third Reich. If they have a purpose beyond profit it is that they keep the glimmer of a past frightfulness flickering.

Of the countries annexed by Germany prior to 1939, Czechoslovakia is, arguably, the more infamous in terms of the fate of its children. A few details should suffice for an understanding: By

Jewish Solution

1945, 700,000 Czech children exhibited the consequences of malnutrition. Sexual imbalances were detected. Otherwise-fertile Czech people were menaced with sterility if infirmities and tendencies were not counteracted early. A lack of milk gave tuberculosis free rein. Sanatoriums became overpopulated. Within a year of war's end some 890 Czechoslovakian children were still missing.

From the Czech village of Lidice, razed by the Germans for the assassination of Rhynhard Heydrich, leader of the SS and proponent of "The Final Solution of the Jewish Problem," prior to Himmler, only 15 children of an original 90 were ever found. Some older, returned children believed that 82 from Lidice who'd accompanied them to Poland, had been gassed. This, their fate, was confirmed later from the meticulous documentation for which Nazi Germany became curiously renowned! Six of the 15 survivors (all of whose parents had been shot or burned alive in Lidice barns), were recovered from a German creche in Prague. Today, a small memorial tablet on a Prague wall is dedicated: "To the Memory of the Unknown Child."

Europe-wide, the atmosphere in which children existed was a mixture of violence and trickery. Memory and power of concentration were poor. Emotional stunting became a feature of children exposed to extreme shock and grief. Normal responses to every-day events were lacking. From Poland, a violently invaded country as compared with one passively annexed, Germany demanded 1,000,000 workers. Of 750,000 earmarked as agricultural, half were women. Mothers and pregnant women were not spared. Children saw their mothers seized and taken away. Whole households were taken, then replaced by German families.

As the penalty for resisting invasion troops in Britain, is this what my own mother would have been subjected to while I remained mutely in America? From what we now know, there is very little doubt that Germany's leaders would have gleefully stripped the country out of pure, unadulterated spite and a vengeance repressed for a quarter of a century. Assuredly, I would have beheld my mother for the last time as she stood outside that Liverpool docks air-raid shelter. And I would have had no liveable country to which I might have returned. And I *would* have become an American, but with an uncomfortable, lifetime of guilt. Notwithstanding that, as a family, we were spared, my mother could not bring herself to converse with a German until the 1960's when she and my father would holiday in southern Austria and Italy. She still shrivelled when the language was heard on radio programmes. Such involuntary responses remained a little-known product of six years of German harassment via air waves that reproduced Hitler's harangues and the mouthings of Goebbels, propaganda minister. Add to that, the gut-churning terror every time my mother heard "Lord Haw Haw's" theatrically silken tones announcing the decimation of an Atlantic convoy and

The American Option

her isolation would be complete. Had my father's ship been among the twelve or more claimed to have been sunk? There was a church at the bottom of our road. She would end up inside it many times.

The desolation of service wives who, with few exceptions, were drawn to listen to the British traitor, William Joyce, broadcasting from Germany, was enhanced by the mixture of truth and lies that offered listeners a skewed credibility. The naming of bombed streets and perhaps a familiar tobacconist shop or pub on the corner, gave the lie to official assurance that a "fifth column" network of informers did not exist in Britain.

Joyce, American-born who chose to identify himself as British, was caught in Denmark, tried and hanged—as British—late in 1945 under little-used treason laws. A bad Joyce choice, one could say. Irish members of his family tried desperately to secure witnesses to his American birthright and so strike out any residual legitimacy which his fake British passport might still have given him. Ludovic Kennedy, attendee at the Nuremberg Tribunals trying Germany's war criminals, put it rather well in 1975. Describing Joyce, he wrote: *"The man who was born American, Lived a German and died a British traitor will, at the end become what he really was all along—an Irishman from Comnemara."*

Of the spin-offs from German occupation, the indiscriminate execution of Polish children, was one. Soldiers used them for target practice. Hollywood's *Schindlers List* was not an overplay, as some film makers stand accused. Finally, illness, their resistance lowered by lack of nourishment, cold, homelessness, strain and grief were multiplied over the land. Influenza, typhus, anaemia and tuberculosis found ready incubators. No Poles except farmers were allowed to buy underclothes or shoes. But, everything that Poles suffered was inflicted with even greater remorselessness on Jews. Yet, amidst all this, around 80,000 Warsaw children received some education, in secret.

We can extend this exercise in comparisons, i.e. my life to the bare existence of humans regarded by German Nazis as sub-human, with a quick check of Greece, Yugoslavia, Norway, France, Rumania with its Gypsies and the Jews of all these sovereign states. Atrocities against the Russians must be left as a composite of all while, in that country's vastness it must be said, the German soldier's lot was little different when the tide of war changed direction.

The following bald notes, extracted from Dorothy McCordle's book, together with the foregoing will, I feel, best enable the reader to make his/her own deductions regarding one's prospects in "The Thousand Year Reich." My prospects and destiny in America will, sadly, never be known. But, one could look at the average American male of around my age today and, I suppose, get some idea. At the end of my two years in Montclair I was probably well on the way to becoming indistinguishable.

Jewish Solution

So, in Greece... A head count gives 91,000 executed. That could mean shot against walls or burned in houses. Eighteen-year-old German youths used knives to rape and mutilate. The country seems unique for babies born without nails. Those that lived beyond a year often could not grow teeth. A beginning to the end of life was marked by mental deterioration, scurvy and decomposition of the human system through undernourishment. Few children under four survived.

Yugoslavia, by 1945, is notable for having half a million destitute children living in forests.

Norway was special for having defiant children although certain groups of mothers were less so. The children they bore for German invader fathers became known as the "Tyskerbarnas" or German children who would become Norway's legacy of the occupation years. In the *New Zealand Herald*, July 6th 2002, Kate Connolly, reporter for the *Observer*, London, revealed that Abba vocalist, (*Knowing Me Knowing You*) Anni-Frid Lyngstad, was one of those children. She has recently become a role model for 122 compatriots pursuing claims via the European Court of Human Rights. How many millions have similar rights? All such children would be ostracised in their villages. Many have been driven from the country in little understood misery and desperation. Anni-Frid drifted across to Sweden, initially reclusive and somehow picked herself up there. But in very many cases a discovery that "father was a German" was indictment enough to send children to mental hospitals where many were tortured and raped. They were deemed dangerous and thus disposable because of their "Nazi genes," capable of forming a fascist fifth column. And so, with the exception of Quisling collaborators in their midst, much of the Norwegian's especial wartime loathing for Germans and their local partners is explained. In official circles a peacetime reserve is studiously maintained.

France became a place in which men seized children and carried them off and put them to death, but the fight-back went on underground, as portrayed in print and film. Again, malnutrition effects took their toll, i.e. height loss, weak spines, narrow chested, memory, irritability over small things. Children would burst into tears; cry for a long time. They might never recover. And hereditary defects would be their long-term legacy.

A legacy of a different order is Oradour-sur-Glane, a new town, built adjoining ruins of the old. Just how long the horrors accompanying the removal of buildings and village people from the face of the planet extend *after* a war, now occupies the minds of survivors. Sarah Farmer, in her book: *Martyred Village* (Berkeley University Press), enquires: *"Does memory just turn into history?"*

She is well qualified to answer the question. An assistant professor of history at the University of Iowa, she developed, in research, what appears a passionate sympathy for the handful of survivors.

The American Option

Four days after D-day, 120 soldiers of the Waffen S.S. tank division Das Reich, torched the small farming town and murdered 642 men, women and children. A kind of record for sadism in Germany's four year occupation of France. Unlike Czechoslovakia's Lidice, it was not a reprisal massacre. So why? With the politicking of a post-war period in the offing, with elections, revenge executions, calls for French revival and the energy wasted on rationalising a national conscience, it seems that Oradour, as an incident, was both used and mis-used as a symbol of something. *"The town's own chosen identity was as innocent victim; its emotional stance, however, proved weaker than political expediency. When twenty-one German soldiers involved were brought to trial in 1953, fourteen proved to be Frenchmen forced to join the SS after Germany annexed the province of Alsace. They received light sentences and were subsequently amnestied."*

Again, unlike Lidice, whose demise is now blessed with a degree of closure, Oradour remains a supperating sore with debate continually on the boil over France's role in sending 78,000 Jews—give or take a thousand here or there—to the death camps. And this, notwithstanding that such an affront to the human ethic is customarily attributed to occupied France.

Taking that sad, proud nation further as a case study: "Post-war students were intellectually changed from their pre-war counterparts. They seemed excessively skeptical. Unsurprisingly, they had developed an immunity against optimistic promises or ideals. Inexplicably, many seemed eager to turn their backs on their country and upon Europe. Those capable of hard study preferred factual subjects such as science, economics or town planning. They looked to the future without anticipation or happiness or peace. Their deepest resolve appeared to be how to survive in a world which gave them nothing in which to place their trust yet the spirit of resistance burned intensely and in secret. And they buried home-made Tricolours in metal boxes for a liberation to match their dreams.

Even during the occupation, France appeared to have a multiplicity of services for mothers and children. In 1944, the resistance movement with the Red Cross, co-ordinated with the Comite des Oèuvres Socialés des Organisations de la Résistance. (COSOR) Funds came via parachute. Households whose breadwinners had disappeared or where children had been left alone, were helped. In that year, various organisations brought hope to 2,584 vagrant minors whose status was masked by such terms as Displaced Persons or Unidentified or War-Handicapped or...supreme understatement covering total bereavement and desolation... "The Unaccompanied Child."

By war's end, people on COSOR's register included relatives of more than 29,000 patriots who'd been executed. 47,000 had been deported for opposing their German occupiers and died in Germany. 106,000 had been deported for racial reasons, and died somewhere.

Jewish Solution

Few of the invaded countries had been so tragically undermined in every respect of national life as was France. When Dorothy McCordle published her book in 1949, barely four years after Hitler's suicide in his Berlin bunker, *"...malnutrition and depression continued hand-in-hand despite a brave parade of high spirits. Children were found to be well-mannered and gaily dressed while living in sparsely-furnished orphanages. An equal number remained almost destitute for whom no satisfactory homes could be provided. Such children, without relatives, were swelled by returned deportees in 1945, but 25,000 from that source had already died. Few, if any, had been able to retain any knowledge of their origins or knew their family names. French families whose homes had been destroyed in bombing numbered about 5,000,000 which produced an unenviable, mobile segment of the population in the immediate postwar France."* Thus, the experience of the French child which might fairly be replicated across Europe with the one exception of Rumania.

In that Balkan State of oil-wells, art, Transylvanian myth, one-time granary of the Roman Empire, *"...the loss of child life through infant mortality reached 80% in some regions, from a pre-war 38%. In 1947 a diplomat, visiting Geneva, advised relief organisations not to send, to certain parts of the country, anything for children under five, because none were alive. Rumania experienced no national recovery as applied elsewhere. In the summer of 1947 an estimate put 17,000 children as still starving. There would also be an intense move to de-Nazify children and students who'd been caught up in industrial centres. Outside the German Nazi world, most discovered another, wider one in which it was pleasant to survive.*

"Soon, American schools, in recovery mode, sprang up in Eastern Europe and both the USA and Britain sponsored individual towns, twinning them with towns in the home countries. The Boy Scout and Girl Guide movements sent their members into the field. The Guides were given drastic training for the work and care of some of the most distraught and wretched human beings on earth in the displaced persons camps. Many children were deformed with misshapen heads—and who never smiled."

Back at base, in Germany-Austria, where all these sickening effects were propagated, The United Nations Relief and Rehabilitation Administration (UNRRA) discovered, via the German penchant for leaving paper trails of intentions and deeds, orders relating to the disposal of the unwanted. These turned up in a place called Aglasterhausen, near Heidelberg, synonymous with the melodious voice of Mario Lanza in *The Student Prince*. From that film's picturesque portrayal of German university life, learning and Teutonic cultures, we hear again of blood with honour, dripping from the prized facial cuts gained from students' fencing duels high on principle; low on reasoning. Akin, some say, to self-mutilation by New Guinea tribesmen—with ladies always somewhere about. The carefully signed orders were found in a private home. Defective children were to be killed in groups. A quota, at regular intervals, were to be processed by injections. Some of the children who made up the quotas were physically handicapped. All, were found to be mentally sound.

"Beyond Europe, the injuries purposefully inflicted upon children by war, persecution and occupation, was not fully realised, even by relief workers for long after hostilities ended. New governments lacked workable bureaucratic machinery to complete surveys and publish findings. A shortage of newsprint curtailed reports, journalists were unable to penetrate where distress was most acute. Finally, when at length some accounts were published, they made such appalling reading that many people took refuge from this demand on their sympathies under a blanket of incredulity. This left the more sensational disclosures, like Belsen and Auschwitz, to stand alone while dense confusion and ignorance hid a vast host of sick, lost and suffering children from the world's view."

Some figures now. *"In a six month period, children kidnapped for Germanisation throughout greater Germany and Austria were: Lower Bavaria, 1,000, the rest of Bavaria, 5,000, Silesia/Austria, 800 (mostly Polish). A useful half yearly total of 10,000. Sixty thousand names fill a list headed:* Missing Parents & Children. *In the postwar rehabilitation hostels, warped and hardened children unleashed barbaric and vengeful behaviour on any and everyone. Collectively dubbed: "The Wild Children of Europe," they could ineffectually defend the bad conscience of a whole continent. A vast multitude of children learned in their hopeless misery to use the mean weapons of the weak: lying, stealing and blackmail. Dangerous tendencies that can simply emanate from a humiliating lack of acceptable clothing, became features of the dispossessed—and the 'Unaccompanied Child.'"*

In the worst hostel scenarios, children lodged in them became stricken with apathy; stupefied from monotony and restraints or just fretted for a one-to-one understanding with a sympathetic adult. Preferably, we may imagine, one not wearing a uniform. In times of illness or just loneliness they would dwell upon all they had lost. Even those without memory of a mother or of any close, tender affection, became oppressed, as they grew older, by a sense of something missing from their lives to which they had a right. Eventually, the rebuilding of towns and cities went some way to satisfying the nervous and emotional needs of the young who'd witnessed only wreckage and waste. Some appeared emotionally retarded; others disconcertingly mature. Later, special "villages" were built to house those according to needs, maladjustments and skills. Two, at Civitavecchia, Italy and Longueil-Annel, France, catered for small groups of 10 to 15-year-olds. By that time, teachers were in short supply, partly explained by a murdered 1,055 Czech and 6,000 Polish teachers and professors culled from the thirteen countries annexed or technically invaded. Of Europe's children, 13,000,000 lost one or both parents.

Finally, with these depressing yet highly salutary revelations of the misfortunes of children compared with those of adult citizens and soldiery, I hope I can place in appropriate juxtaposition, the sufferings of Jewish and German child populations of annexed and invaded nations. Partly as a result of the re-drawing of frontiers following the Great War, German nationals were to be found on both sides of Polish, Austrian, Hungarian and Czechoslovakian frontiers. They represented "The Greater Germany," as Hitler was fond of saying before acting out his pretexts to stomp in with his black-suited elite and acquire a bit more territory. The Jewish people had and still have a far wider choice of country. The Romany people, Gypsies, likewise roam wherever opportunity beckons. Hitler had intended to pay special attention to the offspring of these Middle East and East European races. They were to be liquidated from within the sphere of National Socialism. A tall order, one might say. For they remained numerous beyond his orbit.

In the German solution of the Jewish problem, as espoused by Rhynhard Heydrich and then equally zealously by his successor, the bespectacled, sinister, former chicken farmer, Heinrich Himmler, 2,000,000 German-Jewish children died variously. 1,000,000 were murdered by a German Government Ordinance. *"The systematic slaughter of innocents surely must stand out in history as the most coldly, vicious proceeding ever to emanate from human brains."* (Dorothy McCordle—*The Children of Europe*)

But the deliberate killing of Germany's children began in Germany before the war under the guise of the Euthanasia Commission headed by Rudolf Hess, Hitler's deputy. A State programme to remove the mentally defective from aspiring, pure Aryan blood stock, was in place. Intravenous injections or poisoned chocolates were used for older children. Nazi doctors and officials were taught to accept the measures to improve the German race and were able to overcome any repugnance of killing children since it was the general feeling among so-called natural men.

Half the German-Jewish population under sixteen, about 30,000, escaped from Germany and Austria before the war and the s.s. *Baltrover*, London, was one ship that aided their survival. *"Back on the continent of Europe, menaced children wandered, hid and lived like terrified, hunted animals. Groups and swarms of frightened children gathered in forests or desolate places which were safer than inhabited areas. Much, much later, in the security of an Israeli State, some Jewish survivors were encouraged to record their experiences and which now form the most pitiable archives in existence of childish misery and fear. In 1948, Jewish children had no enemies in Palestine. Arabs came with gifts and said: 'May Allah be with you. You are now the children of mankind.'"*

And what of Germany, the ordinary people...of Hamburg, Cuxhaven, Kiel, Emden, Berlin, Essen, Dresden, Cologne...and those killed or maimed, as Londoners had been killed or maimed in the London Blitz? The anticipated, fearful retaliation by the Royal Air Force, swelled by crews from the British dominions, and the U.S.

Army Air Force, saw German cities demolished to a degree where few buildings remained higher than two floors in the wake of 1,000 bomber raids and the fire storms they generated.

In early postwar months a flotsam of Europe's young waited for the emergence of United Nations agencies to lock on to desperation and bring a semblance of order and hope. UNRRA, already mentioned, The United Nations' International Children's Fund (UNICEF) and The United Nations Education, Scientific & Cultural Organisation (UNESCO) added their weight to human recovery. For Britain's NSPCC, The Royal Society for the Prevention of Cruelty to Children, it was all way too late.

And as a 20-year-old Merchant Navy cadet in 1948, ashore for an afternoon's stroll, I would see a small girl walking along without arms to swing. In the evening, I drank Schnapps for the first time from correct, liqueur-size glasses in a subterranean beerkellar fashioned from a mound of rubble. I remember being impressed by the improvisation and by the spotless, meticulously-darned white woollen stockings of another small girl who, observing me with some curiosity, finger in mouth, was sliding along sideways, against a wall as small girls do. The photograph I took of her is the aid to my recollection of Emden's near-levelled landscape. It was quite a walk. I was glad when it ended, with a cup of tea and buttered toast back aboard a ship inaccurately named the s.s. *Granview*, whose cook may well have included mutton chops and mashed potatoes in the dinner menu, as he had done for breakfast. I remember, it was that kind of ship.

Our shore nightwatchman, thin, greying "Otto Reigen" had, pre-war, served in the Deutsche Ost Afrika Linie. We had things in common. In July 1945, my second ship served in as cadet, had been the s.s. *Urundi* of that company, then a German prize of war. Three months before she'd been a prison ship for the merchant seamen survivors of ships sunk by surface raiders. "Otto" had been her pre-war captain. After learning his story I always addressed him as Captain "Reigen." And why not? Aboard our ship, unthreatened then for three years by German submarines, he seemed well content to have a warm, coal-driven, galley fire to keep stoked up and sit by until daylight came and he went somewhere to sleep. It seemed all a sad, desperate price to pay for being on the losing side of Hitler's war.

But German victims were not the innocents of occupied territories, the subject of this chapter. German children, killed or mentally destroyed, have already been indented in an earlier paragraph. They, if you remember, were the 2,000,000 plus 1,000,000 German-Jewish children already done away with. Their perverse and ghostly imagery would stick like napalm to the recollections of the living and ultimately create a Jewish solution to the German problem—for at least one thousand years.

"...observing me with some curiosity..."
A small girl of Emden, Germany 1948

Emden, Germany
"...where few buildings remained higher than two floors..."

12   Many People Don't Know This

The cue to commence this chapter could, conceivably, come from the first three pages of the previous one. In them, if the reader will recall, I touched upon the British response to the imminence of invasion by German forces in 1940 with a government-sponsored, second evacuation of children to rural areas. This was to clear south coast beaches and resorts as a first line of defense and free up the cities for the savage and bloody house-to-house street fighting that, if Churchill was to be believed, could eventually ensue throughout the British Islands. Remember, the second most memorable of Churchill's 1940 speeches?

"...*we shall fight on the beaches; in the fields; on the landing grounds...we shall never surrender...*"

I would like to believe that no quarter would have been given and none asked and that the defense of Stalingrad still three years away would have its premier on the British mainland. The scenes around London, for example, could be similar to those in and around the Ukrainian city, subsequently to be shown to the world on cinema screens. Other of our cities would follow and become sites to emulate the German defiance to come, born of desperation and recognisable fear.

Why does it seem important to conjecture on the British reaction to having its borders crossed by a state hostile to its way of life or to settle old scores? Unlike other European States with land boundaries, the British Islands have only crossable coastlines. The English Channel and the North Sea would become untenable as avenues for retreat once invasion forces had gained south coast bridgeheads. Beyond, to the north and west, lie the Arctic seas and Atlantic Ocean. Effective enough walls, one would think, for 50,000,000 members of Churchill's scorched earth, nil surrender advocates to put their backs up against.

Hypothesising whether one's country possesses psychic stamina to stand and fight has real value if a track record exists. Since Britain does have one of those hope also was present. Angus Calder reminds us that only the very wealthy or highly placed had access to the truth of our predicament and in consequence lived with pessimism in June, 1940. Short on facts the middle classes and the poor shared their optimism in the food queues and the pubs gleefully bolstered by caricatures of Hitler, Göring, Ribbentrop and Goebbels, our washing to be hung out on the Siegfried Line—and Mr Churchill, through the wireless, intoning his trenchant disgust, incomparable exhortations and joyful ridicule.

Many People

Now, with stirrings of regret, I would not be one of that 50,000,000. Bill Brown, John Moore Jr., Bob Mapletoft, "Red" Jacobs and myself, were persevering with our Seventh Grade schoolwork at Montclair Academy and patiently preparing ourselves for the grand crossing of one of our own frontiers. This would be the highly significant ceremony attending our graduation to the Upper School and eighth grade. No longer could we allow ourselves to be termed "kids," just in case anyone had the temerity to try it. We would soon let them know who we were; that only another four grades separated us from twelfth grade and adulthood. For four brief years we could just about endure being called "the in betweens."

Reference in the last chapter was also made to the mental destabilising of individuals—particularly the young. Mind corruption, "mindset" and "mind-cleansing," were terms used. This last might fairly cover the "de-Nazification" of millions under a special programme instituted by the allied occupying powers at war's end. For, in the six years of a sadistic German domination over Western Europe, National Socialism, as then practiced, had employed a near Frankenstein intellect. As a role model for twenty-first century sadisms against whole populations, it can hardly be bettered. The methods of counselling and reversing pagan philosophies instilled into young heads, must be left outside the scope of this book. Some, liken the "de-briefing" of Germany's citizens, to the downloading, then deleting, of a tyranny out of sinc., with a civilised world and needing a bit of editing out. Yes, the process would have unquestioned merit were it not for the contradiction that Germans were already among the most civilised and cultured of all the western nations. Now, for some reason, the wheel had turned to a point where it all needed resurrecting after taking an inexplicable fall.

Whatever the term, German and Russian medical and scientific fraternities, delving deeply into electro-magnetic phenomena and the parameters of radio frequencies, were "into" mind-control in a big way from the word "go." And their medical and scientific fraternities had, at their white-coated elbows, ready practitioners and "testers" in numbers undreamed by most doctors of medicine: Psychologists, anthropologists, hypnotists, theorists or simply cranks. When World War II commenced, studies, experiments and the writing of learned papers by notable men and women in all the western countries, on ways the human brain can be made to react in electromagnetic fields, were already eighty plus years into the past.

Where all this information fits in a book about the survival rate of children in the European war is perhaps more in the context of America fighting a war on its own soil. Who, where or what might be *its* enemy? In the previous chapter, I wrote: "What manner of hostile power could possibly exist that might compel America's politicians to scratch their heads then come up with solutions?"

The American Option

Coincidentally, they are doing that as I write. The world knows of a limited invasion of America on September 11th 2001. "Brave," special forces of Al Qaeda utilised three aeroplanes-full of ordinary people to demolish three buildings filled with more ordinary people. The selection of a soft target to make a statement? Hardly! In the light of all the other soft options attacked around the world since then, an effort by Islam to coerce the world into believing what it believes is a moral lifestyle, is now taking place. America, it believes, is the nastiest nut to crack, so go for it first. Other nations will fall into line.

If world domination in the name of Islam is the goal, maybe adapting the little publicised science of mass mental programming, is in the cards. If, at one time, official America regarded Arab nations with disdain, albeit in ignorance, it cannot do so now. In Britain, we are fortunate in having, at bedrock, a different relationship with present and former Arabian kingdoms but, allied to America in a world war against terrorism and its principles, old Arab friendships may not save us from attacks on our cities in the name of terror groups waving Islamic banners. And what might be the new weaponry used in place of unwieldy, cumbersome field artillery, tanks, massed troop movements, aircraft, warships or the colossal expense of rocketry with nuclear warheads?

Judy Wall is editor and publisher of *Resonance*, the newsletter of the MENSA, Bioelectromagnetics Special Interest Group in America. We can use the views of a journalist to introduce a subject of immense diversity of application in both the positive and negative sense yet is accorded little credibility by the public at large. There is some evidence that a conspiracy of silence exists in western official circles and that private persons are weaned into believing that the manipulation of the human mind by electro-magnetic impulses are the mind-wanderings of already-effected, mad scientists. Not so, argues Ms Wall, impressively supported by a host of medical and scientific academics—serious thinkers all.

I have decided to initially quote from her article titled: *Military Use Of Mind Control Weapons*, which appeared in the October/November 1998 issue of *Nexus*, having its head office in Australia and published in the U.K., U.S., N.Z., and the Netherlands. The magazine devotes its pages to "Behind The News" subjects on health and scientific research. Its topics appear on TV's Discovery Channel and the magazine's readers, like viewers, are left to draw their own conclusions. Readers of this chapter may do the same for I am a novice reporter on a little-discussed subject and I submit the findings of others in an attempt to discover what America's politicians are scratching their heads about and what the "futurists" can produce from their imaginings. Under the subheading: "Towards Global Mind Control," Ms Wall writes (and I paraphrase):

Many People

"The secrecy involved in the development of the electromagnetic mind-altering technology reflects the tremendous power inherent in it. Bluntly, whoever controls this technology can control the minds of men—all men.

There is evidence that the U.S. Government has plans to extend the range of this technology to envelop all peoples, all countries. It can, and is, being accomplished by utilising the nearly completed HAARP project for overseas areas and the GWEN network (of radio beacons) in place in the U.S. for internal nationwide coverage. The U.S. Government denies this."

Dr Michael Persinger is a professor of Psychology and Neuroscience at Laurentian University, Ontario, Canada. His findings, that strong electromagnetic fields can affect a person's brain (and physical condition), are contained in an article titled: *"On The Possibility of Directly Accessing Every Human Brain by Electromagnetic Induction of Fundamental Algorithms."* It gives weight to his claim that, *"Temporal lobe stimulation can invoke the feeling of a presence, disorientation, and perceptual irregularities. Within the last two decades a potential has emerged which was improbable, but which is now marginally feasible. This potential is the technical capability to influence directly the major portion of the approximately six billion brains of the human species, without mediation through classical sensory modalities, by generating neural information within a physical medium within which all members of the species are immersed."*

Well, that is imponderable enough, but for me, still scary. He concludes:

"The historical emergence of such possibilities, which have ranged from gunpowder to atomic fission, have resulted in major changes in the social evolution that occurred inordinately quickly after implementation. (One supposes he's referring to the 20th century's four major wars.)... *Reduction of the risk of the inappropriate application of these technologies requires the continued and open discussion of their realistic feasibility and implications within the scientific and public domain."*

As Ms Wall remarks: *"It doesn't get any plainer than that! And we do not have open discussion because the U.S. Government has totally denied the existence of this Technology."*

Well, speaking for me, I wish it all was plainer. The following comment and extracts lifted from the learned papers of those to whom it does seem all perfectly plain, must suffice for readers of this book. Recently, I acquired from private archives, a large body of material which, even if spot-read by those who disbelievingly read certain comic strips, could still develop a perplexed frown.

Unclassified technology is tabled on three pages of Ms Wall's article in *Resonance* and is conveniently identified for those interested, in a list, edited here for space, of twenty-seven U.S. patents issued to inventors of appliances utilising radio and electromagnetic resonance techniques. What of other nations' patents? An introduction explains that:

"The technologies may be combined for use in direct or subliminal

mind-control systems and urge they are mainly private inventions intended for positive uses, but could be applied for negative purposes. We have no idea what the government has in classified research."

The stuff, presumably, that doesn't exist!

Here, selected out, are several U.S. patents whose purported functions will:

1. Afford a silent, subliminal presentation comprising a silent communications system in which non-aural carriers in the very low or very high audio-frequency range, or in the adjacent ultrasonic frequency spectrum, are amplitude-modulated with the desired intelligence and propagated acoustically or vibrationally for inducement into the brain. (The last four words provide the clue to this nasty little machine's potential.)

2. Provide an Auditory Subliminal Message System and Method, e.g. an amplitude-controlled subliminal message may be mixed with ("Piggy-backed" onto) background music via chosen carrier frequencies. Useful, it is claimed by another source, to induce warnings into the minds of those on shoplifting expeditions. (I'd buy that!)

3. Offer a combined subliminal message generator for use with a television receiver that permits complete control of subliminal messages and their presentation. Also applicable to cable television and computers. (Now that sounds a bit nasty!)

4. Provide a method of changing a person's behaviour. (That surely could be one of the more positive uses of the technology!)

5. Give combatants a Psycho-Acoustic Projector, being a system for producing aural psychological disturbances and partial deafness in the enemy during combat situations. (This puts us more closely within the orbit of military weaponry. BANG—you're deaf!)

6. Advance the treatment of Neuropsychic and Somatic Diseases with heat, light, sound and VHF electromagnetic radiation. (I give the U.S. patent number in this example: Number 3,773,049 held by messrs. Rabichev, Vasiliev, Putilin, Ilina, Raku and Kemitsky–November 20th 1973.)

This is the patent–unclassified–for LIDA, the infamous Soviet brainwashing machine. But it all gets nastier than that.

How the inventing fraternity came to a conclusion that tampering with brainwaves by externally induced ones provides links to physiological cures, is unclear to me at this time. But, as I read through well-researched papers and articles variously titled as: *Military Use of Mind Control Weapons*, (Judy Wall), *Microchip Implants, Mind control, and Cybernetics and Microwave mind Control: Modern Torture and Control Mechanisms Eliminating Rights and Privacy* (both by Dr Rauni Leena Kilde, MD, former chief medical officer for Finland), *Radio Frequency Weapons and The Infrastructure* (Lieutenant General Robert L. Schweitzer, U.S. Army (Retired), *Scalar Electromagnetic Weapons* (Lieutenant Colonel T.E. Bearden, U.S. Army (Retired),

Many People

Timeline of Important Dates in the History of Electromagnetic Technology (Ms Cheryl Welsh), it is easier to understand that the "Doctor No's" of the neuroscientific and biochemical world in whose shadow we all live, are not all quite mad. But understanding some research continues to stretch our credibility. The *Nexus* magazine carried an article in 1996 titled: *Soul Catcher Implants*, by its author, David Guyatt. It claimed that: *"British scientists (were then) developing a concept for a computer chip which, when implanted into the skull behind the eye, will be able to record a person's life-time thought and sensation. This is the end of death,"* announced Dr Chris Winter, of British Telecom's artificial-life team. *He predicted that within thirty years it will be possible to relive other people's lives by playing back their experiences on a computer."*

I've just delved a bit more into the piles of files in front of me on my work table. For some reason I become uneasy reading about people being "implanted," i.e. having things stuck under their skin, for either good or bad reasons. It seems an arcane subject and, for that reason perhaps, a little more space ought to be given it before we get further into what has become a totally unplanned chapter in this book.

Let us look at what Dr Rauni Leena Kilde, MD., has to say about implants. A reference to some of her work has been mentioned here. As former chief medical officer for Finland, the doctor's more specific views and warnings can be respected.

The Finnish language journal *Spekula* is published by North Finland medical students and doctors of Oulu University, Olk. It had, when her article went to press, a mail list circulation of around 6,500 sent to medical students and doctors. In her October 23rd 1999 contribution to this journal, Dr Kilde writes on a questionable subject under title: 1 *Microchip Implants, Mind Control & Cybernetics.* She tells us that brain implants were first surgically inserted in 1874 in Ohio, USA and also at Stockholm, Sweden. Babies were treated in 1946, both humans and animals in the 1950's and 1960's, prisoners (Sweden) in 1973, nursing home patients in the 1980's. In 1995, *The Washington Post* speculated that Prince William received an implant at age twelve, as protection against kidnapping. And people have heart pacemakers implanted and assorted spare parts. The procedure is not, in itself, earth-shaking. Opportunity for its perverted use is, in the absence of a general public awareness.

We do not know, for example "that every newborn could be injected with a microchip making them taggable for life, brain functions can be monitored by supercomputers or altered by changing frequencies. *"Today's microchips,"* Dr Kilde warns, *"operate via low frequency radio waves which can target them. Satellites ensure an implanted person can be tracked anywhere on the globe...a person's privacy vanishes for the rest of their life."* Even more Frankenstein, she explains how emotional changes can be press-buttoned into aggression or lethargy. Sexuality, even, may be artificially influenced. God! Is there no end to this?

The American Option

Of course, the technology can be used or misused by military forces. Dr Kilde claims certain NATO countries have used it. A "cyber soldier," can be created. Chemical methods have been developed using mind-altering drugs. Different smelling gasses affecting brain functions can be injected into air ducts or water pipes. Bacteria and viruses have been tested this way.

Has that way already been the Saddam Hussein way? In that case, I've changed my mind about a career as a weapons inspector.

Dr Kilde believes the reason why all this Big Brother stuff has remained shadowy in our minds is partly the result of the prestige given to the psychiatric *Diagnostic Manual-Vol. IV*, produced by the U.S. American Psychiatric Association (APA), and printed in eighteen languages. It is believed that psychiatrists, working for U.S. intelligence agencies, helped re-write the manual. Thus the psychiatry "bible" is a bible no more and now conveniently covers the secret development of microchip (MC) technologies by labeling some of the effects experienced by patients as mere symptoms of paranoid schizophrenia, a condition with which we are all more comfortably familiar.

Except that in 1997—and after this chapter we'll all be pleased to learn this—former moon-walker, Senator John Glen, was not comfortable. "*All international human rights agreements forbid non-consensual manipulation of human beings, even in prisons.*" But, notwithstanding this, the senator tabled the issues dealing with radiating civilian populations. More recently, *Nexus* magazine reports in its February/March 2002 issue, that on October 2nd 2001, Dennis Kucinich, U.S. House of Representatives introduced a Bill... "*To preserve the peaceful uses of space for mankind....prohibiting basing weapons in space by the U.S. and to require the President to take action to adopt and implement a world treaty ...,*" etc., etc.

A term, "exotic weapons systems," appears in my reading for the first time. It seems that all of the "dangerous toys" described herein come into that exotic category, e.g. "*weapons that could damage space, natural ecosystems, the ionosphere and upper atmosphere, climate, weather, tectonic systems ....all with the purpose of inducing damage or destruction upon a target population or region on Earth or in space.*" (Source: *Secrecy News,* January 10th 2002)

I thought it would be nice, at this point, to insert evidence that, apart from President Bush, the United Nations and custodians and implementers of the Geneva Convention, other people are getting worried about what a few schizophrenic nuts can come up with after an hour or so in the unique chain of America's "Radio Shack" shops. I swear by "Radio Shack." It was the only shop in the West that got my 240 volt typewriter going on America's 110 volt power supply. And the machine cannot be modified to emit a masonry-crumbling, radio frequency beam from a hotel room.

The LIDA machine, mentioned above in Ms Judy Wall's list

of patented radio-magnetic appliances, "was built in the 1950's by the Soviets. The CIA purchased one through a Canadian front for a Dr Ross Adey. Its purported use was for medical treatment, but the North Koreans used it as a brain-washing device during the Korean War. Big question...what did they do with the technology? An electrician, noticing Dr Adey's "experimental" machine commented that as a prisoner of war in Korea, one like it had been used on him. Interviewed later by the Red Cross, the former POW responded with what had been read to him while under the influence of the device. He seemed to have no control over the answers he gave.

Dr Kilde explains that "Dr Adey has since discovered that by using 0.75 milliwatts per square centimeter intensity of pulse modulated microwave at a frequency of 450 MHz, it is possible to control *all* aspects of human behaviour! Also, microwave radiation excites the hydrogen bond in the cells and can interfere with meiosis–which leads to tumours.

"It is possible," she warns, *"the U.S. will ignore resolutions which could curb its research and development of the Alaskan HAARP and other projects that touch upon the manipulation of human beings (and the atmosphere). The dangers were already revealed at an expert meeting of the International Committee of the Red Cross in Geneva, in July 1994."*

"The LIDA machine is patented in the U.S.," states Dr Eldon Byrd, psychotropic researcher who funded Dr Adey's work on the LIDA machine. *"Why? They are not sold in the United States. The only one I know that exists is the one that was at the Loma Linda Medical Centre, near Redlands, Southern California–where Dr Adey used to work."*

Is the machine, or similar, clinically in use at the centre to treat patients suffering from hypertension, neurotic disturbances or psychological problems–and what name might it now go under?

I will not go further with this technology's disturbing research except to offer the comment that this chapter is a scratch on the surface of scientific realities rather than fantasies.

"British Telecom, Britain's giant telecommunications enterprise, has a long history of involvement with the intelligence services," states David Guyatt. He gives his source as the London *Daily Telegraph*, July 18th 1996 indicating how, piecemeal, the general public are, line-by-cautious-line, being made aware of what is going on beyond the garden gate. But the world is full of skeptics. Not a useful condition for anti-zap planning.

A Ms Cheryl Welsh produced, in 2000, her *"Timeline of Important Dates in the History of Electromagnetic Technology."* It serves to collate the works of scientists and authors from 1942 on. She writes: *"It is interesting to note that two scientists with connections to the American Central Intelligence Agency (CIA) classified mind control and psychic research, have contributed to this study (Timeline). They are, J. West, MD, Director Emeritus, Neuropsychiatric Institute, University of California and Los Angeles (UCLA) School of Medicine and Behavioral Biology and*

The American Option

Edwin May, Ph.D., Science Applications International Corporation (SAIC), Physics of Consciousness.

"This timeline," goes on Ms Welsh, *"demonstrates how classified the electromagnetic and mind control technology is. Scientists have been killed (in process of) revealing this technology. They have lost government funding. They can be prosecuted and/or lose their jobs if they reveal national security secrets. And some scientists have been targeted with the technology and been unjustly labeled mentally ill.*

A similar analogy," she explains, *"would be The Manhattan Project, the U.S. government programme to build the atomic bomb. The project used the highest of national security precautions and few knew of its existence. Mind control technology is the currently classified weapons programme and national security methods are even more entrenched and developed."*

Ms Welsh pin-points 1942, New York, as a date when discussions at the Josiah Macy Foundation were devoted to problems of central inhibition in the nervous system. She writes of German experimentation on human volunteers unknowingly exposed to a low-intensity, 10-Hz electrical field demonstrating how fluctuations of the earth's magnetic fields may cause undesirable behavioral changes. Dr Norbet Weiner, subsequently attached to the Massachusetts Institute of Technology (MIT), the originator of cybernetics, was involved in the German experiments. About Dr Weiner's book, *Cybernetics*, the *New York Times* said: *"One of the most influential books of the twentieth century, judged by twenty-seven historians, economists, educators and philosophers to be one of those books published during the past four decades, which most significantly altered the direction of our society."*

Dr Weiner worked with colleagues under the assumption that Extra Low Frequency (ELF) internal rhythms in the brain were determinants of behaviour, and that pulsing external fields could "drive" these internal rhythms, thereby altering behaviour.

From Ms Welsh's calendar for 1953 we read of the irradiation of persons in the U.S. Embassy, Moscow. On November 15th 1992, *The Washington Post* reported: *"The Russian Government is continuing to bombard the U.S. Embassy with microwave radiation, according to U.S. officials. The pulsed emanations originate from a residential building across the street that is believed to be staffed by Russian security officials."* Then, in 1976, the *Globe* reported that Ambassador Walter Stoessel developed a rare blood disease, suffered headaches and bleeding from the eyes. Two of his irradiated predecessors, Ambassador Charles Bohlen and Ambassador Llewellyn Thompson, died of cancers.

In 1977, Paul Brodeur published his book: *The Zapping of America*. He wrote: *"A report published in the New York Times, October 30th, 1976, revealed that in recent months a mysterious broadband, short-wave radio signal had been broadcast intermittently from the Soviet Union. The signal was so powerful that it disrupted radio and telecommunications throughout the world."*

There was grave concern that such an encoding, when impressed onto carrier wavelengths, could effect the central nervous system. But, who would wish to zap America?

Well, there we go...we creep a little closer to this chapter's topic concerning America's vulnerability as potential victim of a technology it is, itself, developing. There are clues to the present Bush Administration's seeming obsession with the level of know-how acquired by Iraq's former leaders and the nasty things which the world knows they've been responsible for, and their erstwhile president's suspected alliance with the Al Qaeda terrorist network. It does not take great effort, in light of the above, to appreciate American preoccupations with so-called Weapons of Mass Destruction. There can be no better form of mass destruction than irradiating—burning out—the brain matter of one's adversaries from a great and safe distance. And the subjugated lands and infrastructure would remain non-toxic and intact. As for the human work force, it would be mindless, mute and malleable. It is believed this capability has been reached. It is one reason why the western world should follow Washington's lead in a fight against terror weapons. America's options may truly be limited by time.

At which point, a few notes from a discussion on HAARP may be of interest in conjecturing what America might do to resist an invasion of a mind-bending character in a World War III, War-Of-The-Minds. HAARP stands for High-frequency Active Auroral Research Programme and its facilities are chiefly based at Anchorage, Alaska. In Judy Wall's list of 27 U.S. patents which she sub-heads: *Technology To Boggle Your Mind*, the machines and appliances, with some exceptions, require a nearby power source. HAARP limits itself to the ionosphere! From its transmitters and computers, there is hardly a place on earth for me, the reader or anyone else—to hide.

HAARP: Vandalism in the Sky?, is the title of *Nexus* magazine's excerpts from Dr Nick Begich and Ms Jeane Manning's book *Angels Don't Play This HAARP: Advances In Tesla Technology*, contained in Volume 3, Number 1 (December '95-January '96). *Nexus* introduces the article with the following: (paraphrased)

"Technonet is the protest vehicle for 1990's picketing on the information highways. For example, a fast-growing assortment of men and women worldwide are using the Internet. The Internet was developed by the U.S. military as an information transfer tool supposedly secure from interference. Technonet, however, draws attention to HAARP's questionable military applications capable of being projected from the Alaskan facility. These Internetting, e-mailing, faxing folks are blowing holes in the U.S. Department of Defense secrecy wall by using the government's own system, the Internet!"

Dennis Specht, an anti-nuclear activist living in Alaska, sent a news item to *Nexus* discussing HAARP. Dr Nick Begich read the magazine, noticed a reference to his home town, presumably Anchorage, dug out documents cited in the article and then co-authored the book with researcher, Ms Jeane Manning.

The American Option

Despite the amount of research with 350 footnotes the book, at its heart, is a story about ordinary people who took on an extraordinary challenge. HAARP transmitters will impact the upper atmosphere with a focussed, steerable electromagnetic beam. It is an advanced model of an ionosphere "heater." The ionosphere is the electrically-charged layer enveloping the Earth's upper atmosphere like a soap bubble. (What happens if it gets pricked?) It ranges between 40 to several hundred miles above the surface. HAARP's super-powerful radio beams purport to lift and heat areas of the ionosphere. Electromagnetic waves bounce back to Earth penetrating everything—living or dead. HAARP's publicity machine puts out that theirs is an academic project whose goal is to manipulate the ionosphere to improve communications with submarines!

The Alaskan protest group's fears centre on the enormous radio frequency power's potential for driving the ionosphere to unnatural activity. Reasonable, one would suppose. Dr No tampering with things again? However, the military give seven beneficial effects from their trials. One, is an innocuous tool for geophysical probing for oil, gas and mineral deposits. Another, with similar altruistic motives, would provide wide-ranging, Earth-penetrating tomography which, if combined with the computing capabilities of super-computers, could be used to verify many parts of nuclear non-proliferation and peace agreements.

Slightly more sinister, HAARP could wipe out communications over large areas while keeping intact the military's own systems. According to some scientists, any of the effects from the reckless use of these power levels in our natural shield, the ionosphere, could be cataclysmic. An independent assessment describes the unforeseen effects of the HAARP "skybuster" as acts of global vandalism. Begich and Manning refer to: *The big boys with their new toys.* And what could be the eventual outcome of the Bush Administration's near desperate bid to "come up with solutions" in a fight against global terrorism—and America's vulnerability to being hit, nation-wide, from radio-beam weapons remotely controlled?"

American President, George W. Bush's current predicament and continuing dilemmas leading the West against global terror, Middle-East style, echo those of President John F. Kennedy in 1962. Almost, since bluff and spin are no longer substitutes for strategy. Nicolai Khrushchev's bluff was called when Russian ships, Cuba-bound with missiles for speculative deployment against America, were hurriedly ordered back to Russian ports. At that time, a fairly clear-cut message had been made—and cleanly parried. America had threatened a retaliatory response, assumed to be nuclear. For loosening the newest Arabian Gordian knot there are no manuals.

The word Scalar is a measuring term used to describe a charged-up state of vacuum energy. The vacuum can be destroyed or "exploded" electromagnetically. This was the Scalar EM super-weapon which in January 1960, Khrushchev announced could wipe out all life on earth if unrestrainedly used. The *New York Times* carried part of the story of the later Soviet development of large, Scalar EM beam weapons capable of deployment from Russian soil. Frightening stuff. After a time lag, America also has the technology plus HAARP. One has to ask, at this point: who can win?

In 1991, as the Persian Gulf War with Iraq was winding down with the en-mass surrendering of Iraqi ground forces, world media conjectured on probable reasons for the Iraqi collapse. A body of opinion, undisputed, suggests that types of electromagnetic and radio frequency weapons were in use with American forces. Wholesale cowardice fails as an explanation.

A March 26th, 1991 ITV News Bureau (London) wire service brief stated that at the centre of U.S. war planning operations at Riyadh was "an unbelievable and highly classified PsyOps programme utilising Silent Sound techniques, (SSSS: Silent Sound Spread Spectrum) which, more simply put, is a mind-altering mechanism based upon a subliminal carrier technology. Such weaponry is referred to as "non-lethal" weapons in military jargon. Tests with experimentees indicate that among debilitating effects likely to plague groups of people are fear, anxiety, despair, hopelessness. Add the capability to induce permanent, chronic fatigue into populations (Lupus?), and we have reason to question the integrity of afflicted Iraqi leaders–at this point in time.

Finally, HAARP's Alaskan facilities are credited with the potential to manipulate weather systems. In 1958, chief White House adviser on weather modification, Captain Howard T. Orville, described how the U.S. Defense Department was studying ways to harness charges of the earth and sky to affect weather by using electronic beams to ionise or de-ionise the atmosphere over a given area. In 1996, a Professor Gordon J.F. MacDonald, associate director of the Institute of Geophysics and Planetary Physics at UCLA, was a member of the President's Science Advisory Committee and later, a member of the President's Council on Environmental Quality. In his book *Unless Peace Comes*, he wrote a chapter titled: *"How To Wreck The Environment."* It describes weather manipulation, climate modification, polar ice-cap melting, ozone depletion techniques, earthquake engineering, ocean wave control and brainwave manipulation using the planet's energy fields. He claimed these (potential) "weapons," when used, would be virtually undetectable by their victims.

Is HAARP that weapon? The military's intention to do environmental engineering is well-documented. Leading-edge scientists describe global weather as not only air pressure and thermal systems but also as an electrical system.

Did someone know about this in biblical times when the children of Israel were saved?

13   America is Life. Imperfect, Essential

P hew! Coming into possession of the material that built up the last chapter then trying to digest it, tends to draw me away towards the more pleasant, visible; tractable phenomena of the planet, and what's above it.

Noisy miner birds, the size of crows, perched in nearby Pohutakawa trees (New Zealand's flame-red Christmas tree), or strolling impudently over spikey, newly-mown grass, do not quite succeed in disturbing my morning revery as I look out to sea across parkland. Leon, the Lodge owner, observes certain signs...my "up-and-about" signal...the blue bath towel drying in the sun, draped on a stressed-out cane settee outside the sliding glass doors. He announces: "knock knock" with the chumminess of a reformed navy chief petty officer. Timing is impeccable so he enters confidently. We drink coffee. Iraq is pushed aside while I'm briefed on the day's coming and goings of tenants. For a consideration, I've been appointed volunteer manager while he gets on with building work at his new home in the west—Ahipara at the southern end of Ninety-Mile Beach. I am complimented for saying *Ahipara* correctly the first time and so I am an approved asylum seeker. When I drove into this region some months ago, during winter, road signs read: "Welcome To The Really Far North." Both are real.

If what we breath hereabouts, is not 100% air, then its oxygen-nitrogen content only has to compete with additions of salt, wind-driven off the sea and the scent of the flowering shrubs at this time of year, which is December. There is no chain reaction from picking up a sea shell or scooping a hand-full of the pure white sand. I do not feel concerned over linked electromagnetic impulses that may be floating around. My radio cassette player cannot attack my brain and America's beloved chain of ye "Radio Shack" shoppes are a couple of oceans away.

After the tractor, with its lawn mowing appliance, has completed its runs over the adjoining park, it takes but two or three days for the wild flowers to spring up and bloom again: dandelions, daisys, buttercups, columbines, clover, the exact range of virtual weed seen in England's meadows, twelve thousand miles to the north west. Children, whose parents have been renting units in the nearby Taipa Beach Resort, run around or sit in groups on the grass, making innocuous chains by knotting the stems of flowers together. Funny! But just now, they are the only chains I feel I want to care about. At least they are breakable, needing only a slight tug.

America is Life

Worryingly, the stuff discussed in the previous chapter seems, by comparison, irreversible and, once applied, has none of the benefits of daisy chains. It was not the most pleasant of subjects to dwell upon at length and induces a certain pessimism—even hopelessness. What can we mere mortals do when governments of peoples clash, threatening planetary vandalism. Is Armageddon around the corner? And whoever/whatever it was that parted the Red Sea to save the children of Israel, it certainly wasn't a couple of battalions of kilted, shrieking, Scottish infantry, high on wee drams of their national beverage, brandishing cold steel bayonets. The "women from hell," as their Great War, German opposite numbers dubbed the Scots in 1915–B.H. Before HAARP. Earth's saviour or wielder of retribution's sword?

So I say, Phew!, again, in preparation for bringing into the story some experiences of a Mr Justin Cartwright who, like myself, attended an American school as an English evacuee during World War II. In his article, titled: "*Another Country*," published in a 2001 magazine supplement of the *London Times*, he writes poignantly of the feelings and responses aroused by attending a reunion of the school many years later. He describes the occasion as motivator of a subsequent novel titled *Leading the Cheers*, based on more detailed research into American life and mores. But it is the contrasting of his long-ago attitudes while in high school with his later perceptions, all sparked by the reunion, then socialising with greatly changed former schoolmates, which I find interesting. I too, can empathise with that. As a grown-up of many moons, I cannot identify with me in 1941 except in almost fictional terms. Back there, it is an age of innocence long gone. Only old photographs show I existed.

It was also a nice age to be in America. Prohibition had been reassessed and abolished, The radio character, The Shadow, was weeding out crime, the 1930's gangland boss, Al Capone was being chased for the lesser felony of diddling the Internal Revenue Service. Errol Flynn, in *The Sea Hawk*, had repelled boarders and would soon be winning most of the current war's battles. Walter Winchell was providing pithy war comment and in consequence, his sponsor, Jurgen's Lotion was selling well. Paul Robeson was singing African canoe songs—effortlessly and melodiously with panache as he wrestled a steering paddle. Long, blonde-haired Veronica Lake, actually had two eyes but showed only one. Al Jolsen was on his knees at mom's feet, Fred Astaire and Ginger Rogers would surely marry, Humphrey Bogart and Lauren Bacall did and Roosevelt was still a president not at war with anyone. Al Qaeda, then, could have been the name of an enthusiastic group of Bedouins modelling themselves on Baden Powell's Boy Scout movement. And flying schools were turning out fighter pilots who really did want to be able to take off expertly and land, wheels down.

"Language is life" writes Mr Cartwright, in his defense of fic-

The American Option

tion whose characterisations can often offend or otherwise hurt those who feel identified with a composite character. He would have been around the same age as myself in 1940, when, as he describes it "*I passed through the Mid-West (of America) at an impressionable age, but that somehow I seemed to have forgotten a lot of important detail.*" Apparently, a girl nicknamed "Mouse," was unremembered as a student from another school whom the young Mr Cartwright had taken to his school's "prom." America-speak for the end-of-term ball. American high schools have definite protocols. Their equivalent in Britain may now have similar though perhaps less defined or adhered to. Britain's schools were famous for adhering to punishment often applied with sadistic pleasure by some beast of a prefect in training for the Hitler Youth. In America, one did not, I now learn for the first time, invite girls from other schools to own school social events. The potential wall flowers might rise up, seeing their chances spiked by "new Americans" like young Cartwright. And given the chance, I would certainly have been in trouble.

Speaking for myself, I seem to be able to recall rather more about my relatively short time in an American high school albeit not a co-educational one. In my life, girls seemed non-existent, apart from Audreta, who was rather like a sister, therefore sort of sacrosanct, and Paula Dean who, secretly at least, was the opposite. There were the end-of-year plays we put on jointly with the Kimberley girls' school, but its twelfth graders, one had good reason to suppose, had dipped their painted, (in teen defiance of parents), toenails into the racy world of the theatre and were sexually aware and closely chaperoned by our own twelfth graders. Those, who we seventh graders had been able to glimpse on stage, had been wearing bras since eighth grade anyway.

The sexuality of the sexes seemed very unevenly distributed at that time. Paula Dean, however, would remain my chief luminary. Otherwise, my life in America was asexual. That was not a difficult condition. I was barely a teenager and one was constrained by a variety of things. In those days, one simply did not get bad or good girls into "trouble." Shame and parental sanctions were deterrents, church and law-enforced. We seem to have been a happy bunch of kids withal. Most of us observed the basic courtesies toward each other and our elders and we said "please" and "thank you." Which brings us to another of Mr Cartwright's observations: "*Although I had almost become an American, I now see America as Europeans see it, distorted by the mirrors of television. How was it, that the America I'd lived in now meant so little to me while the America of fiction and film was so familiar and real? The authors and many of the films I love most, are American. Our lives, are shaped by America (visually?) but not, I think, by America as it is.*"

"By contrast," he claims, "Americans out in the middle of the country are barely interested in other peoples of the world except insofar as they may derive amusement and colour from, say, certain members of the British royal family, our wacky fashions or quaint habits and ritual. Gradually, he explains, he began to appreciate more, the gap in perception between the America, as it exists in the vastness of the hinterland and the America as we, in Britain (and other countries), perceive it to be.

Conversely, the other "peoples" gain false impressions of America whose traveller citizens get on aeroplanes and land in the crowded cities of an older Europe from where many of their kith and kin hailed. Emigrants by choice. The nineteenth and twentieth century flood is now but a trickle.

Notwithstanding greater awareness of what lies beyond its boundaries, chiefly through an involvement in two world wars, its exposure to global economies, participation in world events at political levels, etc., there remains a body of otherwise inquisitive, interested Americans, who would will the world to be just like home including holiday venues, resort facilities, cuisine, and supermarket produce. Some, have an involuntary disapproval, dislike even, of anything which is not recognisably American, and say so. Which is boring. Why, for example, the French or British system of motorways should be replicas of California's clearly sign-posted Freeways or New England's equally sensible Turnpikes is not for me to say. Americans tend to. And personally I wish British road and rail planners were American. I would be able to drive down an off-ramp when I make mistakes, which I often do, and not forced to drive twenty or more miles in an unchosen direction wasting gas until I can re-route. We, in Britain, can thank American visitors for establishing trends toward en-suite hotel rooms instead of the standard washhand basin. Failing that modest provision it was, down the hall to the communal. For many years the *Cumberland Hotel*, at Marble Arch in London, was probably the only hotel in the country offering a private bath and toilet in its bedrooms. American friends, I remember, made for it like a muddy, Saharan water hole.

For anyone sitting in an hotel room in the United States today and switching between thirty or more TV channels, the message of American goodness and rightness comes across clear. For some reason it fails to convince us in the wider world. We will not be seduced by Larry King's avuncular earnestness or Bill Cosby's family values or Oprah Winfrey's ongoing search for them. What, I wonder, can be missing in the message? Newscasters, political analysts, talk-show hosts and radio's *Voice of America*, frequently sound mystified, hurt, indignant, scathing or derisive in turn, when their country's generosity with aid to countries afflicted by famine appear to go unappreciated; her motives misconstrued as self-seeking. Yet, why bite the hand that offers to feed? And can a tall poppy help being tall?

Has all this a faintly familiar ring? Are the roles of America and Britain curiously turned around from the desperate urgencies of 1940 when we needed not ten allies but one; when American leaders were obliged to take heed of public opinion before lending an official hand; when Pearl Harbor not the electorate gave us unstinted American support against the Nazi terror machine? Now, in America's own war against a more global terror we found a dearth of unified, independent European backing for a march to Baghdad. The issues are not clear-cut. In Britain we do not have a significant, vociferous Moslem or Jewish vote sufficient to turn us isolationist. Neither do France or Germany. America is not threatened with imminent invasion by ground forces. So what fearful event will become Great Britain's and Europe's "Pearl Harbor" before America can expect unqualified support? History repeats while Annabella Churchill parrots her grandfather's postwar reflective phrase: "Jaw, jaw is better than war, war." And can a tall poppy help being tall?

Americans are programmed from birth to grow tall in a society favouring success above most things having the tools and opportunity to succeed. All this, generated from less than three hundred years of blood, toil, tears and sweat in a virgin, wild, beautiful, often hostile land. And aid is not all about money. American volunteer aid workers, doctors, biologists, teachers, are at least as numerous in the former Belgian Congo as are Belgians, French, German or British. American Methodist Missionaries were as numerous in Korea in the nineteenth century as were the German Lutherans spread over the archipelagoes around New Guinea. And was that such a bad thing? Inchon, in South Korea, has the largest Methodist cathedral I have seen anywhere. What all this says, I think, is that there are numerous ways of influencing for good. The word "subtle" comes to mind. It is unsubtle to be over-zealously patriotic or religious. Christianity and Islam are inherently good. Only certain of their practitioners make them less so.

Ambiguity, perhaps contradictions, in Anglo-American relations are at least comprehensible. We–explained Churchill, in another of his visionary summations–are two countries separated by a common language. Easily explained. And it works, sometimes haphazardly. In an increasingly English-speaking world America should have little difficulty with international relations. For some reason it does. Oh...that blood-brother thing that Britain and America are supposed to still have? But America is the great cultural melting pot of the globe. Every American is an ambassador for their land of origin. Maybe a first-year, university student of psychology could volunteer an answer. Beggars, the undergraduate might say, have their own unique brand of self-esteem; behaviour codes, that sort of thing. The poorer peoples of the planet do not beg, in that sense, and do not want to be patronised. Their pride is negotiable but only to a point–and not with America. If forced, resentment is strong. Psychological gymnastics?

Statisticians have their own methods to account for the world's love-hate relationship with America. Hate of a magnitude which compels haters to fly passenger planes into New York's and Washington's buildings. The British Empire, in its 400 year history, had also to deal with unrest. An enigmatic British India suffered a genuine attention lapse when it defiled sepoys' rifle bullets with pig fat. It led to the nastiest mutiny ever. And there was that "black hole of Calcutta," too, but the French did that to us. Then we were in Egypt and the Sudan, which culminated in the murder of General "Chinese" Gordon at Khartoum and of course, Irish hatreds that call murder a political necessity. And we've been in a couple of other hot spots here and there. The British have had it all. Are having it. Except that in more recent times only real pilots flew aeroplanes and suiciding was what people did in garages or from bridges or in bed.

The *New Zealand Herald*, December 6th 2002, heads a piece from a Washington website, http://people-press.org/, as "U.S. Loved, Hated Around The World." Statisticians have been at work. The Pew Global Attitudes Project reveals that, among Russians, U.S. popularity had surged from 37% two years ago to 61% now. In the same period Germans, who favoured America, have dropped from 78% to 61%. Similarly, among Uzbeks and Nigerians U.S. popularity was up 29% and 31% respectively. It all seems about as dependable as certain free and fair elections, yet antipathy is detected in otherwise friendly nations such as Canada and Britain. World citizens admire American technology and culture, but reject the spread of U.S. ideas and customs and decry its influence on their societies. (and politics?). Canadians, Germans, the French, Egyptians, Jordanians, Pakistanis, Lebanese, fall into that category. On the musical front, all of these countries were pro-American in the Pew poll and on West Africa's Ivory Coast, very American with an 84% vote of approval. *Maybe Elvis really should come back.*

The most common criticisms unearthed by the pol were that the U.S. acts alone (suggesting ill-advised arrogance in its leaders?), that it pushed policies which widened the gap between rich and poor nations *and didn't do enough to solve the world's problems.*

Many Americans make themselves highly visible by word, style or deed. An ebullient, over-zealously conveyed patriotism effused by some, in or out of their own country, sometimes grates on those whose dynasties might well be longer and with less need to push. The pushing of good or bad foreign policies, however, makes little impact on Americans at home and where international terrorism now has a reach. Policies will mean nothing to the girl in the Riverside, Southern California's Western Union telegraph office, where I once went to send a fax to a Guernsey, Channel Islands address.

"Where is Guernsey?" she asked. Reasonable question, I thought.

"It's one of a group of islands off the European mainland," I explained. But she continued to probe: "Well, where's that?"

The American Option

As there was no wall map of the world handy, I gave up then. I wondered if geography, outside the United States, was taught in Californian schools. Didn't Western Union offer in-house staff training before appointing their branch managers who telegraph people's cash around the world? But what would it matter? America is self sufficient, self-contained and understandably self-centred. Is that a part of its problem? An old *Reader's Digest* witticism comes to mind: *"People who are wrapped up in themselves make small and uninteresting parcels."*

I know! Why don't we all paddle off to a library or bookstore and get a copy of Bill Bryson's *The Lost Continent–Travels In Small Town America.* It's all in there! I was lucky. I obtained one recently from an unexpected source. Here's a little taste, page 45, of Bryson's small-town America by courtesy of his car radio driving through Mid-West states:

"I twirled the dial. A voice said, "This portion of the news is brought to you by the Airport Barber Shop, Biloxi." There was then a commercial for the said barber shop, followed by thirty seconds of news, all of it related to deaths by cars, fires and gunfire in Biloxi in the last twenty-four hours. There was no hint that there might be a wider, yet more violent world beyond the city limits. Then there was another commercial for the Airport Barber shop–in case you were so monumentally cretinous that you had forgotten about it during the preceding thirty seconds of news."

For more profound and deeper stuff, try the same chapter number as this one in Bill Bryson's book, Chapter thirteen, page 127.

One gets an impression that America is a world within a world. Seemingly as detached as one of its satellites. In September 2001, in tragically authentic, theatrical style, it became just one more frontline battleground against a new force intent on subverting western democracies to fundamentalist Islam. But who and where is the new Hitler this time round? And where will Americans go as refugees?

From the same source, about midday one day, I was loaned a book titled *Strawberries with the Führer–A Journey from the Third Reich to New Zealand*, by Helga Tiscenko, Shoal Bay Press Ltd, N.Z. publishers. I was gripped by its contents and put it aside at around quarter past midnight. Mrs Tiscenko is a German-born, naturalised New Zealand citizen. With the battlefronts driven deep into Germany by 1945, the infrastructure that keeps nations tick-tocking nice and regular was about to collapse. Anarchy, everyone for oneself, would replace it until the occupying forces and administration scrabbled things together again. Her personal account of the mêlée in which she and her family, with other German civilians, found themselves fleeing from their own military by the few means at their disposal, even incarcerated in Dachau by error, provides searing commentary on a regime disintegrating. In the last hours of the Third

America is Life

Reich individual officials were hysterically conforming to chains of command which were no more. Lines of authority made suddenly obsolete, were being used by one general against another. Himmler threatened one lieutenant general with execution. Next day, or the day after, he'd donned a pair of workman's overalls to merge with his country's refugees. He did not make it of course.

Mrs Tiscenko, who married a Russian in post-war Germany was, with her family, a committed Nazi at age twelve in 1939. My own age at the time. But I had not eaten strawberries and ice cream with Hitler one fine day on the steps of Berlin's Air Ministry building. For her, the spontaneity of the experience turned the dictator into a God she admitted she would have died for–and nearly did.

After coming to New Zealand with hundreds of other Germans who'd effectively displaced themselves, she describes her painful struggle re-assessing National Socialism as decreed by Hitler. Rationalising loyalties inculcated via school and the girls' equivalent to the Hitler Youth, to her father, a Wehrmacht general and to her mother, an automatic follower, had taken her half a century. To me and this book, as we near the end of chapter thirteen, the plight of ordinary Germans, as all the normal, every-day things about them fell in on themselves, offers an enlightened, unexpected perspective on a society about to be extinguished.

Is that a scenario which today's vulnerable, family America can relate to or prepare for? Or can the violence of military conflict be kept at bay, as has so far been managed behind sea defenses thousands of miles in extent, excluding Mexican, Canadian and Alaskan borders? Have the alternative options already been decided by America's supposed adversaries? And again and again and again, why should America have any adversaries if the stuff its television and radio presenters continually tell us, is true? That is: America is not a great satan but the world's benefactor.

And listen to this: In the immediate post World War II era, when Europe's devastation was many times that of present-day Iraq's, General George Catlett Marshall, America's chief of Staff, 1939-45 and Nobel Peace prize winner, 1953, gave his name to the Marshall Plan offering long-term financial help in return for the purchase of American goods. Help in which Britain and her Empire would become a major beneficiary. That much is emphasised in Nick Clarke's all-but forensic biography of the late Alistair Cooke who, after some 65 years until his death at 96 in March 2004, had remained steadfast as "reader" of his celebrated *Letter From America* beamed out by weekend radio to Great Britain and the world. I would regret missing a broadcast because each week it served to re-enforce my faith and trust in America and Britain as "family." Therefore, I understand Nick Clarke when he writes: "*Many in Britain resented the idea of a rich uncle offering largesse with strings attached–especially one who had grown prosperous in the very war which had impoverished them."*

As he says: *"This provoked accusations in the populist American press of rank ingratitude."* Then, Mr Cooke, born British who'd applied for American citizenship in 1937, quoting a report in the *New York Daily News*, May 1947 a month before the Marshall Plan was agreed, explained: *"It would seem just as well for the British that we are a young, vigorous, optimistic or, as they put it–childish people. If we were ageing, sour and pessimistic like some other peoples we could name, we'd never have supported the British Empire in 1917-18 and 1941-45."*

Nick Clarke sums up Cooke's analysis as being no more serious than a family feud. Quoting Cooke: *"Americans and Britons are rather like in-laws and what is really humiliating in this relationship is just when you want to get very grand and announce you will shake off the dust from their house forever, is the maddening knowledge that they have a standing invitation for Christmas dinner."*

It seems that old Anglo-American "family" feuding had become a driving force behind the wartime and life work of Alistair Cooke. By then a new American having two feet resolutely astride the Atlantic Ocean, he strove, in his broadcasts, to further the interests of two continents and at least two cultures, nailing misconceptions before they had time to proliferate. His *Letter From America* would become a trans-Atlantic institution while his talent for arbitration and conciliation gave him near full employment.

In a London tabloid, *The Daily Mail* for October 11th 1997, Professor Paul Johnson headed a piece: *A Schizoid Nation.* What's a schizoid? Oh yes...the professor was flying a kite for the book he was publishing the following week titled *A History of the American People.* He wasn't being unkind, just confessing to a difficulty in coming to terms with, "crime, illegitimacy, divorce, violence, the horrific exploitation of sex and depravity by Hollywood, now going through the worst cult of immorality in its history. *"Yet,"* he writes, *"if I attend a family meal in places like Dallas or Houston, Atlanta or Kansas City, my host says: 'Professor Johnson, as our guest, will you ask a blessing please?' In how many British homes today is family grace before meals still said?"*

And I do like a 1929, Sinclair Lewis comment on what he suggests could be typical, simplistic, no-frills logic that aids Americans like nothing else. Lewis says: *"I like Vermont* (and so do I!) *because it is quiet, because you have a population that is solid and not driven mad by the American mania...that mania which considers a town of 4,000 (people) twice as good as a town of 2,000, or a city of 100,000 fifty times as good as a town of 2,000."*

Personally, I prefer the word "laminated" to Professor Johnson's "schizoid," which sounds suggestive of brittle fragmentation, frailty and therefore weakness. America is a laminated culture as is Great Britain and, like plywood, is the stronger. We have undergone fifteen hundred years or more of lamination and the layers, as in New York, Chicago and Los Angeles, can be seen walking about the streets of London. And chancing some heated debate, France, Germany, Spain, Scandinavia, Greece, the sub-Continent of India, China, the Arab nations appear homogenous by comparison. I'll take the ply. Like Russia, it will stand a lot of rough, inconsiderate usage.

Lucinda Lambton, historian, writer (*Old New World*), roamed America for 30,000 miles and returned to London with the astoundingly good news that a 1950's England, its graces and styles, manners and conventions, respect for women, marriage vows, the Church and its Christian ideals, is alive and kicking as never before in hinterland America. Vestiges of earlier English practice still cling in the elevators of big cities where real gentlemen still remove their hats, or, in Manhattan's subways, where announcements are preceded by, "Ladies and Gentlemen," and in stores where "Ma'am" and "Sir" come with the packages. "I'll have five sheets of that eight-by-four three ply, if you please ma'am."

In an exhaustive review of contrasts, Ms Lambton laments the loss from Ealing, London to Edinburgh, Scotland of homes built for 19th century, "moneyed merchants." Where once were numerous handsome villas, today they are gone or gutted, transformed into nursing homes, flats and guesthouses. In America, they survive, in use by families and descendants. Taxes? The American system seems to have favoured continuity, like the greenback. My dimes and nickels small change could be the same coins I pulled from my pocket in 1942! Feet, inches, pounds, ounces? Okay! Sovereignty? No uncertainty there. Her message rang clear: To find the best of old England go to New England or, for that matter, to any one of the United States of the North American continent. So much of British culture is under attack while in the New World, characteristics planted by Britain's early settlers continue to flourish. She complains: "*By cruel irony, it seems we British are abandoning our treasured past in favour of the seamier side of the very country that is conserving so many of our best traditions. What proper chumps and Charlies we are making of ourselves in the process.*"

She deplores this country's official stance on conservation. Here, she reminds us, the word has the ring of reaction about it. In America it is associated with progress. In America, good manners do not denote servility.

Just one more choice Lambton shot on the topic of hunting: "*It will,*" she predicts, "*thunder on into the American future long after the sport is likely to have disappeared from Britain.*" And... "*Pink coats in South Carolina are unashamedly worn, in vivid contrast to conditions in England where hunt members were recently urged to adopt a less conspicuous attire.*"

Abraham Lincoln, the greatest of the American presidents found it hard to believe in God, Professor Johnson explains, and never belonged to a church. But during the agony of the Civil War, he turned to the Bible for guidance and called it "the best gift God gave to man." He might have included America, a country which is still a magnet for the world.

"While intellectuals fix on the dark side of America, ordinary people concentrate on the brighter side," he suggests. *"And they are right. At the end of many years studying the history of the United States, I am convinced that Americans are the greatest problem-solvers in history."*

He tells us there are some 3,500 universities in the U.S., part of the continuing dynamism of American life. And it is this sheer dynamism which enables America to solve its problems, correct its mistakes and remain the "City on a Hill" the Pilgrim Fathers strove to build. It all reads wonderful, but it's still a muddle. It may have been Bill Clinton and his eight continuous years of consumerism which has cast Mammon as the friendly silks and lace merchant come to town...his wagon, the shop. Americans were able to fill their closets with goods and appliances they might use only once. An age of commercials and the expectation they generate, unlimited drug abuse from eight to eighty, gratuitous big and small screen violence and explicit perversion via video, telephone and the internet. Yet he never inhaled. And he might have said, in defense of cigars: "A woman is only a woman, but a good cigar is a smoke."

14   Egg in a Teacup

Following the Family's trip to Washington D.C., a final term in seventh grade sped to a rapid conclusion. We were all, it seemed, heavily pre-occupied with such things as, how individual performances had averaged out in the year, who might make the first five places in the school's honour roll and with the graduation ceremonials themselves. These would not only usher us, with due symbolism, into the Upper School, but establish ourselves, in the eyes of the world, as teenagers. Official! Bill said it was a kind of "re-usher" in my case, back into eighth grade.

As the great day approached, my classmates would corner me in the lunch room down in the basement during the ten minute jam-donuts, peanuts and Coca-Cola morning breaks and, with the intensity of schoolboys, quiz me on my vast experience of the Upper School. "You've been there, done it, what's it like, who was the worst master, why, what does Dr Head gush on about each morning in study hall at dedication, is it true he picks on people to stand up and recite Lincoln's *Gettysburg Address?*"

I recognised these concerns as representing major issues in life and would reply gravely and reassuringly. I explained that the worst thing that had ever happened to me—and may I stand forever in penance if I tell a lie, I added, was having a whole, new, unbroken length of blackboard chalk plucked out of its box and thrown at me for inattention.

"You mean," said John Moore with incredulity, "he'd never even used the chalk up to then?"

"Never used, fresh as a virgin," I said, thinking of Paula Dean.

"Well, go on, who was it?" Bill pushed his face closer.

"Mr Barras," I told him. "He was taking us for English before a replacement came for Howard Parker who went into the army."

"What was that for?" said "Red" Jacobs of the flaming hair.

"The war," I replied vaguely.

"America is not *at* war," ventured Bob Mapletoft, a little loftily I thought.

"He would have been a reservist," argued Bill with great patience. "Didn't you ever read Phil's talk he gave to the boarders that time after he came from England? It was in *The Montclair News*. We'll probably go and help England again."

"And Scotland and Wales and Ireland," I prompted.

"Oh, sure. Goes without saying."

The American Option

"Well, I'm as sure as hell not going over there. I get real sea-sick on my dad's boat," complained Red Jacobs, who'd digested a few swear words from movies he'd seen on the sly.

On occasions, I suppose I was "buttonholed" a bit because I was still quite obviously un-American and had a funny accent. But I was not alone. Tony Rooke in sixth grade had come over from England with his older brother Brian in ninth grade, or form two. Then there was Franklin Ernst and John Morris...five all told at that time. We'd all been photographed, back in December 1940, for a write-up in the *Newark Sunday Call*, Christmas number. I imagine it was because of the Season but we were lined up in order of height holding songbooks called *Get Together Songs*. We were asked to hold our mouths open for the camera so it would look as though we were all singing in unison. The effect, I now see, is not entirely natural. In my coat lapel appears the small, British Union Jack given me by my mother before I left home. One day John Moore said in class:

"You have to have one of ours too," and he handed me an American flag of matching size wrapped in tissue paper. I wore both after that.

But no publicity is bad publicity and we overseas "evacs" seemed to have generated some interest over and above the "home" evacuees, who went to rural areas in Britain. As we've learned, many of their experiences were hardly publishable. The lid, as far as it

Five evacuees
"...we were asked to hold our mouths open..."
(*Courtesy:* Newark Sunday Call)

Teacup

Lapel flags
"...I wore both after that..."

could be, was clamped on the more unflattering incidents accompanying a mass exodus. In contrast, our opinions about America would be sought. We would write things home which somehow would be picked up by the press, greedy for any news in the face of restricted war coverage of what was mostly bad news anyway. A piece on page three of the *Daily Mirror* might be headed *Egg In A Teacup,* and go on to describe the way Americans like to eat their boiled breakfast eggs. There was a certain technique involving painstakingly peeling off the shell, then mashing it all up in the cup with a spoon then eating the revolting mess. What's an egg-cup? I might be asked. I cannot remember including that innovative egg eating method in any letters but no doubt I did discuss peanut butter, as the all-American sandwich filler, possibly garnished with crisp streaky bacon, lettuce, mayonnaise, gherkin and eternal catchup.

I would probably have commented on the modified use of knives and forks, i.e. first chop up all the food on the plate, like one does for people in high chairs, then fork it all into the mouth with the right hand. At crowded tables, one's hostess should separate all the left handed diners from the right handed ones to avoid cracking the ribs of one's neighbour. The likelihood of it happening might be weighed against the sickening inevitability that gossip columnists would be fulfilled for ever. As a matter of fact, the style is sensible for crowded tables. In Britain, we all saw away at our food with both elbows knocking our table companion's finely balanced forkfuls into the hostess's flower settings. "Keep your elbows into your sides," my mother would tell me when in training for the business of conveying

The American Option

food toward the mouth, and other table etiquette. Emily Post, the great American sage on the social graces explained to one troubled questioner: "It is quite in order to brush the bread roll crumbs into the hand and eat them." But I've always done that.

Of the Family in nearby Verona, unintentioned tutors in things American, Audreta now lives near Denver, Colorado, USA, with husband "Skip." It may have been around the time of her Skidmore College days in New York State, that she foreshortened her name. Dreta wrote in answer to her receipt of chapter seven. I'd imagined it just might bring to life some half forgotten recollection which I would include in that chapter. It seems, after all, that I have more recollections than she. My dislodgement from home being the more impressionable while for her, I would have remained just a novel addition to the family circle. She did say though, that she recalled the Washington trip we all made and that she remembered looking forward to my coming as offering her chances for being taken about on similar family outings with greater frequency.

She is the only one remaining of the wartime Family. Dear Aunt Elinor, Uncle Roy even Harold, my only "brother," have gone on. Harold's widow, Phyllis, whom I met when I tracked Harold down in 1983 at Poughkeepsie in New York state and who now lives in North Carolina will, I hope, be able to share with me some of her husband's recollections of the period. We have had many phone chats. But it is a long shot. Their grown families plus grandchildren are two new generations of course, having a limited interest in their grandparent's transitory friendships, folklore or wartime visitors.

If I *have* been heard of it could quite possibly be in association with historical, wartime events. One would be the largely unwritten story of American families who offered safe, clean, middle-class homes to British school children and to those of other overrun European countries. For now, I am but a curious, older sample of thousands who took the voluntary routes to Canada, America, South Africa, Australia and New Zealand by sea. There was no other way. I became a participant in the mass movements of European peoples in World War II; ineligible for any American family tree.

I might though, in Victorian times, have got a mention in one of those gigantic Bibles always visible on a damask and lace-covered drawing-room table. Lines and squares divided up the front pages to include a potted family history. One or two extra columns might have been inked in and headed: "Evacuees Taken In." Another: "Dates—Bundles for Britain," a reference to donated clothing for the bombed out, and home-knitted garments, much of it for sailors in the Battle of the Atlantic.

Some of those items would have maintained life on a thread of wool in lifeboats and on fuel oil-drenched rafts. Now, Dreta's and Skip's lives revolve around family and a range of local activity. I suspect I may have acquired an image of one who transported himself to

Teacup

Australia for some years; who turns up on the doorstep to link everyone with high school and college days of a vanished age. Whether that is a popular thing to do, I have no way of knowing. People never say.

Before the day of the Graduation, June 6th 1941, my Aunt Elinor had hired the appropriate outfit to wear. Everyone would be attired similarly, like a uniform: White trousers, blue jacket, black shoes, white shirt, combed hair, clean fingernails and, horror-of-horrors, somebody had rumoured, a black bow tie. A photo shows me looking like a too highly groomed model in a mail order catalogue, aimed at teenagers.

It was all very formal and meant to draw a line between one age of man and another. It was an open-air do, tea and sandwiches on a part of the playing field not too dug up from some earlier, frenzied football savaging, parents and folk saying pleasant things to one another and patting the heads of their young proudly, if a little condescendingly in isolated cases. There is no trace of the nicely rolled diploma tied with red ribbon we all received when our names were called. The next drawing of lines would come in 1946 when we graduated out of high school altogether into the half-adult world of college—or were drafted into the armed services.

Some time after the grand graduation doings, I went to a schools' summer camp in deepest, north Vermont. Camp Wayeeses, on the shores of Lake Seymour, a bare four miles from the Canadian border, undoubtedly did for me all of that claimed, in the camp's brochure, for boys around my age. Obviously, it was geared up to instill the manly spirit. We learned resource, dependability, commitment, a subjugation of self, teamwork as well as independent action and cool thinking to get us out of the minor predicaments contrived for us by camp leaders.

The eight weeks of camp life, which utilised the bush conditions to a maximum consistent with our physical strength, would define much of my future thinking and responses. I can still ride a horse, spin a lasso and do other ropework, track if lost, and survive in the wild forest region of the State and show people how Indians make their damper rise without baking powder.

The wide-ranging agenda was the work of one Charles A. Hill, fortyish, one time science head at Kingswood School, Connecticut and a former 2nd Lieutenant, U.S. Army. A Colonel Philip S. Wainwright, U.S. Army, (Rtd), whom I remember as being then around sixty, was his fatherly camp manager and disciplinarian, as and when needed. There were a number of camp counsellors, possibly twelfth graders or undergraduates from some school or college.

They appeared to be regulars at the camp, perhaps paid a wage, and led our expeditions up rivers or to sleep on the tops of local mountains. A stiff, 3,000 ft. climb was considered high enough for tenderfoots like us. Notwithstanding, one heard moans and groans lamenting foot blisters, scratches and insect bites. The rewards, on such treks and climbs were the fish we caught and sleeping on a mountain top in the open with our basket-type back-packs adapted to cover our heads. Lying in that position, on one memorable occasion, staring upward, the sky was criss-crossed with more shooting stars than I have ever seen before or since at ocean level, during my sea career!

The camp had a sailboat, the *Medawela*, Indian for the indigenous loon bird, said to have once belonged to Katherine Hepburn and we learned to sail it. Sometimes we would get a lift in the colonel's ancient Ford open tourer, to the small township of Morgan on the opposite side of Lake Wayeeses. For some reason, I remember the old car had no paint on its bonnet. Bare steel shone in the sunlight as though it had been sand-blasted. We would all pile in, gears would grind and the dust from the unsealed roads would rise and stay in the still air for a long time. Jack Belvor, our real resident singing cowboy who knew all about saddles and how to secure them to a horse, would most likely be sitting on the pole fence of his corral waving his ten gallon hat at us—or the flies. In Morgan, there was an old, unpainted, timber general store that sold everything, even boxes of chocolate-coated cherries! Once, I made one box last a whole week just to disobey our self-imposed "sharing rule."

We slept in log cabins which had no windows, just fly screens and wooden shutters that could be dropped down over the opening in case of heavy rain. There were seven cabins, spaced out on cleared land gently sloping toward the lake shore but blocked off by forest. From the top one of the cabin's five steps we could make out the few white buildings that pinpointed Morgan across the blue waters. Otherwise, dense forest was on all sides. A track led down through maple, conifer and pine trees to the boat house and the ice pit. A jetty extended out to deep water and our small yacht was moored to it along with assorted dinghies and canoes. One of our jobs was to dig through the sodden sawdust in the ice pit to extricate large blocks of frozen lake ice which had been cut during winter then buried in the sawdust. It was messy work and demanded a quick dip in the lake to wash out of our hair the sawdust we'd thrown at each other. There was always a lot of ice in the pit. It never seemed to melt, but must have done, slowly. It kept our camp lodge iceboxes supplied all through hot Vermont summers. So I learned how to preserve natural ice.

Our bunks and bedding were basic but we pretended we did not need any comfort. We were committed to roughing it. Would we have made candidates for the Hitler Youth? I think so, insofar as we were greedy to test ourselves with all of the camp's activities and challenges. With us, political brainwashing and the setting of loyal adherents against less committed family members would have been a totally alien adjunct to our introduction to young adulthood, as imaginatively programmed by "The Colonel." But the technique remains absurdly simple and, for us, would have required only a basic Boy Scout uniform adorned with arm bands, shoulder flashes and a dagger engraved with "Blood With Honour" to turn us into marching bands of fanatical worshippers of Franklin D. Roosevelt, a pagan god.

Look toward the Middle East for less visible "Hitler Youth" movements. We know they are there. I came away from camp at the end of August, 1941, with a Pro-Marksman shooting diploma and

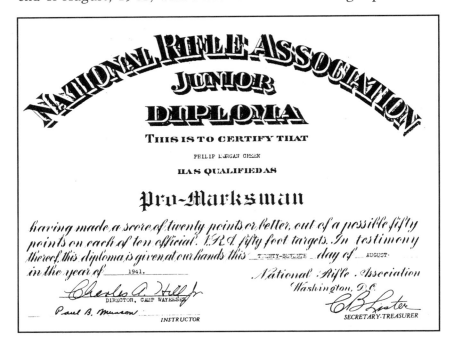

medal from the National Rifle Association, Washington, D.C.

Well, okay...the range was only fifty feet, but on ten targets I'd had to gain twenty out of fifty points. Of all the items I subsequently missed being granted in my 90 Park-style Christmas lists: a 22-calibre rifle and a globe of the world. I have yet to acquire either. But at war's end in 1945, with Hitler dead, I had nobody worthwhile to shoot. As for the globe, I have been around the real one more than once. However, I bide my time for a real school-room model, illuminated by an electric light inside with embossed mountain ranges and sailing tracks. I shall make room for it.

At intervals, letters or postcards from one or other parent would reach me at camp, forwarded on from Verona by Aunt Elinor. They would make a day special insofar as they reminded me how I was linked in to two homes, but that I only needed one. If it was a post card from my mother, she never mentioned the privations and dread that always would accompany the air-raid sirens going off followed by the mayhem of night bombing. I never did hear about that from her. I had to read about it in books after the war. The few that have survived are picture postcards which I stuck into the photo album I was compiling. Surprisingly, one has just turned up, accidentally coming *un*-stuck. It shows a photo of Winston Churchill, black jacket, pin-stripe trousers, trademark white spotted bow tie, gloves held aloft in a wave, confident smile under a black Homburg hat, other hand gripping a walking cane and cigar...emerging from Number 10, Downing Street, the official residence of Britain's prime ministers.

On the other side is the postmark—Bexleyheath, July 16th 1941 and the censor's stamp: "Passed." It is addressed appropriately for the time to: Master Philip M. Cheek. My mother's familiar neat writing says:

"Bexleyheath, July 14th... Here for few days. The spirit moved me while out shopping Saturday a.m... Just felt lost without Dad so got on bus and the folks (friends that we had in Bexleyheath) persuaded me to stay. Billy left for training today (their son, entering the RAF), very thrilled and excited....but not so his parents. Received your lovely long letter with aunty's. You should be seeing Dad in about three weeks. All news in detail tomorrow. Thinking so much of you this hot weather and hoping you are A-1. All here send their love and writing you soon...with much loving thoughts and greetings to all.
-Mother.

I'm glad that one got saved. Billy Ford completed his training in Britain and U.S., flew Lancaster bombers, got shot down and so survived the war as a prisoner. He was killed in a post-war flying accident during the Cyprus emergency.

In Vermont, defining moments would occur in the early mornings of any day we were in camp and not off in the mountains somewhere. From the distant Lodge building at 6:30 each morning a bell would ring out. We would all have been awake for some time. Some joker would always be present to ensure it! But we would delay heading for the wash tubs at the rear of the cabins until the last bell stroke. There, cold natural spring water, piped from source, was tapped into each cabin's ferro-cement tub. The water was icy cold and never seemed to dry up. A visit to the Lodge shower blocks would give us the luxury of hot water. That would mean a sprint across dew-wet grass, soap in one hand and towel in the other. Paula Dean would have loved it.

At the Lodge, we'd crowd around tables jostling for positions, ravenously hungry. The camp cook's response to this condition was never disappointing. The menu, by the "Colonel's" decree, was the all-American breakfast to set us up for the day. Commencing with fruit juice, coffee, a glass of ice water, the list would wander through assorted cereals, crisp streaky bacon, eggs any old way, corned beef and hash, (being a mix of corned beef and potato), sausages and, if there was any more room, fresh baked, bread rolls, sultana muffins, a continually replenished pile of buckwheat pancakes, butter or cream—and jugs of maple syrup from local syrup factories, since about every other tree, in that corner of the globe, seems to be the maple. I cannot go on, the recollections are too painful unless my digestive juices can be satisfied. Perhaps I can settle for a peanut butter, crispy bacon and catchup sandwich! In the camp I began to enjoy my evacuee status.

And about then, in Britain, prospects for most were bleak. I do not remember thinking about it in those terms. I was enjoying life and well pleased by then with the choice I'd made. But I think about it now and try to reconcile how the have's and have-not's live side by side, how the affluent and the deprived are taken for granted by each and how the threatened and the aggressor remain uneasy custodians of our green and lucky planet.

Who would wish to dominate; who would wish to destroy part or all of it for some of the skewed ideologies with which we, in the western, industrialised world, still heavily dependent upon oil, seem perpetually having to deal. What is evil in our system or with its practitioners that certain of our Arabian friends wish so intensely to wipe out—via the right of suicide—a route to heaven so beloved by Allah and his representatives on Earth?

When God made the world in six days it is suggested he forgot to give the Arabs a share of the planet's glorious resources. Reminded, he gave them oil. We buy their oil don't we?

Bill didn't come to the camp that year. He must have done something else. He had so many interests. I must ask him sometime. Almost predictably, at the graduation ceremony he'd carried off the honours for class academic achievement. How do people do these things without appearing to do any homework yet build the most perfect model aeroplanes? Nowadays he sounds just as mystified.

Returned to eighth grade by September 1941, (first form), Bill remained my pal, after-school baseball "coach" and test pilot of balsa wood aircraft. One morning I manoeuvred myself into the study hall desk in front of Art Totten, by then a Senior in twelfth grade, who welcomed me as a co-conspirator. I could almost recite the *Gettysburg Address* backward in case Dr Head pounced on me. I could sing *America the Beautiful* without looking at the songbook and both the Stars and Stripes and Confederate flag of the old South, (some say I am mistaken about the latter flag, but I'm all but positive it was there) were nicely furled with gilt tassels in either corner of the broad stage. Things were almost normal.

In French class once more, this time with Bill somewhere about, he was talking French back to Charles Jaillet, to the latter's delight, with what I can only describe as unfair fluency. It was sickening. In math class it was similar, Karl Billhardt acted as though he'd found a protegé. But I felt I held my own in English with the newly arrived Mr Thoreson. In Science and Chemistry I did quite well, spurred on with expectations that one of Mr Miller's test bench experiments would do something unexpected. When I say, I think I did quite well, I really mean that I liked the subject. It had no bearing on my grades and I wished Mr Miller a long, explosion-free life. Which I believe he had.

Some time in May, 1941, my father had visited, flying down from Montréal to New York. Canada Airline's promotional postcard shows one of its air fleet in flight. The twin-engined McDonnell Douglas, DC3, famed as the versatile "Dakota" of many later years, would serve the world-wide battle fronts of World War II. Then in peace, would come the Berlin airlift and parachute drops to break the Russian's 1950's siege of the German capital, or flying in sacks of flour and rice to break African famines. But in mid 1941, the "Dak" was still a major carrier on domestic routes. In a military transport role it would become indispensable.

During his visit someone at the school must have encouraged my father to give a talk. Perhaps it was me, for he gave it to the seventh grade students. I was still one of the pre-graduating hopefuls. The May 27th edition of the school newspaper, *The Montclair News*, carried a shortened account of what he said:

"CAPTAIN CHEEK SPEAKS TO SEVENTH GRADE'
Expresses Belief That Allies Will Win Present Conflict.

'Captain Cheek, Philip Cheek's father, of the British Merchant Marine, in a recent talk to the seventh grade, expressed his conviction that the Allies will win the war. However, he is extremely anxious for the United States to send effective aid now, and for American warships to convoy the vessels. If this were done, he declared, the war would come to a speedy close. Several of his experiences were also recounted to the boys."

That was page five stuff. The front page leader article is interesting. It was the meat of a recent debating session of the school's Forum Society. Subject: "Should the United States Aid Britain by Declaring War on Germany?"

"On May 7th, (1941) the student body and faculty of Montclair Academy considered this topic in a round-table discussion. The two sides were ably presented by four seniors (twelfth grade), Tom Guthrie, Ben Hamilton, Charles Ebers and W.J. Brown.

The session was opened by a short address by Guthrie who advocated immediate intervention on the side of Britain. Tom mentioned the dangers facing the United States in case of a Nazi victory and stated that we must fight to save the true, free way of life.

My father, Capt. Stanley Seth Cheek, North Atlantic–1941
"...anxious for the United States to send effective aid now..."

The American Option

Mr Ebers, on the side for isolation, then presented the opposite view.
He cited that Britain seemed unreliable. He attacked the past phases of the
present war and said the United States should not become involved in war to
save such a nation.

Ben Hamilton spoke on behalf of the British. Ben said there were
many fallacies, injustices and un-free aspects in the Nazi nation. He ques-
tioned the religious beliefs of present-day German life and showed how life
under possible German control would abolish all freedom.

On the same side as Ebers, W.J. Brown advocated isolation. He
pointed out that Germany had no hostile intentions to the United States and
sanctioned the idea that Great Britain should fight "her own battle."

The debate failed to draw any definite conclusions. However,
it started a new trend of thought in the minds of all about a problem that
must be faced within a few days or a few months."

Reading through saved copies of the paper I grow astonished at the level of erudition delivered in print by the Academy's 16, 17 and 18-year-old contributing journalists of that time! In the editorials of a further twenty-three copies on my worktable, many are the adult points of view marked with a red pen. The breadth and depth of dissemination, grasp of topical matters stemming from an ugly war being fought three-thousand miles off plus an understanding of why it came about, truly impresses. Would our own present-day seventeen-year-olds demonstrate a similar intellectual interest? But then I no longer attend preparatory school debating societies.

Early on December 7th, Japan attacked America at Pearl Harbor in the Hawaiian Islands. I remember the morning of that day quite well. Uncle Roy went out and bought up copies of the national newspapers. Of course, there would have been much discussion between us all. Later, I laid out all the front pages on the conservatory carpet and photographed the four-inch headlines of each. My father must have been around, because I used my new Argus "A" 35mm camera. Like Harold's Argus "C3" they would have been advance Christmas presents from my father to us. Uncle Roy bought the family's first movie camera, projector and screen and we all became silent film stars courtesy of Eastman Kodak.

The night-time comment in my journal, I do remember, went something like:

"They're IN at last!" This was doubtless a reflection on Churchill's constantly voiced hopes, which I'd read about, that America would become a full ally rather than the kind with one cautious arm out front and the other behind the back. As we know, Congress delayed a vote on President Roosevelt's urgent appeals. Inter-war, American isolationism was worryingly established and the New York City German-American Bunde, a political entity, wielded a formidable block vote on behalf of the Nazi party and Hitler. But it seems now the Jewish lobby had been stronger.

Teacup

My journal's page of writing and comment for the day America went to war with an agenda of vengeance and an unscheduled defense of its territorial security, did not survive, as did not the whole book. My father, or someone may have regarded my spontaneous thoughts as immature or just provocative should they have been scanned by the Family. The "In at last" comment printed under one photo in the album, sounds suspiciously like some contemporary newspaper criticism of America dragging its heels, that I'd copied. Either that or some feelings invoked by writers in the Academy's *Montclair News* whose editors, aged around 18 as we have seen, were by no means partisan. I did not start another journal, which now is a pity.

In the same *Montclair News* that carried my father's talk to seventh grade students stressing how American aid (surface escorts with possibly some air cover) would make a difference to Atlantic convoys, plus the previously quoted seniors' debate featuring aid to Britain (or not) we have, on page six, Lewis Townsend's piece headed *Food For Fascism*. Lewis Townsend, *Montclair News* staffer, a Class-of-'41 fifth former, could have been writing about America's 2003 war against terrorism, not an earlier, 1941 edition.

As a prescience pointing up present-day terrorist threats in New York's subways or at some 130th floor level, it grips attention and is offered with limited editing. Lewis Townsend was not a visitor, like me, which his use of the third person oddly suggested, but an all-American high school senior. I've switched him to first person. It was, after all, *his* America. He wrote his piece as associate editor. His comments have the unfazed exuberance of his youth:

May 27th, 1941.

"In the present period of war and panic, two out of every three American cars seem to bear on their rear windows signs reading: 'God Bless America' or (Isn't it great to be an American?) Such signs are evidently an enthusiastic attempt at patriotism on the part of people who display them. To me, personally, they represent a pathetic lapse into mawkish emotionalism on the part of the entire country.

"One of the reasons which has convinced me of the worthlessness of these slogans and pepsongs lies in the fact that England, heroic, bomb-scarred England, sings before all others its own national anthem: 'God Save The King.' Moreover, the only patriotic slogans to be heard there are not tearful or emotional; they have nothing of that 'rah-rah' quality which so typifies the American people; they are rough, strong, defiant. The man in the street indulges in no worthless homilies; he says: 'Beat ole 'itler!'

"Let it not be assumed that I am in favour of America's immediate participation in the war. My point is this: Americans are the greatest advertisers in the world. We love to publicize ourselves and our actions—hence these outbursts of apparent patriotism. We have to publicize ourselves so much, particularly in the last decade, that where once we were strong we are now weak;

The American Option

we have come to think so much of ourselves alone; we have become, in a word, so egotistical that we refuse to concern ourselves with affairs going on in the outside world. The tremendous industrial development in this country has, more than any other factor, contributed to this sense of superiority. Life has become so easy, so soft, that Americans are content to limit their patriotism to singing: 'God Bless America' and then we forget to make ourselves worthy by action or principle. When an emergency comes, therefore, we experience a sudden flood of emotionalism and give vent to it by singing emotional songs. That is the way we expect to combat Fascism, while through our own refusal to interest ourselves in outside affairs and our own unwillingness to take an active part in reconstruction, we allow totalitarianism to come closer and closer.

"My contention then, is that these songs represent a degrading factor to true patriotism not only because they possess a rather cheap emotional quality, but also because they do not in any way quicken co-operative, constructive action. I do not mean to say that they are the sole cause of inactivity and mental weakness; there are too many other factors in this invitation to Fascism. I should be glad to be convinced of any error in my reasoning for I know that England sings: 'There'll Always Be An England,' a song akin to our: 'God Bless America,' However, judging from the lack of intellectual fortitude prevalent in a large portion of the American people, I believe we could adequately demonstrate our love for America and at the same time effect a return to sincerity at least, by a wider use of our own national anthem. It would be a step toward preparing ourselves spiritually for the dangers of Fascism."

This *Montclair News* extract must be read now in the context of there being, at time of going to press, just over six months to go before America declared war first on Japan, December 8th, 1941, to be followed by similar attentions toward Germany and Italy—twin hearts of Fascism. Taking up Lewis Townsend's invitation to pinpoint errors in his analysis, one month earlier in an April 29th issue, an older Townsend is quoted, perhaps a relative; father even. His words, to a gathering of Academy students and parents, serve to nicely moderate the younger Townsend's outraged sensibilities and concerns about an unprepared, lethargic citizenry—as he perceived it within circles close to him. Yet, he would have been right, had he known, to have spelled out the existence of a vibrant "Fifth Column" of Americans bent on subversion and industry sabotage.

But the "Bundles-for-Britain" ethic was certainly alive and kicking well in 1940. Haven't I already told you? ...I lost my Beckenham College school gear to the cause! And of purely passing interest, when my second voyage as cadet came round, I found the standard Russian convoy outfit—on loan, officially—of naval duffelcoat, knee-high leather boots, sheepskin mitts, one thick government issue blanket, were all supplemented by hand-knitted long underwear and socks. Attached to the knitwear were the names and addresses of the knitters...U.S.A., Canada, Australia, New Zealand...you name it. Sewn to my sewing kit roll I can yet just make out the address of the Toronto, Canada, Red Cross depot, carefully written in indelible India Ink, by some kind lady long ago. Sometimes, I like to try, in varying degrees of lighting, holding the cover this way and that, to pick out the fading letters. It is the most livable evidence I now have of my small wartime world at sea. Well, that and the blanket, which somehow arrived home with me from the Archangel run. It came in useful on the twelve-hour chilly train ride from Dundee, Scotland to Cardiff, South Wales in that spartan, far off age.

Colonel Dallas S. Townsend, who was chairman of the defense council of Montclair and commissioner of public safety, had astutely chosen his venue and a receptive audience. It was, in effect, a pre-war speech to concerned Americans of all ages. Titled: *The Average Citizen and National defense,* he spoke in layman terms of the average person's attitude toward defense preparedness and of a willingness of people to co-operate in all worthy moves toward security through adequate defense. He disclosed the activities of a "Home Guard," foreseeing its need in the event of war. His co-chairman, Mrs Bethel, told of the many ways women were helping in defense and first aid work, taking special courses in ambulance driving, etc. Finally, answering one of our headmaster's questions, Commissioner Townsend was firm in his belief that any attack on New York would be an attempt at demoralization.

On that first day of America at war, at home; at 90 Park Avenue; in and about Verona and Montclair; in the school's study hall; on the sports fields; in the gym; the swimming pool and, of course, the lunch room, there seemed a good mix of emotions, positive and negative—if one may put it like that. There was a great and fierce spirit of: "right, let's get back at the Nips," even though, details of the attack and damage caused were still incomplete. Roosevelt's scathing response and declaration of war against Japan meant an automatic inclusion of Germany and Italy. Treaties of alliance existed between all three. It was "in for a penny, in for a pound." For pound, read "buck." There may not have been an equivalent approval for America being landed in another European war. But that would come later as the full significance of Germany's territorial land grabs and future intent became recognised among "man-in-the-street" Americans. Maybe, after all, it was something the American "doughboys" of the earlier show had not quite finished and that now, it was time to.

Note:

News item—The *Montclair News*, March 13th, 1942
   "Lewis Townsend has joined Delta Phi at Columbia University.

The American Option

Senior year at M.A: Rostrum, Dramatic Club, Montclair News, *Red and Black Society, French Honors Course, English Honors Course and Editor of the* Octopus." He was 18.

My study hall pal, Art Totten, tapped me on the shoulder after Dr Head had finished making one of the more arguably solemn announcements of his career. As a Great War veteran, he would have been thinking of the seventeen and eighteen-year-old twelfth graders dotted throughout the hall before him. Early candidates all, for the draft, he would acknowledge with sadness.

"What're you going to do Phil," he whispered, "go back to England and join the Navy?"

"Don't be silly, Art, I've only just graduated back to this desk!"

"Yea, but as a "limey," they'll need you." He was in one of his teasing moods.

"Well, looks like you'll be going before me– heh, heh."

"Oh, I guess I don't mind really...give me a chance to see Great Britain and your little home town." He was being serious now. Soon after I'd arrived, a year before, he'd asked me countless questions about school in England, Chelsfield Village, Spitfires and Messerschmitts (ME-109's), battling it out overhead. The lump of shrapnel I'd given him may have stirred something. Now, I replied: "Anyway, Art, it's good that you're in with us. We'll really strangle them now...and Art..."

"What?"

"I'd better get this sketch done of Mr Miller's electric-arc machine or *I'll* get strangled."

"Yea, he sure loves demonstrating that old thing. We had that stuff four years back."

Art was in his senior year by then or twelfth grade, two full terms to graduation. Then, college–or the military?

Letters from my mother and to her would have been full of optimism, hope and, I suppose, tinged with a certain relief. That Britain was no longer a duelist, feigning and slashing in a corner. The "cavalry" had arrived. And what a "cavalry" America turned out to be. We suddenly had more of everything, including a morale boost. American factories had already begun re-tooling for war production. The change-overs were now accelerating and soon, the great Bethlehem Steel Corporation and the wide-ranging shipyards of Henry Kaiser would be recruiting and training women in the relatively new steel welding techniques.

Ultimately, the yards prefabricated the bits of one new "Liberty" merchant ship; then stuck the pieces together, around every ten days! Ships that soon formed a supply bridge across the Atlantic which, with the increased naval escorts available, would overwhelm enemy war production. American shipping, as neutral, would not be indiscriminately sunk off the Eastern Seaboard of the

Teacup

United States. The "Libertys" bristled with armament, bow, stern and amidships, shaming the British Ministry of War Transport into protecting our own people a bit more. Thus, some good flowed from the shock of December 7th 1941 and many of the ships "sewn" together by American ladies, continued trading well into the 1960's. Others, would remain mothballed well up America's great rivers.

The fact of America being at war, appeared not to affect our daily lives. I was still the family-elected procurer, by bike, of our Sunday dinner, litre of chocolate-mint-chip ice cream conveyed home in the handlebar basket. Church attendance was not a regular thing but, when we did go to the United Methodist Church in Verona, it would be followed by lunch at a large, magnificent old wooden private home turned into a restaurant. There, the speciality was the establishment's home-made, chicken and mushroom pie. Mouthwatering!

Those were also occasions when dinner conversation might turn to family or domestic matters concerning our small world. If my curiosity was aroused, perhaps in consequence of some remark concerning local history, I would volunteer a question. It was how I came to learn a little of the Cranes of Montclair, Aunt Elinor's family. It appeared they were prominent in the very early days of the settlement when it came to be known then as Cranetown. A Crane House museum exists. My youthful imagination was stirred by stories of individual endeavour among American Indians–friendly or otherwise. I was pleased to be thus associated, if only peripherally, with the great doings of my adoptive American family. Doubtless, that lunch would have been given over to the heroic origins of Audreta and Harold. I forget now how the present name, Montclair, came about. Maybe there is a mount named after a family of Clairs!

Apart from the famed White Castle hamburger drive-ins, fore-runner of McDonald's or Kentucky Fried Chicken outlets, fast-food-sidewalk-dining hadn't arrived. No one ate their food in public. Chicken was something we still stuffed, roasted in an oven, basted every so often then carved at table and ate with Sunday reverence. The sidewalks were also clean of trampled fries and patches of blood-coloured catchup. A novel exception would doubtless have been the sidewalks of New York City and the steps and platforms of the city's subway train system. Over the century, their cement-covered miles have received the chewed-to-death chewing gum of millions of meditating New Yorkers. Their trampling feet have produced an art form. "Skins" of dalmatian dogs cover the metropolis. Some things never change.

15   A Midsummer Madness

Christmas 1941 came up, then receded accompanied by exhortations from the nation's leaders for Americans to show a united front. *Tchaikovsky's Piano Concerto* which had been top of the Hit Parade for three or four weeks was being whistled or hummed by just about everyone. The melody, played over and over on assorted radio stations, began to take over my brain after a while. It was a relief when *Elmer's Tune and Tangerine* got back into the top ten. But before that Audreta, practicing her accomplished, *On Blueberry Hill* piece in a far corner of the lounge, had succeeded in rubbing out Tchaikovsky, for a limited time, giving me a blessed humming alternative.

The beginning of 1942 also heralded the war's fourth year. By its end, much lackluster progress toward wearing down Hitler and Mussolini would be dramatically reversed except in the Battle of the Atlantic. In that often fierce, turbulent ocean, an enemy in its own right, sinkings by U-boat wolf packs would peak in that year and I would have left America.

In the Pacific, principal theatre of America's conflict with Japan, the picture grew grimmer as, aided by the surprise fall of Britain's Singapore and Hong Kong bases, the Japanese spread west toward India and south toward Australia and New Zealand. Rapidly, they overwhelmed the French, in Indo-China and the Dutch East Indies but, as in Europe, America's industrial output, millions of men and women and a Russian winter, became a decisive factor in the defeat of all three territory grabbers, Germany, Italy and Japan.

As I worked through my second term in eighth grade I was immersed in handling the comparatively small, everyday priorities of a fourteen-year-old. I have been digging deep into my memory to recall—which doing this book has aided as nothing else could—but there seemed to have been no great problems to battle at school or home. Perhaps notably, I can remember no peer pressure being applied to sign up and compete in the Academy's sporting events. I seem to have been left in peace. Cricket and soccer could not readily be adapted to baseball or gridiron football and I played those in incidental fun sessions and not competitively. The famed school coach, Van Brunt, may have assessed me as poor material for football warfare. I cannot recall any time when I donned the American sporting armour for that game or the uniform baseball attire. Along with Brian Rooke, by then in tenth grade, I was coached in tennis. He went on to gain for the school some local tournament credits. I was doing okay on local ice skating rinks and probably would have gone for ice hockey as "my game" if my school career had not once again been interrupted.

For the moment, I was satisfied with membership of Mr Carroll Howe's Photographic Society and doing candid camera work for the 1942's edition of *The Octopus*. I was also maintaining a somewhat ambivalent viewpoint about academic brilliance being the yardstick of success ensuring I had a lifetime meal ticket. I sensed there could be other ways of doing it after reading a paperback edition of Dale Carnegie's, *How To Win Friends And Influence People*. How that came about makes a nice little story.

You may remember that in late 1940 I discovered the attics and the arts and craft workrooms of Montclair Academy. Up there I'd designed and produced for Howard Parker, (English literature) the posters for the school play, *The Hottentot*. I'd done similar for the December 1941 production of, *It Pays To Advertise*, with our Jim Prescott and Kimberley High School's Mary Caldwell in the lead parts.

I occasionally climbed the four flights of stairs to this sanctum just to look out over the castellated parapets toward the always spectacular New York skyline about twelve miles off, as the crow flies. It appeared as a distended mirage atop the smog bank with the Empire State Building always visible above its 75th floor, a kind of floating Eiffel Tower. And when the U.S.-commandeered French liner *Normandie* [5] was allegedly sabotaged during conversion to an aircraft carrier, the oily black smoke carried on downwind for days. I seemed always to have the Academy's roof to myself.

The attics were also utilised to store unwanted school furniture, mostly the old-fashioned desks of yesteryear replaced by the handy chairs with their attached, versatile writing arm. Lifting the lid of one of these desks one day I came upon the copy of Carnegie's book. In the remaining time I had left, possibly a lunch break, I read a few pages before replacing the book and returned downstairs to either a study hall period or a class. In the pages I'd read there seemed to be things that might be fun to experiment with or apply to different situations. When opportunity offered I would return to the attics to read a few more pages.

Eventually, of course, I finished the book. In the month or two it had remained in the old desk no one had claimed it and, like as not, no one ever would. It was conserved by a British evacuee attending the school and, over the years which have since elapsed, can have been the only reason why I am where I am and have always

---

[5] A hearing later determined that a welder's ember created a spark that engulfed the ship in flames while in New York Harbour. *Picture History of the Normandie* by Frank O. Brayard, Dover Publications 1987.

Audreta Maree Sheldon
Skidmore College, Post-Graduate Nurse 1946
(Courtesy: A.M. Pape-Sheldon)

been able to afford to eat. Moreover, as I have never met anyone else who's read it, I can feel confident that my influence over people like Dr Head, Montclair Academy teachers, my superior officers aboard ship—especially captains, marine superintendents to whom I've applied for jobs and anyone else concerned with my survival, has been paramount and probably attributable to Dale Carnegie. I will go further and suggest the book be required reading for parents and their primary school-age offspring. I was a late starter. I have moments when I think I might donate it back to Montclair Academy, as an icon. I have now inwardly digested its contents.

I don't believe either Audreta or Harold read the book or would have benefited from its fundamental teaching. They were doing all right scholastically and succeeded in their later college and lifetime careers and had lots of friends and well-balanced offspring. So I think it was me who would have derived the most benefit from the guru of thoughtful and considerate behaviour upon which so much of a civilised world and happy community depend.

Easter came and went, a third and final eighth grade term commenced, my fifteenth birthday passed in May, letters from and to my parents would have been numerous, but only one from my Aunt

Madness

"...a final eighth grade term commenced..."
Bill: *third row standing, second left*
Me: *second row seated, first left*
John Moore: *first row, second from left*

Elinor to my father survives, still in its envelope with the Clipper air mail stamp. It is heavily annotated with ballast or cargo or fuel figures. My father must have carried it around with him for a bit, finding it useful for back-of-an-envelope calculations. Maybe the figures helped his own survival. Today, I find there are far too many blank spaces in the happenings of that time, but the few photographs and bric-a-brac resurrected are an enormous help to memory which, in itself, Bill now claims, is not too bad!

At this time, my sights would have been firmly fixed on my elevation to ninth grade in the forthcoming Christmas term. First would come the Class of 1942's graduation and all the excitement which the events associated with it generated. I was already shooting rolls of 35 mm film at everything and everybody for the Photographic Society's year book selection. This was the beautifully bound volume called *The Octopus*, dedicated to the Upper School's achievements through the year but also carrying the individual photographs and write-ups of each graduate. Every student from eighth to twelfth grade inclusive received his copy of a prestigious document each time the twelfth graders were ejected into the cruel world of college or job-hunting. By tradition, graduates were hunted down and button-holed for short, individual write-ups under their photos that would evoke fond memories down the years.

I think the high school year book must be an American insti-tution. Certainly, the friendly use to which it was thus subjected is identified with America's way which, in school life, translated into an absence of stultifying oppression between students and teachers. Recognition of and respect to a faculty hierarchy that chooses to dis-pense a benevolent authority, was referred to in lunch room banter as being rather better than tolerable. A form of American understate-ment. Mr Avery Barras's box of chalk ammunition springs to mind. The frank and open discourse which I had enjoyed with my teachers had helped me pick up on weak subjects. In *The Octopus*, the auto-graphs, wisecracks or simply good wishes became a measure of both sad separation between school buddies–often for ever–and a determi-nation to follow. It is possible to collect five year books from one's Upper School years. Bill has his five. I proudly own one.

My life was punctuated with a desire to do reasonably well at the Academy, an involvement with the similar achievements of Audreta and Harold, both attending the co-educational, Montclair College High School, significant war events, talk of my mother coming, my father's visits, but no pre-occupation with my long-term future. Any ideas I may once have had in England about a lifetime vocation had been replaced by a vacuum. I had no obvious bent and I leaned toward nothing. I must have been resolved to take one year at a time. Maybe even a month at a time, but I can't remember get-ting much advance warning that my days even, not months in America, were now numbered.

My father had arrived somewhere, probably Montréal or Halifax. I have a recollection he flew down, had some discussion with me, Aunt Elinor and Uncle Roy a short time after the summer holi-days had begun. They would oversee my departure from America to Canada. I was told very little more, but I was aware there had been some disagreement with my father's wish to take me away to wher-ever. My Uncle Roy, as guardian exercising an opinion, appeared to have disagreed and then more strenuously on meeting my father's insistence. I sense that Uncle Roy agreed most reluctantly to help process the required emigration documents with his signature of release. No doubt the argument went on lines that the move would not be in my best interests, etc., etc. But it is all speculation and I seem never to have enquired about the reason for the decision. I accepted my lot as being just a product of the war. That made it easy. For the moment, I looked forward to the adventure of an excursion to Canada by whatever mode of transport and whatever might follow.

I think I had about a week at the most to prepare. Uncle Roy took me into New York City, to the Customs and Immigration building situated near the Battery, at the tip of Manhattan Island. I imagine my passport was stamped for a return trip to Canada. Reason: to visit my father aboard his ship on compassionate grounds. Otherwise, American immigration officials were not empowered to assist civilians to leave America. The country had been at war for seven months. By this time I would have known, or suspected, that it was not going to be just a visit, then return to Montclair. The unearthing of my brown trunk gave the lie to any such hope. What might it be like to be a Canadian, I wondered?

The trunk was pulled out of the closet in my room and Aunt Elinor helped me pack with many of the things I'd brought with me two years earlier plus newer clothes bought for me. My black, Beckenham College blazer with the green edging and school badge on the breast pocket, had gone to a place collecting Bundles For Britain. In any case, the school was no more. Bombed and burned, my mother had written once. The gas mask case was used to carry something else. The bomb shrapnel had long since found places in American homes. I carefully packed *The Octopus*, whose pages included a number of my candid camera shots of school activities and the people I'd come to know so well—faculty and fellow students.

Farewells...were there any? They would, in any case, have been minus the customary expectation of meeting again in September, in ninth grade, form two no less! But if I can approximate the words of Jared Sibley Roberts (Wasn't he the tall one with a shock of unruly hair?), there must have been some. He'd said "Don't forget us back in old England." Did I cycle up to 63 South Mountain Avenue to tell Bill the news? We must have said our farewells somewhere. I can't remember. I discovered a long time ago there exists in my head a mental mechanism that excludes certain memories like goodbyes yet sharpens others. It is as old as the womb I once lived in. In it, I probably heard my mother's sobbing on the uncarpeted stairs of her and my father's first home in Wales. Great, stair-shaking sobs they would be, that he never knew about. He'd left, to endure another human rights violation. An eight or twelve month voyage and gut-destroying food. Although rights and their violation were not something Merchant Navy wives knew about. And still seem not to. And food didn't improve much until post World War II. So goodbyes I like to forget.

As for the here and now, I was in and out of New York City government offices for this and that. I would not develop the letter writing habit as I now have, for contact with those outside the immediate family. Where would be the impetus for such a thing. I was leaving one world and going to another. One, bent on destroying all. Clearly, I was experiencing failure adjusting to the situation. Months later, small incidents showed I still hadn't.

One day I would see north Vermont's Lake Seymour again. Camp Wayeeses itself had vanished without trace, except for one

The American Option

relic. The large, slate slab that had formed a step to the camp lodge, was gracing the home of one of the ageing camp counsellors who'd retired to the area. When it was pointed out to me I saw it was tastefully embedded among the tiles of the vestibule floor. Sometime in 1942 or 1943 apparently, Colonel Wainwright had died and one day Charlie Hill, owner, just turned a key in the lodge's front door, walked away and enlisted.

After a good while, one supposes, the clapboard lodge house, cabins, boat house, ice house, would have fallen down and nature run its course. Forty years was apparently enough. The ice may have lasted for two, before melting into the earth and draining back into the lake from whence it had come. But I'd learned enough at camp to deal with most crises in life. I still use the knowledge gained. This time I would see no one in my class again until Bill and I met up some forty years later. The cut-off was dramatic, if not brutal had I not already been inured to family moves and changes of schools. At fifteen I was already an itinerant. Looking back, I seemed to have taken the newest upheaval in my stride, only this time I was not being invited to make a decision. This time I was not with my own family. My growing feeling of attachment to things American was, in the days that followed the news of my impending departure, modified to visitor status and not, as I'd come to believe, for the duration of the war.

One afternoon in early July 1942 , I and the Family were all standing in Pennsylvania Station, New York City. A Pullman express train was waiting to depart for Montréal. It would be an overnight journey and the Pullman sleeping cars were in the middle requiring one to walk a distance from a day compartment. My brown trunk was already in the luggage van and I was wearing a new wide check, fawn sports coat, brown trousers, an Arrow shirt and rubber-soled saddle shoes.

Harold and Audreta were also wearing some of their best gear and our usual jokey demeanour became difficult to sustain. We lapsed into the tongue-tied shyness of our first meeting when I'd landed amongst them all on a Boston wharf. Pea whistles pierced through the overlaid station noise, flags waved, guards hurried people along trying to answer a hundred queries. It was time to go aboard. Aunt Elinor gave me a warm hug and a kiss. For the rest we shook hands all round. All that had to be said had been said back home, in Verona. What I'd said is beyond recall, but I hope I'd been able to say, "thank you" to four wonderful people who'd cared for me for two years as one of their own. Today, two years passes quickly. Then, as I stood on the high steps of the carriage holding the hand rail; looking down at them flashing me encouraging smiles, it had become a small lifetime. Soon it would be joined with the past. Now, what lay ahead?

Smoke, steam and shrieks from the giant locomotive ushered in my immediate future with gusto. Huge driving wheels spun on rails before they gained traction, the train shook and rattled, more pea whistles sounded their coded signals and the guard came to close the door. I stood back a little, waved a little and felt more than a little miserable and desperate as the significance of everything filled my mind. The express snaked its way out from under the huge semicircle of glass and iron, a roof discoloured like Liverpool's Lime Street Station by years and years of smoke and bird droppings. In no time at all we were across the bridges of Manhattan Island, grey smoke from the pulsating locomotive in front marking our northward course. This led first through New Jersey then followed the great Hudson River into New York state, skirting Connecticut, New Hampshire, Vermont until we reached the Canadian border at Alburg on the American side and complemented by Foucault on the Canadian side.

Up to the point of being aroused with the station's name being called out, for the passport checks, I'd slept well in one of the top bunks of the Pullman sleeper. I approved the curtains which I could draw around for privacy in the twenty or more berth rail car. The cheery black attendants attended everyone, making sure older ones could climb to the top tier, each of which had a window to look out at the racing scenery, and generally fix things that needed fixing for one's entire convenience. The bed linen had the nice, clean smell of the laundry. White pillow cases, on which the name Pennsylvania Railroad had been embroidered, not merely stamped, had been ironed. The creases were like one saw in hotel bedrooms. The berths were large enough, if one was fairly nimble, to undress and then sort of half dress in the morning, sufficient to venture along the central gangway to the women's and men's bathrooms.

A permanent feature of the journey was, of course, the swaying and rocking of the train as it sped along the permanent way at around eighty miles an hour. The thick, black, bunk curtains suspended on brass rings from rails, developed their own motion, sometimes outward, sometimes inward toward the slumbering occupant, sometimes in a forward or backward direction. Bare arms would appear, their attached hands and ringed fingers re-closing the curtain joins over a vanishing seclusion with unconcealed haste.

I thought it was all very educational. I wondered what Bill would make of it all. The atmosphere, with half-clad bodies moving about in fairly close company, fitted well into my memories of air-raid shelters. I thought that Americans could take to air-raid shelters quite well, all considered. Theirs, if they were ever to have any, might be a lot better than ours in London and suburbia. They would probably improve on my Anderson shelter's lighting arrangement. As for the upturned flower pot with a hole in the bottom and a lit candle to boil water, they would almost certainly improve on that!

After the passport checks by officials moving through the train like friendly sniffer dogs which deceived no one, I, and most others

The American Option

probably, returned to our bunks for a final snooze before taking turns at the several washhand basins in the bathroom as we chugged, hissed and rattled across rail points, closer and closer to Montréal's Central Station. There was time to enjoy the luxury and leisure of a classic North American breakfast served in motion on starched, white, damask table-cloths with again, the Pennsylvania Railroad's logo on the hem. Set out, the company's embossed, sparkling silverware, coffee pots, china cups and teaspoons were ready for action. And the action arrived in the form of white-coated waiters, their silver trays filled with orders, hovering and maintaining balance like ships' stewards.

I say like ships' stewards because I have a feeling that neither could operate in the other's work place. The movements of train and ship being dissimilar. Train waiters, with full trays shoulder-high, their torsos and waists countering the lateral swings and forward or backward jerks of the floor beneath their feet, would be unprepared for the whole thing to sink twenty or more feet then rise up, twist and spin like an albatross. Now, as a sailor of a lifetime, I cannot stand for long with a sense of security, in a train. The only souvenir I removed from the Pullman was a black card that hung from a hook on a triangle of string. It reads on one side: QUIET IS REQUESTED FOR THE BENEFIT OF THOSE WHO HAVE RETIRED and on the other: DO NOT DISTURB. No rules. Just options you might say.

Somehow, my father and I met on the station's platform, we recovered my brown trunk and decamped to the Windsor Hotel where my father was staying for a night or two's respite after the latest Atlantic crossing. I had no idea what type of ship he now commanded, but I hoped I would get an opportunity to go aboard for a look around. I doubt if I asked him any questions in the taxi to the hotel. I hardly ever asked people questions. Maybe I'd been told too many times: "Don't ask questions."

My mother had interesting and workable ways of avoiding giving answers. She might say: "Ask me no questions and I'll tell you no lies." After all, one merely desired the truth. Better still, she would just say: "I don't know," and hardly anyone would risk impoliteness by responding with: "Why don't you know?"

I would hear my father call out from the bedroom: "Gwen! When are you coming to bed?" and the reply would come: "I don't know." My mother did her ironing around midnight and sewing until two. But I probably did enquire over morning coffee in the hotel's lounge about my immediate future. It might have gone something like this: "Dad, what is my immediate future?" And he would have told me no lies and doubtless said, as any sea captain might: "We sail for England in three days." And I may have answered with: "What, me as well Dad, honest?" "Honest!" was Father's reply.

Again, the conversation is sheer speculation. What is fact, however, is that after one night at the Windsor, we got into a taxi and drove to the docks area on the St Lawrence River at that point. We got out of the taxi and I looked along the full length of my father's latest ship, as there had been several others. I could see no white-painted name on the bow. We went aboard, climbing a steepish gangway to the main deck, a sailor lifted my brown trunk onto his shoulder and made for the series of accommodation ladders leading to the bridge deck. We followed, deck by deck.

The ship seemed to be covered from truck to keel in a white powder and looked very, very old indeed. Every bit of steelwork was painted dark grey. Even the brass portholes of the deckhouses, once polished bright, were now coated in the same grey paint. The single tall funnel carried no company colours. Once white-painted lifeboats were grey. Everything was grey except the decks and they were red-dish brown, with a deck paint that was showing signs of lifting with rust that crumbled underfoot. For as long as I could remember, the only ships I had laid eyes on were the smartly painted ships of the United Baltic Corporation with their varnished teak bridge fronts, ladders and gunwales that topped a ship's bulwarks.

"The ship looks a bit dirty, Dad," I exclaimed trying to think of something to say. I still felt as though I ought to wake up at any moment. The problem was that I knew I was awake and things weren't fitting. What kind of ships was Britain sending on its war missions now? They weren't looking like this one in the 1940 convoy.

"Dirty?" exclaimed my father, with mild indignation. "She's really a pretty good ship, when the lads get her washed down. It's only flour. See?" He pointed to a dozen bags of flour in a rope sling. A dockside crane was swinging the load across the ship toward an open hatchway. "There's a bag in that lot that's been holed on some sharp obstruction in the rail wagon." I could see that a fine trickle of white powder was steadily changing the dark grey ship to light grey.

"What's her name?" I asked, "when was she built?

"The *Essex Lance*," my father replied, "er...steamship...built in, er, 1916."

"1916!" I exclaimed, panting a bit. My father took two steps at a time. "Gosh, that's old!"

"The *Baltrover* was built in 1921, a bare five years later," replied my father, a little defensively. "Yes, when you go around, you'll see she's quite a strong ship, not pretty, more of a work horse. It was what they wanted at that stage of the Great War when sinkings were threatening to starve us out. Yes, cut off by the yard these were."

"Howd'ya mean?" I said.

"Well," my father went on, "the shipyards of the day were given a kind of quota, to turn out so many a month, to save our bacon. They built the midships sections, then bow and stern and tacked them on to each other."

"Like the Liberty ships we're hearing about?" We'd stopped climbing and were approaching a doorway.

The American Option

"Not quite...no welding in those days, all riveting and pretty basic, but strong. No shaping at the stern, just a triangular end section right down to the rudder stock. A bit ugly I suppose but, as I said, just looking like they were cut off by the yard. Go and have a look. I've got a few things to do. That's your cabin, there, see. This is mine. You're in the pilot's cabin."

We were on the deck beneath the ship's navigating bridge. The deck rating had put my trunk in the cabin and left. On the door frame at the top, was screwed an inch-wide brass plate with the letters "Pilot" stamped in. Across the alleyway, above my father's cabin doorway, a similar brass plate read, "Captain."

I stepped over the two-inch high step capped by a brass plate and entered. The cabin had just a single, cot-like bunk with no drawers, a table beneath the single port hole facing aft toward the stern, and a chair. A varnished, teakwood rack, fixed to the bulkhead over the bunk, held a heavy, wide-based water bottle and two glasses either side. A square of coconut matting covered the deck planking with their caulked seams. The bulkheads were old-style tongue and groove with twenty-six years of successive coats of white paint covering the joins. A cockroach scampered back into an uncovered crack. I would not be lonely.

The deckhead steel plates, frames and rivets had been coated with a mixture of cork granules as an unsuccessful treatment for condensation. A wooden tray, affixed to the deckhead, held a cork-filled lifejacket wound about with its securing tapes and a small red light bulb. Salt water would activate the battery. There were arrangements of pipes, large and small, without clues to their functions. A paperback novel was stuffed behind one, just over the bunk. My brown trunk was on the deck. I divested myself of the gas mask case, slung over one shoulder, and set it down on the bunk. I was now using the handy container to carry passport and other travel papers. I stood there, looking down at the trunk.

Well, here I was, about to commence a voyage in another ship, two years after I'd come to this huge continent of North America. What had happened in between? I was already regarding my experiences as part of my past. Only two days ago those days had been the present. No, that could not be right. *Today* was the present. I was not going back, I'd known that, but why I'd entertained an idea that I would be staying in Canada I couldn't fathom. My passport was stamped for only a visit. What would all those officials, who'd boarded the train the day before, be saying when I failed to reappear?

The visa had been for two weeks, I seemed to remember. Strictly speaking, it was not my worry and, as I try to remember what I really did think and feel sixty years ago, I find that I was merely in a state of excitement. The feeling of being with my father aboard ship again, however old and dirty, didn't matter. My mind

Madness

was being restored and my world was as it should be. Here, among the smells and noises of a ship, with her inevitable mix of crew whose accents identified with every corner of the British Isles, was where I appeared most to belong. Perhaps, if I'd thought about it, I would have been surprised by this realisation but, at fifteen, I wasn't into realising much about anything. The word, fatalistic, comes to mind. As to the future, its horizon was now utterly devoid of any specific goal. Graduating from Montclair Academy, in 1946, four years into the future, was already in the past.

Suddenly as I stood contemplating the trunk with its TO MONTREAL train-sticker label adhering to its brown surface, and no longer new-looking, a figure appeared in the doorway. A boy, not much older than myself, wearing a whitish coat, was holding a whiter cup and saucer. A biscuit was in the saucer, absorbing some of the slopped liquid. The liquid in the cup was a deep orange-brown colour.

"Wud-ee lark a coop-a-tay?" He asked.

With those words, I was already back home!

16 Return to War

The strength of the tea was such that a teaspoon might have stood upright in it. But it was hot and its provider, the young cabin-boy, was welcoming. I'd made my first contact with the crew of the *Essex Lance*.

"What's your name," I asked him, "where d'you come from?"

"Alec Boles, Newcastle. Are you Philip? The old man, er the captin, yer dad, said to make up this room for you. 'Ope it's all right...um, we 'ave lunch at twelve—pork chops, mash 'n gravy, followed by spotted dick." I was getting the full menu in typical British, Merchant Navy terms. "Spotted dick" was a kind of suet pudding with currents. Lyle's Golden Syrup, warmed to make it pour better, made the delicacy more edible. In later years I would come to actually like this dessert, a staple in the culinary repertoire of Merchant Navy cooks of the day.

"Yes," I said, "everything's fine." It was then just after eleven in the morning and I followed up my father's suggestion to look around the ship. The *Essex Lance* was a flush-decked vessel of around 7,500 gross tons and could carry about 6,000 tons of general cargo in her five cargo holds. After six days in port she was already nearly full to capacity. When I regained the main deck via internal stairways and alleyways, meeting a large tabby cat being kicked out of the saloon pantry, I saw that bags of flour were going into holds four and five and army trucks into the 'tween decks of two and three. Number one had already been battened down and on top and at the sides, right to the bulwarks, more trucks had been jammed in and secured by chains, wires then tightened with "bottle screws," sometimes called "turnbuckles."

Deep in the holds, well below the waterline under bags of flour and a Heinz 57 variety of general cargo, were stowed cases of shells and boxes of ammunition. I learned all this from the chief officer when I poked my head inside the tiny ship's office. A man was bending over a small desk fixed to one of the bulkheads. A smouldering pipe lay in an oval ashtray that had once held another mainstay of ship fare—herrings-in-tomato-sauce—a frequent Sunday special in the foreign-going trades.

"Ah ha...," he said looking up from the ship's cargo plan laid out on the desk. It was held down by two books and he was entering figures in one of the squares that depicted blocks of cargo. "You must be the captain's boy, right? Heard you're coming across with us this time." He turned around in the chair to look at me.

"Yes, I think so," I replied. I saw a man whose greying hair suggested he might be sixty but whose face, much younger though lined, said forty. The eyes looked tired and he blinked often with a nervous little nod of the head.

"I'm Mr Reynolds, your dad's number one on board. You're Philip?"

"Yes, sir," I said, choosing a safe form of address. Mr Reynolds demeanour, while still sitting, was courteously authoritarian and the "sir" bit came curiously out of the sub-conscious, as though I'd never left England, where schoolmasters demanded it on pain of some pointless punishment. All that was now in my future, the more relaxed relationships formed with Montclair Academy teachers, a mere two weeks into my past.

The chief officer, wore the blue, serge patrol jacket with epaulettes that could be buttoned to the neck with a single row of brass buttons and thus needed no shirt or necktie. It was, in fact, derived from the white, "Number 10," tropical uniform worn in ships of the top companies. The dark blue serge version had become a popular working rig among Merchant Navy officers serving in cargo ships that demanded a hands-on approach to the job. It was a preference only, where no passengers were carried. My father, however, wore the Merchant Navy's "square rig" uniform, a double breasted jacket having eight brass buttons stamped with the Merchant Navy anchor and crown, plus four gold rings around the sleeves denoting captain's rank, a white shirt, collar and black tie. The tip of a white handkerchief was always visible in the breast pocket. It had been a fashion icon before uniform-wearing in Britain's Merchant Navy had become largely a casualty of shipowner economies, reduced crew strength to danger levels, the exchange of uniform for white (maybe) boiler suits or weekend, home gardening gear, plastic hardhats and a liberalising of former displays of legitimate shipboard authority. An isolated concession in the 1980's might be someone's hand-painted, "1st Mate" on the front of his hardhat. Even that, among the curious socialistic, growing egalitarian trends of the era, might be seen as ostentatious, a hark back to the bad old days when the very worst that could be said was that officers were officers and seamen ratings were seamen ratings.

But whether patrol jacket or "square rig," neither style, in 1942, could look smart or neat if they'd been slept in on a cabin or chartroom settee during a two or three night U-boat alert. In lulls, a bath or shower might be taken, the crumpled uniforms of choice again donned. So much for dress protocol in the Battle of the Atlantic. If the *Baltrover* was still afloat at this stage of the battle (and I would learn, years later, that she had been), she would now be painted wartime grey from stem to stern and her captain and officers doubtless still keeping up their "square rig" appearances.

I excused myself to continue my walk around the ship. Mr

The American Option

Reynolds had explained that when the after holds had been filled and hatches battened down with the three basic tarpaulins per hatch, four steam locomotives would be loaded on either side and more trucks on the hatchcovers themselves! I looked over the stern railings and gazed down at the flat, triangular cross-section. What ugly ducklings these Great War economy ships were. I noticed the wind-frayed edges of a British red ensign in the flag box at the base of the flag staff. The country must be in grievous state to keep these old ships going, I thought.

And by mid-1942, things were reaching critical levels re-supplying the bare necessities of British national life. Germany's U-boat arm under Grand Admiral Karl Dönitz, was now hunting merchant shipping in packs of eight to twenty submarines with increasing thoroughness and success. In convoys of 35 or more ships, bound east for British ports, 11 to 15 sinkings was becoming a fairly common tally. Some of the remainder would deliver their life-sustaining cargoes in a sinking condition with tanks and crated aircraft only just saved. About this time, Churchill was verging on despair. After the war he would write that the U-boat menace was the only real one he feared which could bring about Britain's defeat.

I often wonder how I might have felt if I'd been privy to such statistics as I was about to set out on another wartime Atlantic crossing at now fifteen years of age. Certainly, I have failed, following many, many attempts since he died, to discern my father's feelings and determination to play a kind of Russian roulette with a revolver virtually handed to him by the Nazi admiral. The gun being pointed at *my head* in this case. The enormous risk of my mother losing both husband and son and being left destitute, was real enough. What was so important that I should have been returned to my homeland at such a perilous stage in the Battle of the Atlantic?

It seems pointless. I cannot fathom it. Now, I can only conjecture, never to know. The fact that I am here, to write this story is not because I, my father, the ship, the crew, had some special dispensation from on high. Possibly more than one U-boat would, during fifteen days, hold us in the cross-wires of a periscope's sight. My adolescent senses, however, would not then allow of any such possibility and faith in my father's judgement, whatever the motive, was implicit. In fact, I was more than satisfied to be around the smells and sounds of a ship again. Particularly one that was getting ready to sail. The frightful consequences of the ship collecting a torpedo and the horror content of the telegram my mother would read, weighed not at all heavily on my young conscience or affected the stimulus of my new surroundings.

I met my third member of the ship's company on the way in to the saloon with my father. We came up to a cabin, its door latched back and a curtain half drawn over the entrance. A uniformed figure was standing, discussing some matter with someone who could have been the chief cook.

Return to War

"This is Mr Larkin, Chief Steward...er, my son." said my father, making the introduction.

"Hello, Mr Larkin," I replied. Then, for something to say, "Is it going to be a smooth crossing this time?"

"Not a ripple," the chief Steward said, glancing at my father. "Ask your dad."

I might have put Mr Larkin's age at around thirty back then, if I'd thought about it at all. He had a modest, ginger moustache and wore the standard Merchant Navy uniform with two zig-zag gold bands on either sleeve.

"I've asked Mr Larkin if he'd mind taking you on a sightseeing trip ashore this afternoon," said my father. "I'm going to be a bit tied up with completion of the cargo. We'll see you back around five, for tea." Looking at the chief steward, he added: "You could take him up Mount Royal in one of those horse and buggies they have standing around."

I imagine the reference to a "trip ashore" would have been the first Mr Larkin would have known about his unusual mission but all he said was: "Yes, sir...back for teatime, I'll just tell the cook I'll be ashore. He's had the menu for this evening's meal."

We went in to the saloon with the smell of food all around. The soup course had commenced I noticed. My father pointed to a place near the end of the long table which was covered by a white table-cloth. Over its centre, a large, brass oil lamp was suspended unlit, since the room was illuminated by four electric lights.

"There," my father said, "next to the young 'Sparks,' not much older than you, I think, eh Mr O'Harney?"

"Come to think of it, sor, I wouldn't mind a bit being your son's age again." There was subdued laughter from the other soup-eating officers. I took my place next to the wireless operator who had two wavy gold bands on either sleeve with green felt between plus the gilt diamond, marking its wearer as the holder of a First Class Certificate of Competency as wireless telegraphist in Britain's Merchant Navy– a commissioned rank. The motif signified radio waves and electricity! Wireless operators were traditionally nick-named, "Sparks." The term was descriptive, harkening back to early marine wireless sets which required a spark to be generated between terminals before a message in Morse Code could be tapped out.

Everyone had looked up and said hello to me, all strange faces, some stern, some youthful, some interested, some not, just men eating a lunchtime respite before a variety of duties took them back to the many corners of a merchant ship whether in war or peace, it made no difference. Lennie O'Harney was probably not more than nineteen, dark haired with a David Niven moustache struggling on his upper lip and a devil-may-care countenance. Probably a devil with the girls, I thought. Eventually, he and Alec Bowles, the cabin boy were the two I chatted to mostly. I don't remember the third officer or any of the engineer officers although there would have been at least four in those days. I took a photograph of the second officer taking a sun sight with his sextant. He is wearing a P & O uniform jacket with that company's distinctive gold shoulder tabs denoting rank instead of bands on sleeve cuffs. In the Merchant Navy there could be many employment moves between shipowning companies in one's career. In the second officer's case it was doubtless economy that had caused him to wear his former employer's uniform and not sentiment for the company's identifiable livery.

Mr Larkin and I went ashore. The gangway already seemed lower with the cargo putting the ship deeper in the water. We turned a corner by a cargo shed, walked to the dock gates, got a taxi and were soon standing near the row of black painted buggies near the base of Mount Royal. The jet black horses waited patiently between their shafts contentedly munching from nose bags of feed fixed to the harness. Steel and brass accoutrements clinked with the occasional toss of a head. If it hadn't been for the chief steward's uniform, I might simply have dreamed the whole two day's events.

I took one memorable photo of Mr Geoffrey Larkin, leaning over the parapet of the Mount Royal Pavilion. He is gazing at the camera with a slightly bored expression. The peaked uniform cap with its Merchant Navy badge very correctly worn. We'd reached the lookout and pavilion building. The two black horses had pulled the four seat buggy up the winding mountain road at a leisurely pace and the chief steward dutifully and kindly followed me around the exhibits as I clicked the shutter of the Argus with a growing professionalism.

I do not remember another excursion ashore before the *Essex Lance* sailed from Montréal on a voyage to somewhere in the British Isles. Photographs show I was busy with the camera from that point on. I do not remember writing a letter or sending a picture postcard to the Family back in Verona, New Jersey. In later years I formed a great habit of sending people picture postcards of wherever I found myself in the world. Letter-writing too, became a major responsibility and obligation as my sea career developed. I just hope that I did send *something* to Aunt Elinor even if pushed by my father as a continuance of my formative years then taking hold as a day-by-day process. Everything I saw or did from this point made its impact and impression.

The ship anchored off the small river port of Sorel, thirty miles up river from Montréal and next morning, as the St Lawrence River widened, we steamed in convoy with several ships and a naval escort. This was because U-boats had been spotted operating that far down the great river and, it was said, being re-fueled by French Canadians disenchanted with British resolve to fight the war and which could only lead to delay in French Canada's play for independence from the British Empire of the day.

"Sparks" and s.s. Essex Lance*–July 1942*
"...it is clear we were in a danger zone..."

"...Some had quite possibly survived an earlier sinking..."

The American Option

The small convoy reached the mouth of the St Lawrence, rounded the Gaspé Peninsular, each ship disembarked its river pilot then headed for Sydney on Cape Breton Island, a part of Nova Scotia. Like Halifax, farther south, Sydney had blossomed into a major convoy assembly and dispersal destination for the big Atlantic convoys. A photograph shows the *Essex Lance* topping up her coal bunkers from the lighter alongside. Being a twenty-five-year-old ship, she would have consumed about forty tons of coal per day at eight or nine knots in her declining years. For an average fifteen day passage plus five days for bad weather and convoy diversions before either a smudge of Ireland or Cornwall was sighted, our coal bunkers would have been filled with nearly one-thousand tons of coal! It's quality, 80% combustible producing 20% clinker, was always something the "black gang" (stokers) in the stokehold would always argue over, with the choicest of curses heard only on the stokehold plates above the clang of shovels, slicers and rakes. It was they who had the task of slicing and clawing out the clinker from boiler furnaces at the change of each watch and sending it up in the ash hoist, to be dumped into the sea. It was they, working with fire on two-hour shifts, synchronising the shovel-loads of coal into the flames as a mate threw open a furnace door then slammed it shut—then the next stoker and so on—they who faced the greater hazard, war or peace, with no "safety net" from exploding boilers and escaping saturated, super-heated steam. They, who were lowest down the payroll, remained classified as "semi-skilled."

All this activity made lots of black smoke—a signal to U-boats always alert to the phenomena of a diminishing era between sail and diesel-powered ships—the coal-burner. Illustrated is the ship s.s. *Granford* before sailing from Cardiff, South Wales about 1948 for Galveston, Texas. All the designed bunker capacity had been filled. Then number three cargo hold, with its 'tween decks was filled. Removable bulkhead plating to the stokehold gave access to the coal. The wooden hatch boards and tarpaulins were then replaced and, for a bit extra measure, the coal wagons had been ordered to dump more coal on the hatch! The pyramid's angle of repose as it formed, gave a visual signal to stop pouring—to anyone watching—as the first stray lumps of black gold began to tumble over the side into the coal-stained water of Cardiff docks—and the Notice-to-Sail was hitched to the bottom of the gangway.

We remained anchored in the Sydney roadstead for two days. When my father had to go ashore to attend the naval convoy conference, he took me with him. The outer harbour was studded with large and small merchant ships at anchor awaiting sailing orders like ourselves. Supply boats and bunkering craft moved constantly among them in a general mêlée of effort and purpose. A constant movement to the eye and the audible sounds of myriad diesel and petrol engines and voices amplified by hand-held brass or tin cone megaphones. A communications era that preceded battery-powered amplifiers and walkie-talkies. And flag signals! Every ship was flying a hoist meaning something. Occasionally the rattle of a ship's small armament could be heard in the distance as gunners cleared obstructions or just practiced for something to do. Sometimes the piercing flash of an Aldis signalling lamp would draw the eye to a distant ship. The dots and dashes of the Morse Code, laconically answered by the letter "T" from another ship, suggested either urgency from the sender, practice or just a bored officer-of-the-watch alone on his navigating bridge wanting to chat with someone. I suppose the scene could have duplicated one a century earlier, of a fleet at anchor off Spithead or in Scapa Flow.

I imagine I would have passed some of the time sitting or roaming corridors in the building housing the Naval Control of Shipping until my father and all the other captains had been briefed by the convoy's commodore. If thirty merchant vessels were to make up our eastbound convoy there would have been thirty merchant captains re-emerging from the conference room clutching briefcases, uniform caps or bowler hats and brown envelopes containing sealed orders—should something go badly wrong beyond one's imagination. There would always be a few of those "things." In that manner, every contingency was taken care of. Years later I discovered that my father had his own ideas on how to get out of trouble.

My father thought it would be a nice relaxation to go and see a movie. No doubt we ate lunch somewhere then bought tickets and sat on hard, unyielding wooden seats. The film was *Gulliver's Travels*. The latest release. About two hours later we eased our cramped bottoms from the seats and hobbled toward the exit. A taxi set us down near the ferry wharf and we climbed aboard a motor launch. My father recognised several captains who'd attended the conference and somehow we ended up touring the harbour putting these men aboard their ships before we finally reached the *Essex Lance*.

A wind had sprung up and a choppy sea was sending spray over the cabin roof. When finally we reached the bottom of the accommodation ladder it was a slippery business getting aboard but there was the chief steward to give us a hand. Our spell ashore was over and I would not stand again on the North American continent for several years. The trip ashore to Sydney, effectively drew a line under my American experience, the unconscious endorsement of a new identity and parting from the old. I would not now ever become an American.

By now the ship was moving about her anchor cable in swings to port and starboard and seemed to be saying: "All right, the captain's aboard, let's begin the voyage and get it over with." But we had a night to ride out some wild weather in the open roadstead. Ships might have dragged their anchors and it could not be certain that the convoy would still be in its previously assembled order in the morning.

s.s. Granford *at Cardiff, South Wales—1948*
"...the pyramid's angle of repose..."

I do not remember the actual departure of the convoy. Being an old ship capable of about ten knots, maybe eleven if the chief engineer was told there was a U-boat on our tail, we had been assigned to an eight knot convoy. Morning after morning I would wake up, throw off the uncomfortable lifejacket my father made me wear at night, wash in the small basin with the hot water Alec would bring up, and gaze through the porthole at the ships steaming in line from horizon to horizon. The smell of the bacon and egg breakfast drifting up from the saloon would drive me down there before I did anything else.

I had plenty to do. Quite soon, I was helping "Sparks" pulling flags from the flag locker, bending them on to acknowledge signals from the commodore ship and perhaps make a reply. Unlike the *Baltrover*, we had no naval yeomen-of-signals "bunting tossers" aboard. I was happy to be a de-facto yeoman and re-splice broken halyards, watching my father in the chartroom and maybe even being a small nuisance at times although no one said so. I was busy most days with the Argus camera and the photographs today help to bring events back into focus as nothing else could. I had no wide angle lens but I experimented using the ship's telescope, reversed, to get pictures of the ship's decks, cargo, superstructure and the tall funnel. Larger exposure settings were needed to compensate for the long tube which starved the lens of light. Perhaps the shot of the convoy, sprawled over the ocean in late afternoon sunlight, is the more dramatic.

At some point, about midway across the Atlantic, my father switched me from the pilot cabin to his and, for some nights, I slept in his bunk wearing the lifejacket. Where he slept I don't remember but, with my awareness today, it is clear we were in a danger zone and he just wasn't sleeping at all, apart from cat-naps. It really is remarkable how trusting and unquestioning one is at age fifteen. Or did I sense rather more than I wished to admit? If there *had* been isolated comments from other officers or crew members to whom I would surely have spoken concerning our increasingly hazardous location, I have no memory of them. Obviously, the convoy's dangers were not topics of conversation at mealtimes or around the decks. Some, had quite possibly survived an earlier sinking, and were back at sea doing the only job they knew which provided a living for families at home. To live, they had to taunt death in the blast of an ammunition ship, the fiery inferno of an oil tanker or just succumb to drowning, when no ship dared stop to pick men up.

Thirty-eight ships. "...sprawled over the ocean in late afternoon sunlight..."

"...no wide-angle lens but I experimented..."

The rules of engagement had been learned, at cost, early in the sea war. Grand Admiral Dönitz did not encourage his U-boat commanders to delay ordering: "fire one, fire two, fire three" torpedoes at a naval escort or rescue ship picking up swimming men. And even though unarmed, becoming a prisoner of war was rarely a feature of service in the Merchant Navy. Even if there was space in a submarine, inclinations did not match those of the combat soldier in pure military confrontations. In that sense the Atlantic war, including the Russian convoys, was not a conventional war where the Geneva Convention rules held sway. The *Athenia* sinking, hours after the outbreak of war, bore testimony to modern Germany's intentions toward its non-combatant enemies in merchant ships. Civilians all—with a pea-shooter on the stern for defense.

A number of alarms had gone off on board, day and night, alerts possibly emanating from the commodore's signals or my father's double check on a situation as he saw it. At night, a distant explosion somewhere on the convoy's thirty-mile perimeter announced, in a way known to all, that a distant ship was no longer in line or a straggler had paid the price for having missed a boiler-clean at her last port. (Or maybe, just conserving coal as ordered?) Night or day, the double thuds of depth charges fired in quick succession with their displays of white-plumed waterspouts, proclaimed an angry escort's response to an Asdic contact with a now deathly silent enemy below. Most U-boats were killed this way, their end marked by debris and fuel oil. Our ship, of course, was totally blacked out with only a blue stern-light for each ship to follow, each line of ships a bare sea-mile apart. It needed almost a miracle to keep station in those conditions and collisions did occur.

We sighted the northwest coast of Ireland on the thirteenth day. Surely we would make it without the convoy having to scatter under attack. But now, the convoy was in range of the Royal Air Force's Coastal Command flying-boats sent out to spot submarines below

"...deathly silent enemy below..."
A "thumbs-up" from my father.

the surface and acting as spotters to aid the hunt by corvettes and destroyers. Depth-charging the submarine would often bring her up to face the concentrated fire of warships and merchantmen.

One bright, sunny afternoon, having spent the morning on the bridge watching the Western Isles slide past on either side, the convoy approached its destination seemingly intact. A small loch on the Scottish mainland opposite the Isle of Skye named Loch Ewe, was then being used as a dispersal point where each ship would learn its final haven. As for the *Essex Lance*, she would be routed, through minefields, around the top of Scotland to an east coast port. North Sea coastal waters had been dubbed "E-boat Alley," a happy hunting ground for the German version of Britain's fleet of fast coastal motor torpedo boats. Like our MTB's, the little fifty-ton German craft were floating gun platforms having perhaps six torpedo tubes, quick-firing Bofors-type, main armament, mounted heavy machine guns and small arms. The latter were for the use of a typically swashbuckling captain and crew whose sometimes quirky, pro-active personalities had singled them out for more unconventional, close quarter action and perhaps the final boarding of a subdued merchant ship. In fact anything that might be shot up for exercise, brandishing side-arms and maybe even the odd cutlass. Predictably, having first hitched a ride across the Atlantic in an equally unconventional fashion, and having got me thus far toward the fields of Kent, my father opted to land me with the naval staff at Aultbea, the base's administration centre.

The afternoon of our arrival at the anchorage, I said goodbye to my father, officers and crew of the *Essex Lance*, my brown trunk containing my worldly goods and souvenirs was lowered into a launch manned by a sub-lieutenant and two naval ratings, who then deposited me aboard a yacht moored close to the Nissen huts of the administration block.

The yacht, whose pre-war pristine whiteness had become wartime grey, was the *Iona*, named after one of the Hebridean islands and a proud possession, I was informed, of a Scottish laird. The small stateroom into which I was bundled, reflected the opulence of her owner whose current employment may well have been as colonel in a commando unit for the duration (of the war), his yacht, commandeered by the Admiralty. Presumably, he got his yacht back after the war.

I remember eating breakfast in the small, beautifully furnished saloon before being ferried to the shore where I imagine various people helped me with the trunk. There seemed to have been few formalities to delay me being put aboard a bus. My father, before the *Essex Lance* had sailed that morning, had obviously "squared" everything with the authorities, as they then existed at Aultbea.

I could only surmise what the authorities back in Canada had been thinking over the past fifteen days since leaving Montréal. I had, in a manner of speaking, absconded from two countries in wartime. At the Canadian border crossing, Master Philip Morgan Cheek had not reappeared on expiry of his visa to visit his dad on compassionate grounds. Is an amnesty in the cards?

On the bus, as it droned its way laboriously up the steep roads overlooking Loch Ewe, I may have thought about all that. On the other hand I may not have. Certainly, I would have had a lot of things on my mind. I appear to have been put in the charge of the bus driver. After some two hours of weaving through the North West Scottish Highlands, with gorse and heather in July profusion from horizon to horizon, I fancied I was at sea again.

The "ocean" this time, was mauve-heather with the white fronds of cotton grass creating an illusion of white, wind-flecked wave-tops in a force-3 breeze. The roads, thereabouts, called for stops to allow rare vehicles to pass at specially widened sections but finally, we rolled to a halt near a small building and a single track railway line. This was, and still is, the little railway station named Achnasheen from which one train departed for Inverness each weekday and returned. The service may be more frequent now.

Someone probably deposited my trunk on the platform and I

Achnasheen Railway Station

waited for the train. It came eventually, blowing steam and smoke. I got into one of the two carriages and perhaps an hour later I was standing on a platform at Inverness Railway Station having travelled that day from the west to the east coast of Scotland through a land strange and beautiful as any that might lie atop Jack's beanstalk. Then I climbed down.

I had sufficient money to buy a ticket for London from The London Midland and Scottish Railway Co.; somehow got the trunk and myself onto the correct train and relaxed in the small, third-class compartment for the first time since waking up aboard the Laird's yacht around five that morning. It was then about eleven o'clock and the journey, in wartime, would have taken around seven hours, maybe eight. White-coated ladies sold tea in thick, white china cups from food trolleys. At that time you took your cup of tea, *with* its saucer, into the train compartment. The chinaware had some distinctive logo of the train company glazed-in–LMS–and would be collected up by staff at some other stop. A bit like the circulation of money. I don't remember coffee being sold. Sacks of coffee beans earned no priority shipping space in 1942.

I bought a cup of the uniquely flavoured railway tea, kept hot in the chromium-plated, copper tea urn which had a tap. At intervals the top lid would be lifted off, fresh tea leaves sprinkled onto the almost toxic liquid inside, a large kettle of recently boiled water poured in, the lid replaced and it was business as usual. Tea bags had not been invented. I also bought a cheese sandwich and an apple whose combined chemical actions may have neutralised the tea, for I am here, writing this.

It may have been an express train for it didn't seem that long before it was rattling over points and threading its smokey way past the backyards of London's railway residences, under networks of bridges and finally trundling into the great Euston Station protected from the elements by glass and ironwork. Tiers of sandbags protected doorways and paper strips, pasted on glass, reduced splintering.

There would have been some arrangement made with my mother to meet the train for I was gazing expectantly out of the carriage window, ignoring the notice that warned of the dangerous practice. When the giant locomotive, hissing and steaming, was halted by the buffers, eight carriages down the platform, I opened the door, got out, and fancied I saw my mother standing with a group searching for familiar faces. Now, people were descending rapidly from the train's doorways soon to crowd the platform with bodies and baggage. Yes, it was she, looking about anxiously, little changed it seemed and wearing her customary pill-box hat and carrying the handbag my father had bought her on one of his Montclair visits to see me.

"Hi! Mother," I called, making toward her, "it's me." But she looked past me to someone else, to a boy about my age who looked more British in a wartime utility suit than did I, in the new, wide check sports jacket and brown trousers Aunt Elinor had bought me. The white and brown saddle shoes and outrageously coloured socks would also have served to isolate me if my new accent hadn't. On the second try, she accepted me as the son she'd said goodbye to in the air-raid shelter in Liverpool's docks two years earlier. It seems I'd effected a remarkable transformation, a new, inexplicable yet transient identity, an interloper in the wrong nest. But the strangeness soon passed. In the welcoming there would have been some limited demonstration, a hug of sorts. My mother was always restrained in public. It was stiff-upper-lip time and I would freeze inside if displays of affection were obligatory. On that occasion, I believe she would have probably handled things with her inherent wisdom saying, simply: "Did you have a good journey, did you have a meal on the train? No? You must be hungry ...come along then," as though I'd just come home from some school trip. Then we were in one of London's black taxis, driving up the Strand, to be deposited outside the Strand Palace Hotel, then eating dinner whose government-controlled cost of five shillings per person could not exceed the subsidy. At that time the exchange rate was around four dollars to the pound. Five shillings was therefore one dollar. We dined well on that.

"Would you like ice cream?" enquired my mother when the waiter hovered awaiting a decision on the dessert.

"Yes please," I replied.

I remember there'd been something strange about the ice cream. My mother was eating hers. There appeared to be specks of chocolate all through. In the paint trade it might have been called oatmeal in the colour chart. It was pleasant to the pallet but I could not place the flavour. My mother watching but not watching said: "I'm afraid this is the ice cream we have nowadays in England. It's made of flour, not much milk, water and um.....a few other things."

"What are the specks?" I had to wait a little for the answer.

"We now have what's called the "national loaf," Philip, made of standard, part refined flour. It produces a light brown loaf of bread. Quite good and actually more nourishing than the white loaves we had when you were here. The specs come from the flour."

I would have to get used to numerous other changes to our daily life but none stand out as being remarkable. Great Britain had been at war with Germany for three years and food rationing had begun earlier than it had in the Great War with the Ministry of Food better prepared. We would endure serious shortages of citrus fruits but somehow Vitamin-C was acquired from other sources.

Children would grow to seven years without ever handling an orange, lemon or a banana although they'd seen pictures of them. Scenes depicting domestic situations in American movies might show an American family sitting down to breakfast with a jug of freshly squeezed orange juice on the table, a banana being peeled by a child and a lemon sliced up into quarters to re-appear with the fish course at dinner times.

After our dinner at the Strand Palace and the start of my re-education, my mother and I went home to our small house in Chelsfield, Kent, last seen one morning early on August 30th, 1940. I seem to have lost track of my brown trunk. I assume it had been put into the luggage van of the Inverness-to-London train. On the other hand we certainly did not have it with us at the Strand Palace Hotel. Perhaps, after all, my father had kept it aboard his ship to bring home when he came on leave? It would certainly have been an encumbrance on the Scottish bus. And now it is strange how, thinking intently about that small matter, the fogged past has cleared, permitting a glimmer of recovered memory to resolve the question. Yes, it does come back.... The *Essex Lance* reached Newcastle a week later; my father and the trunk arrived home at 38 Malvern Road some days after that. There had been a large, canvas sea-bag also, I remember, filled with canned foods and of course very heavy for the ancient taxi's suspension whose driver always fretted about our unsealed, rutted road. In our house we had made a shallow basement under the structure having a trap door concealed by the carpet. It was best to be discreet in wartime and not arouse envy. Anyway, chocolate-mint-chip ice cream and White Castle hamburgers would not be tempting people in *our* road.

Alec Bowles, Cabin Boy, late of the s.s. *Essex Lance*, also arrived at his home—6 Argonaut Street, Gateshead, Newcastle-on-Tyne—and everything was complete and as it should be.

Epilogue

W e live in a world of everyday options. All of us have used them. First choices become second, even third choices. I have yet to meet a man or woman who will not own up to even more. They are indeed lucky people and Americans have been luckier than most. In the years since 2001 they will have studied their options with intensity. In this book I have tried to review just a few in the light of what we know of war, modern weaponry and the responses of either pacifists or non-combatants caught up in it.

I began with my own choices and experiences as a British evacuee to America in World War II. Wrestling with memory in efforts to recall words and events of more than half a century ago has not distorted them. Time has opened up new perspectives, given them new meaning. From post World War II re-evaluations of that conflict via the writings of others, fresh appreciations emerge. Quoted passages are a way of saying that paraphrasing could not possibly have improved them. Fresh insight compares with the restoration of a dusty oil painting. With so many images of the safety and comfort of a Verona, New Jersey home and of Montclair Academy itself to accompany me, I have marched along, in the literary sense, line-by-line with side flashes on the war's progress. I hope this device has enabled the reader to contrast and evaluate my good fortune with the misfortunes of others during perhaps the last old fashioned war on Earth.

Of the options touched upon in their different contexts, America appears, with unhappy hindsight, to have tossed one aside at Teheran in 1943 during a Stalin-Roosevelt-Churchill conference. There, Roosevelt's marked preference to overtly trust Russian military objectives while mistakingly assigning purely imperialist motives to Winston Churchill in the latter's advocacy of a postwar confederation of English-speaking peoples, is regarded by many historians as misplaced. Yet today, there is something to be said for Churchill's concept..., i.e. the unrestricted movement of peoples within the western bloc, for residence and trade. Some forty years later, Churchill's former private secretary, Jock Colville, thanking Alistair Cooke for reviewing his World War II diaries, spoke of the first months of 1945 when American leaders viewed Russia as a progressive democracy. Britain was regarded as wedded to Empire. Colville writes: *"Great men like Roosevelt, Eisenhower and even to some extent the greatest of all, George Marshall, were so imbued with their own pride in being descended from successfully rebellious colonists that they equated colonialism with repression.*" He maintained this to be a simplistic view and wondered what these notable Americans would have made of the way independence for colonial nations so often led to the very suppression of desired freedoms?

In the New Year of 1945, Cooke dwelt further on the current Anglo-American spate of hang-ups in his BBC, *American Letter.* (Only much later would it become his renowned "Letter From America.") *"Behind these talks,"* he says, *"is a simple and unchanging belief—it is the belief that, no matter how much we scream and kick at each other, we cannot break up the home. Not for any sentimental reason—not for any persuasive moonshine about our common origins—but because it simply isn't realistic any more to consider breaking up. We may dislike each other heartily, but we can no longer afford the luxury of acting on that dislike. Whether they like it or not, Britain and America are mixed together in a test-tube—the irreducible elements of a working peace on earth. And in case anyone should forget,"* he added, *"May I remind you that I'm speaking to you as a native Briton, who years ago decided on a career that is still understaffed: the interpretation of the United States to the people of Britain."*

Thus, an Eisenhower, seemingly prejudiced toward empires of any kind, suspected Churchill's offer to deploy a surplus British force in the Eastern Mediterranean stuck without sea transport for joining American forces, yet available, to secure the Aegean-Black Sea sector. At some point, between February 5th and 12th, at a Black Sea, Crimean resort called Yalta, Stalin, Roosevelt and Churchill met to discuss the peace, fumbled and, it is said, produced the ingredients of the Cold War. Churchillian prescience foresaw Stalinist long-range intent. Roosevelt, ill, who would die in a month, tragically could not—and lost the plot. It would take another forty years for a later American president to term the Soviet Union: "The Evil Empire" and posthumously vindicate the British statesman.

Options?

I recall the summer of 1942 in England as being not unlike that of 1940 with its blue skies over Kentish wheat fields and ripening fruit trees in endless orchards. The garden of England. By then the blueness was smudged by swarms of American B-17 "Flying Fortress" bombers by day and our mighty Lancasters by night, carrying the war deep into German and occupied territories. There was almost no anti-aircraft shrapnel or the spent cannon shells from battling fighter aircraft to pick up. Red poppies now bloomed among maturing sheaves of wheat undamaged by the wreckage of fallen aeroplanes.

The harvest promised to be a good one. Combine-Harvesters and threshing machinery would be left undamaged by chunks of Spitfire or Heinkel bomber. Around our house it was a souvenir desert. There was almost nothing lying about to be saved for posterity! I walked along familiar paths, again packed hard in the August heat as I'd remembered, and rescued someone's discarded gas mask from a thorn bush, its rubber already perished, its air-tight integrity gone for good. Its presence there made a statement its owner had probably not considered in any depth. War, of an earlier kind, had gone on from this place. Before long, newer enemy weapons and newer defenses would shatter a transient rural peace. A renewed ordeal would come from the V-1 flying bombs and V-2 rockets just two years off. And August 30th, second anniversary of my 1940 departure for America, was coming up.

As it happened, the date would prove to be inauspicious. A third attempt to be accepted by a school had failed. My mother was assiduously studying and comparing the brochures of all those places of learning whose curriculums must surely match Montclair Academy's eighth grade-coming-up-ninth and terminated but a few short weeks before. It was soon evident that my aptitudes fitted no English headmaster's regime and the three I had met in company with my mother had been polite in their rejections. One of these I had met at a school established in 1447 by a group of mercers for their offspring. Mercers could have been latter-day textile barons although any connection with weaving cloth had, by 1942, been retained only as an interesting historical footnote. So, I remember how we had just emerged, from the portals of The Mercers' School, near Chancery Lane in London and I stood at the curbside, seriously dejected and said: "I don't seem to be good for anything in this country," or words to that effect. But the reference to "country" at age fifteen, seems now significant for some reason. Was it, that for the first time, I *had* a second country with which to make comparisons?

As the weeks passed my Montclair days assumed a diminishing relevance. A world and a culture away from Montclair, close associations became blurred or were simply and expediently superseded. Academically mixed up and, it seemed, a year behind other boys of my age, a referral by a family friend secured me a place at William Penn's old school at Chigwell, in the county of Essex near the fringes of Epping Forest.

Founded in 1629, it was hoped, I think, that through the ancient school's association with early English history and great doings, like Penn's Pennsylvania, some of that would rub off onto me naturally, and of course it has. I was of that age. I re-learned to regard my betters with a God-fearing respect. At Montclair Academy there was no "God-fearing" just respect. My new peers included the masters but not certain sixth form prefects who, with threats of sanctions, demanded similar recognition. I never respect anyone who maintains unrealistic expectations. But then I hardly ever go about with my suit jacket unbuttoned or hands in my pockets partly because the recollection of the physical pain produced by slipper-

The American Option

Chigwell School
"...I would never become an isolated Saunders-of-the-river..."

wielding prefects is firmly fixed, and partly because I acknowledge now how damned slovenly it looks. It is almost as bad as seeing national leaders posing in some "think tank" jacketless with the cuffs just turned over. "Look, we are the working proletariat," suggests the lead cynic, "just like what you want us to be."

Kindly Dr R.L. James, headmaster, destined for St Pauls School then Harrow, explained to my mother in an ante-room that recognising just how disruptive of education had been the wartime evacuation of children, he had devised a special class for just such as I. It was called Form Remove-A. It was something like going from eighth to seventh grade all over again. This time, absent would be the cheerfully democratic hubbub of Montclair Academy's lunch-room, juniors and seniors mixed in with jam-filled donuts, Coca-Cola and peanuts to level out stress and the spartan solitudes of a Chigwell boarding student. It was back to the wasteful, often the-atrical disciplines of the English teaching system and the budding authoritarianism of sixth form seniors renamed prefects who, mostly due to immaturity, seemed unable to always handle the role with humanity.

But I was borne up by a snippet of information gleaned, probably from my history master, Arnold Fellowes, that Winston Churchill at my age had likewise shown little academic brilliance while at Harrow excepting the English language spiced with history and fencing. I clasped this fortunate intelligence along with the events of 1066, to my breast like the ship's lifejacket I'd so recently been wearing. A lifesaver, a rock, to sustain morale in the coming turbulence of my Chigwell days. In the young Winston, I now had a secret schoolboy role model whose destiny had seen him, army pistol in the left hand; sabre-slashing with the right at Dervish tribesman from a horse at Omdurman in the last ever cavalry charge. And finally, as Prime Minister of Great Britain. I could dream of nothing better!

And it would aid me when the "ragging" started. The British school phenomenon associated with induction was of the specialised kind to recondition the minds of the over-sensitive and to subordinate the raging individualists to some kind of Chigwellian sophistication and normality. It may still be. Specialised, I mean. It would not return me to English life and mores with the seamless ease enjoyed and remembered in Montclair and the Academy—whatever variations there might be in Wales, Cornwall, Scotland or Ireland. The tone of the "ceremonials" had been wholly and—I am sure—unwittingly set by Dr James himself. Thinking to ease me into life at Chigwell; knowing my recent background he had, it appeared, let it be known to the senior sixth form prefect that a boy from America would be commencing in the Christmas term and how it would do the school, and everyone, credit if the new boy, albeit a kind of American export, could be helped to settle down at his studies quickly and so to fit himself for, well, something.

Americans, in their hundreds of thousands were, at that period of the war, very much a part of life in Britain's towns and villages. I should not have seemed an iconic figure—in the modern vernacular. My mother had adhered as closely as our finances permitted, to the School's war-modified list of clothing. A pre-war uniform which had included the wide, stiff, Eton shirt collar and, I saw from pictures, a top hat, had been discontinued. Thank God for the war! Black striped trousers, black jacket and a straw "boater" or, by preference, a felt school cap were obligatory. I chose the round cap with the school's logo above the narrow peak, a bishops mitre, a hat. The cap would be easier to stuff into one's pocket when "going foreign" on private excursions. It seems to have been excluded from every photograph in which I featured. The foregoing description is more than enough.

I recall Tony Yates as greeter and introducer in every aspect of my initial assimilation. Six foot, friendly and with an easy grin beneath a shock of curly hair, I suspect he'd been selected by Dr James to show me the ropes. He did well which, in one sense, accentuated the later remorseless mimicry by schoolmates of my American accent and an acquired, curious usage of English.

"Come on...let's go," I remember, particularly amused them. "Come on, let's go," sounds (still does) like an army corporal in a foxhole unsure of what his orders were. With chagrin and to my detriment, I would discover much later, that all my friends, no doubt egged on by prefects, had initially held me in some awe and had scrutinised my attire for the tell-tale signs of the couple of hip-slung Colts they'd been warned I owned–and might use if pressed too far! Had I known, I could have played that card for all it was worth until I'd sorted out my tormentors. However, with evidence obviously lacking, awe and respect waned. I was a fraud, an imposter. My initiation became a conduit for frustration, almost a form of punishment. But their disappointments waned. I have to contrast that episode with an imagined reaction of Montclair Academy students perhaps briefed to expect a stereotype Englishman in 1940 wielding a rolled umbrella and uttering a few, "I say chaps." But there, reality was different.

In a way, I would miss out badly with the system. Authoritarian order and the unique British form of discipline and sanctions needed to control the Empire if not to govern it, was becoming obsolete. Just as I was about to come of age and practice what I had learned from my peers at Chigwell, various people were giving the Empire away to various other people. I would never become another isolated "Saunders-of-the-river," colonial district commissioner meting out punishments to dart-throwing African pygmies or head-hunters of New Guinea's Fly River. And there will be few voices as authoritative as Paul Robeson's, Martin Luther King's–and Winston Spencer Churchill's.

My mother would travel across London, to Essex to visit on days set by the headmaster. The flying bombs had not started to come over then. Mothers would not normally be spotted on a campus with a culture dedicated to the weaning away from cosy family security. "A man must do what a man has to do...without women." The truth was a little different. There were sports days and end-of-term days when girls might be seen, usually the sisters of one's class mates and of course parents. So, I would meet my mother at the small Chigwell railway station and we would proceed to Kistruck's tea shop and bakery in the village where she would order tea and all the things I had not seen or tasted for six weeks and I would learn about my father's recent homecoming on leave, his ship and unburden my feelings. Before I waved her off on the train she would have handed over a large bag of her Welsh scones or a fruit cake in an airtight tin along with urgings to do my best. The train farewell scenes were totally miserable and somehow relived each time I opened the cake tin.

On end-of-term holidays I would escape home. I would manage to survive about four terms due chiefly to having joined the school's Air Training Corps (ATC) - to enter the Royal Air Force. It was a toss-up between that and the Army equivalent, The Officers' Training Corps (OTC) as to whether one might live longer in the air or in the mud. I left my indelible mark on the school. A few years ago my name, scratched into the tongue and groove paneling of where my five-by-six cubicle had been, was still visible. The air-raid shelters had been filled in.

Chigwell was, and is, a fine school in its class, then turning out Empire administrators, stockbrokers and the odd judge or two, as it had always done, weaned on former views of the world and world orders and comfortable with their rigidity. Those, however, were fast becoming displaced—and replaced. The flexibility of my developing lifestyle could not mesh. I went to a Polytechnic to try for the matriculation examinations in January 1944 and in June, Hitler's secret weapon, the V-1 pilotless flying bomb, kept the school closed for most of the week. There was no defined target. A gyroscope was unfussily programmed with the co-ordinates of London, in the first instance. Then an upgrade, the V-2 rocket, a ballistic missile you couldn't hear coming, blasted our home. Heralding in the rocket age, it would one day put a real "man-on-the-moon" and cause my mother to polish the surface of our oak dining table more often. She became fascinated by the way the suns rays made the minutest, embedded fragments of shattered window glass glitter like diamonds.

By November, disgusted and 17, I escaped to my sea career, to Antwerp in Belgium then a Russian convoy, to Archangel and back, and seemingly endless navigational swot and examinations over years. The world would be my university; the imponderable, apparently ever-expanding universe, my inspiration. It was better thus. In 1999, the Russians sent me a medal, thanks to The Russian Convoy Club which, for some reason I genuinely cannot figure, makes me proud. Accidentally it seems, I'd joined a special band of Merchant Navy men of the time and had caught up, just a bit, with the father who'd been through the fire and nervous hell of the Atlantic war, for six years. By comparison, my commitment was miniscule.

Attempts to resume an interrupted customary education and re-adapt had failed, miserably and rather shamefully when I remember my mother's strenuous, solo efforts to find me a place in any school at all. A half-forgotten pre-war Englishness had somehow become annealed with a positive American stamp. A return to British life at age fifteen had not been accompanied by self-assured feelings of belonging and, with a sea career thrown in it has not, it seems, been regained.

Thus I remain loyal to two countries and only the tax man holds sway in one. That Great Britain and America are almost blood allies makes today's trans-Atlantic British commuter all-but an acceptable immigrant. For a child of Europe under Nazi occupation, America, as an alternative destination, was never an option. Wholesale kidnapping and Nazification by adoption into "suitable" German families took care of the options. Later, in peacetime, the practice introduced those conflicts in identity and origin that marked the maladjusted teenager of the fifties; who then played no part in the recovery of nations due the wasteful process of filling up correctional institutions!

By contrast, I had been a voluntary 1940's wartime, child evacuee to America and ended the six year conflict against Nazi evil as a Merchant Navy Cadet in 1944. My father was still afloat in the same business and my mother had been unmolested by jackbooted thugs in black uniforms.

From Montclair Academy I acquired a distinctive hallmark and William F. Brown II, (Bill) who, with the Family at 90 Park Avenue, had become my tutors in things American, won a two year personal achievement award he could neither claim nor learn about until four decades had passed. In 1983, when proceeding on leave from a ship in Miami, I visited the Academy for the first time since 1942 and whose headmaster, Dr Peter Greer and Alumni staff, headed by Christie Austin, director, helped me to track him down to a Connecticut address. There, in tranquil surroundings with wife and co-writer Tina, he continues to write and generate the stories for his successful Broadway and state-wide musical shows. It is a friendship forged in a conventional war and since re-dedicated in America's war against the less than illustrious terrorist—and cretinous coward. And on their garden flagpole, common to many American homes where Old Glory is displayed almost as frequently as a house number, Newtown Turnpike neighbours will sometimes observe a two flag hoist flying. The signal, reserved for my visits and professionally bent on by Bill, exhibits, on the single halyard, America's own Stars and Stripes while in the subordinate position, he clips on Great Britain's Union Jack. Sometimes, as aboard ship, the two flags hang down limply with no breeze to reveal the signal's meaning without training a telescope. At other times they curl and dance in merry fashion and the message then is clear. Neighbour comment goes unrecorded but one or two just may wish to keep up with the Browns.

Opening the 1942 *Octopus* again, to check some names and dates, I can still read Arthur Totten's fading message against his graduation photo. The levity of some endorsements scrawled in the heady atmosphere of graduates heading for the unknown, would often at one, demolish and enhance reputations—teacher or student. Both acknowledged it was how the Academy worked in those days. Fearless.

"I may have kidded you all year about the English, but don't take it to heart, because they're a fair bunch. At any rate, I hope you have a very successful life... Arthur Totten. P.S. On the way over to England don't get in the way of a German torpedo."

Well, his "wing-and-a-prayer" caution just may have seen the *Essex Lance* through to Britain all those years ago—without a tor-

"...sometimes, as aboard ship, the two flags hang down limply..."
(*Courtesy:* Tina Tippit Brown)

pedo exploding in her vitals–and with her near desperately needed cargo intact. And now I notice for the first time since then, the message of Arthur Lamborn Hofmann (18) against *his* photo:

"Say hello to that beautiful next-door neighbour of yours. Take it easy here. These masters can't take much more... Art."

He was in line to take care of Paula Dean–in my absence. I hope he did.

Arthur Totten
"...Don't get in the way of a German torpedo..."

Niagara Falls–1947. And the meeting, finally, of two wartime families.
Father, Mother, "Aunt" Elinor, Audreta, "Uncle" Roy, Harold taking the
picture. Me, aboard ship somewhere. (Courtesy: A.M. Pape-Sheldon)

Afterword

SIR ALISTAIR COOKE

One Day In London
(October 15th 2004)

Among Alistair Cooke's early ambitions, becoming a leading theatre director had taken precedence. It was then spectacularly wrecked by the success of his transatlantic journalism.

Whilst the substance of this book strives toward historical and factual correctness, for Americans it must end politically incorrect. Just for this once, the Sir bit in the above heading has no inverted commas. Why this inverted reverence, you may ask? The answer proportionately lay in the music of Alistair's granddaughter, Jane as she interpreted with violin, a Bach concerto which floated ethereally down and around, filling the lofty unseen spaces of Westminster Abbey on the day of her grandfather's Memorial Service. It was all some distance away from New York and the family's Long Island retreat she well knew as a child. It may have something to do with lineage. To my uncritical ear she played the piece to perfection and thus became a worthy follower in Alistair's own footsteps as originator and perfecter of an institution, the two-in-a-room broadcaster who uniquely had just himself and you in there with whom to discuss the week's events. And these words from the Dean of Westminster, The Very Reverend Dr Wesley Carr titled, The Bidding:

"The weight of this sad time we must obey;
Speak what we feel, not what we ought to say."

It's the end of the tragedy of *King Lear*. Albany speaks the final couplet and the play is ended. If there was anyone who spoke what he felt and not the platitudes of the age, it was Alistair Cooke in whose memory we have assembled this morning.

His weekly *Letter From America* was a unique and powerful contribution to our understanding of our friendliest, yet so often to us strangely different, ally.

Jesus said, "Blessed are the peace-makers," those who in their generation bring about understanding and reconciliation. One such

The American Option

was Alistair, whom we remember with Thanksgiving and commend to God in confidence."

So, *Letter From America*, beamed out worldwide on each Sunday for decades plus repeats on other days, informed us of how littletown and bigtown America was thinking and behaving in the seven days elapsing. For Americans on home soil the *Letter* would be digested differently. As when a person is amused to hear stories about him or herself. A gap in the market remains, therefore, to inform Americans about Britain. For that, we need "A Letter From England." Who will write it? For many years Alistair Cook was known to Americans chiefly as host/presenter of television's *Omnibus* series then *Masterpiece Theatre*, also on lecture circuits and in newspaper columns either side of the Atlantic.

I first remember the *Letter* coming on about 9:30 p.m., following the nine o'clock news of those days, which would have been around 1947, perhaps home on leave from the Merchant Navy. The voice sounded more American than in recent years, reminding me pleasantly of my recent, brief American existence, but the intonations seemed always something special so that one stopped doing whatever one was doing—and listened. On this day in the Abbey I would hear our new British Broadcasting Corporation (BBC) director general, Mark Thompson say from the pulpit as part of his eulogy: "Institutions have their own DNA, and if you look deep into the genetic code of the BBC, you will find the rich, calm, beguiling, wise voice of Alistair Cooke."

The late Peter Jennings, anchorman and senior editor, American Broadcasting Corporation (ABC), speaking from the Quire Pulpit explained how Alistair Cooke "used to dismiss any idea of a memorial service after his death. But he might have said: "Ah, the Abbey? Well..." His daughter, Susan, revealed that he had told her he would, after all, like there to be a concert..." at some small church in England."

Political correctness, some say, is predominantly an American preoccupation. We, in Britain, used to fuss more over Royal protocols but P.C. has irritatingly caught on here too. Her Majesty, Queen Elizabeth II, honoured Alistair Cooke for his work in 1974, dubbing him Knight Commander of the British Empire, (KBE). Born English, his eventual 1941 American citizenship— first applied for in 1937—denied him public use of the title. Similarly, former New York City mayor, Rudolf Guiliani and former defense secretary, Casper Weinburger, each for the parts they played, were honoured by the Queen. In this Afterword and, just for the day in question, we will beat the ban on Alistair! So be it.

At twelve noon, I was one of about 2,300 people of London sitting on chairs in Westminster Abbey about to share in the "Service of Thanksgiving for the Life and Work of Alistair Cooke, KBE." He had lived from November 20th 1908 to March 30th 2004. Lately, intermittently confined to a bed from which he could hear the birds in New York's Central Park, just beyond his window, I heard his final broadcast on February 22nd. Then, as though he was still with us, our BBC did the wholly generous, humanitarian thing. From its archives, selected recordings of earlier *Letters* were broadcast each Sunday until June 20th. The chooser was canny too. They succeeded in finding a *Letter* which, having been broadcast perhaps decades earlier, accurately and usefully resonated with current sociological and political events, much as church sermons are meant to do, although I cannot see Alistair Cooke comfortable in that role! However, knowing he was 95, health failing, I began tape-recording his last *Letters* and all of the BBC's subsequent recordings. And so, Alistair lives.

Umbrellas were up. It was raining, street lamps reflecting off paving stones. People hurrying all ways past the Houses of Parliament, past the gilded clock tower of Big Ben, crossing roads, dodging traffic. I reached what I thought was the main door of the Abbey and was asked for my yellow ticket. I didn't have one, I'd seen the newspaper item late. It takes me a week to read my Saturday *London Times*. No mention there of needing tickets.

"Go around to the other entrance, that side road over there," said a kindly porter with impeccable manners. "You just might be lucky." He smiled. After all, we were in the portal of God's House. Everyone around me under umbrellas looked benign, patient, well-behaved and properly respectful. One could be more confident of an afterlife here than anywhere else. The huge edifice of the Abbey fostered a state of mind whoever one was. I could recall queuing up with hundreds to pass Winston Churchill lying in state in January 1965. Everyone was in a state of mind then too.

I went around to the Abbey's "side" entrance as suggested. There, a great crush of people picked their way around puddles. Maybe there was more than one memorial service! Then I remembered. I was climbing the few steps toward the Great West Door through which kings and queens had passed, crownless, then emerged crowned with the glittering, bejeweled emblems balanced, precariously it always appears, on heads. I managed to dodge three red-caped porters by pretending to struggle with my umbrella, moving with the crowd, coming hard up against a 6-foot plus usher in a black cutaway coat, black pin-striped trousers and built like a certain American film star-turned state governor.

"Yellow card sir?" he enquired pleasantly and firmly. Here was an officer of the Abbey of distinctly different mettle and bearing. Physically just barely inside the Abbey at this point, I knew I could not tell a lie. Defeat and a return home stared, and was accepted. It would mean an hour and a half on the top deck of a number 53 bus to Blackheath trying to see out through windows rendered translucent with rain and new-style graffiti scratched on glass. Too many people like to test their diamonds this way.

"Sorry," I replied, "don't have a yellow card...only read about this a couple of days ago...on leave you know, Merchant Navy...been listening to Alistair Cooke's broadcast at sea for years...on short wave–and other bands... I would really like..." I was halted in mid-sentence.

"Any identification sir?" the usher enquired, looking pleasant and forgiving. I pulled out my bus pass and gave him a slightly bent calling card.

"I think you might find a seat somewhere," said he, then turned to continue his cheerful scrutinies of all the good folk pressing up behind me. Furling my umbrella with a suddenly lighter conscience, I walked a good way along the Nave until I spotted one empty seat near the Pulpit. From the seat I retrieved the programme of Service that lay there, lonely and awaiting a claimant. I sat, my feet close to a black marble slab inscribed with David Livingstone's name. Another life story. The Abbey already seemed packed with some eight or nine rows of people. Still a small audience for Alistair, he having built up a global one of millions. But this one hugely symbolised, as no radio audience could, the stature of the man and his lifetime work. That of bringing into British living rooms truer perceptions of America than are possible via the silver screen. Quoting Simon Jenkins in an extract from his book, *Letters: "There may be no one America, single and true. But Cooke's America is the truest we have."*

With the single exception of Alistair's widow, Jane, indisposed in New York, close family were there in some force, I noticed from the programme. There was John Byrne Cooke, Alistair's son, who would read a lesson from the Nave Pulpit and Alistair's daughter, The Reverend Susan Cooke Kittredge, mother of violinist Jane with sisters Phoebe and Eliza. As Pastor of the Old Meeting House, East Montpelier, Vermont, she appropriately led the prayers with:

"Almighty God, we thank you for the life and witness of Alistair Cooke; a man of tender heart, humble soul, and ready laugh, whose brilliance shone across the globe. So let us pray for that world which listened to his voice, for the many countries represented here today and especially for mutual respect between our nations and amity between our citizens. Grant, O Lord, to your divers peoples patience and trust to grow together in understanding, and to our leaders the will and the strength to further that end: that through the wisdom of those whose voice we heed, we both desire and strive for that unity of purpose which is your will."

And, from the Reverend Graeme Napier, Minor Canon and Succentor of Westminster:

"Let us pray for all who share knowledge, who inform and encourage discourse and reflection, especially for journalists, broadcasters and presenters in radio, television and print.

Afterword

"Oh God, whom no human word can fully comprehend, and no earthly image entirely reveals; make your ways known to us, we beseech you, through the labours of those who seek to publish the truth, to expose injustice and to let the voices of your people be heard: that, by banishing fear and ignorance, and furthering our understanding one of another, they may do their part in making the heart of the people wise, its mind sound and its will righteous."

These words surely, could form the basis of guideline notes in any "How To" book on journalism and information technology !

Subsequently, in the *London Times* next day beneath the Court Circular announcements, 266 names quietly claimed connection with American and British Governments, all social classes, ethnic and religious groups, world media, theatre, the arts and sciences. The page editor had been obliged to finish with: "...and many other friends, former colleagues and representatives of other organisations."

I failed to pick out members of his English family. After all, where had he come from? A Salford, Manchester scholarship boy to Cambridge. Of solid British middleclass stock, an engineering-lay preacher father, disciplinarian mother and a brother steadfast in maintaining local roots. Not so Alfred, the name he'd swopped for Alistair for reasons not generally known. Cambridge led to Harvard, Yale and accepted routes to anywhere.

Ah, the programme! I'd leafed through fifteen ivory-coloured pages. Still time, I thought, to read while the BBC Concert Orchestra played *Handel's Messiah*, the *Water Music*, then waltzing with Gilbert & Sullivan, etc. The arrival of the charge d'affaires of the United States only just preceded *Music for the Royal Fireworks*, again by George Frederic Handel. It surged through the special Abbey transmitter loop for the hard-of-hearing and hidden amplifiers, maybe a hundred feet up. It is those which gave to Alistair's spoken voice mischievous intonations from "the other side." Suddenly, the man is saying:

"I am on the whole, not sorry not to be with you today. I believe broadcasters should be heard and not seen!"

They were words Cooke had recorded to be played on a previous occasion when he was given a broadcasting award in Britain and could not be present! I looked about me expecting hair to be standing on end. Instead, secret smiles. Alistair Cooke grins impishly out from the programme's page three, blue sepia photo by Roddy McDowall, hand up to mouth, obviously enjoying a joke, the old rascal. Further in, and having recently read Nick Clarke's official biography, I am reminded of his musical preferences from which pieces would later be played...Handel, Gilbert and Sullivan but excluding, on this occasion, jazz, a favoured Alistair Cooke form of musical expression. Fittingly, with an American flag flying from an Abbey mast for the first time ever remembered, the many pillars, monuments and roof structures resounded to *The Battle Hymn of the Republic* sung with novel and unrestrained gusto for a cosmopolitan London gathering. In this first hour, all were mindful of the prayers.

Alluding once more to the great unknown and permitting Alistair Cooke the last word, so to speak, I recall how at one juncture, down from the Abbey's cavernous upper spaces again wafted recorded words he'd once spoken on the subject of the Big Bang theory:

"Who triggered the Big Bang?" he'd politely challenged in quizzical vein. "Who struck the match? If I were to choose between the Big Bang theory and the words of *Genesis*— 'And God said, let there be light, and there was light' —I'd plump for *Genesis*."

Alistair, a sometime doubter, would surely have been clasped to the breast of Westminster's dean—if he could have been clasped at that moment.

–PMC

GLOSSARY OF COMMERCIAL PRODUCTS, MEDIA & INSTITUTIONS

ALDIS LAMP, Marine signalling appliance
ARGUS, Camera manufacturers, U.S.
ARROW, Branded American shirt with attached, stiffened collar
BENTLEY CARS, Premier automobile product, U.K.
BERKELEY UNIVERSITY PRESS, Publishing House, Berkeley University, California, U.S.
BETHLEHEM STEEL CORPORATION, Manufacturers and ship-builders, U.S.
BOEING CORPORATION, Aircraft manufacturer, U.S.
BOWDITCH, Manual of navigation, U.S.
B.B.C., British Broadcasting Corporation, London, U.K.
BROWNIE, Kodak camera model, U.S.
BRYLCREEM, Branded hair preparation, U.K.
BURBERRY, Branded raincoat manufacturers, U.K.
CADBURY, Manufacturers of chocolate & food products, U.K.
CASH'S NAME TAPES, Identification product, for clothing, U.K.
COLUMBIA UNIVERSITY, New York City, U.S.
COSMOPOLITAN, Periodical, magazine, USA
CUNARD, Premier London ship-owning company, 1940 owners of RMS *Queen Mary* and RMS *Queen Elizabeth*
THE DAILY MAIL, A London newspaper
THE DAILY MIRROR, A London newspaper
THE DAILY SKETCH, Former London pictorial newspaper, U.K.
THE DAILY TELEGRAPH, A London newspaper
EASTMAN KODAK, Manufacturers of camera & photographic products, U.S.
ELASTOPLAST, A first aid, adhesive bandage product
ELLERMAN & BUCKNALL STEAMSHIP CO., LTD., British shipowning company. Now trading as Ellerman Shipping Ltd, U.K.
ESQUIRE, American magazine, popular for centrefolds featuring stylised female "pin-ups" by artists Varga and Petty
FOKKER, Aircraft manufacturer, Germany
FUNK & WAGNALL, American dictionary
HARRIS TWEED, Renowned, woven, wool material, clothing, U.K.
HENRY KAISER CORPORATION, Shipbuilder, U.S.
HOVIS, A quality bread loaf, U.K.
HOWARD JOHNSON, Popular chain of roadhouses and hotels, U.S.
THE ILLUSTRATED LONDON NEWS, Former pictorial newspaper

The American Option

J. LYONS & Co., Ltd., Café and restaurant chain, U.K., (No longer trading)

JACOBSEN'S, Retailing store, sporting equipment & apparel–Montclair, New Jersey, U.S.

JURGEN'S LOTION, A branded toilet product, U.S. Sponsor of one of 1940's America's acclaimed radio newscasters and commentators, Walter Winchell

KFC, Kentucky Fried Chicken, branded food product, U.S.

KIWI, Branded shoe polish (New Zealand origin)

LEICA, Camera manufacturers, Germany

LIFE, Periodical, magazine, (Time-Life Corp.), U.S.

THE LONDON TIMES, A London newspaper

LYLE, Lyle's Golden Syrup, food product, U.K.

MARMITE, Spreadable, concentrated health food product, U.K.

McDONNELL DOUGLAS, American Aircraft manufacturer

M.I.T., Massachusetts Institute of Technology–university, U.S.

MOLOTOV COCKTAIL, World War II improvised weapon

THE MONTCLAIR NEWS, A former, free-speaking, student-produced 1940's newspaper of Montclair Academy, New Jersey, U.S.

NESTLE, Manufacturers, chocolate and food products, Switzerland

THE NEW YORK TIMES, American newspaper

N.Z. HERALD, A New Zealand daily newspaper

THE NEWARK SUNDAY CALL, Former 1940's, Newark, New Jersey, newspaper, USA

NEXUS, New Zealand scientific journal

OVALTINE, Cadbury's brand, malted health drink, U.K.

P & O, Peninsular & Oriental Navigation Company, Premier London shipowners and operators, U.K.

PACKARD, Renowned automobile manufacturer, U.S.

PATHE-GAZETTE NEWSREELS, Cinema news programmes, U.K.

PEARS SOAP, Soap products, U.K. Publishers of *Pears Encyclopedia*

PENNSYLVANIA, Railroad company, U.S.

PIPER, Aircraft manufacturer (Piper "Cub," "Comanche," etc.), U.S.

PLAYERS, English brand cigarettes

PRINCETON UNIVERSITY, New Jersey, U.S.

PULLMAN, Railroad passenger car manufacturers/operators, U.S.

RADIO SHACK, Chain of electronic/radio supply shops, U.S.

READER'S DIGEST, Periodical, magazine

RESONANCE, Scientific publication of MENSA organisation, U.S.

RITZ CRACKERS, Food product

RMS, Royal Mail Ship

RUTGERS UNIVERSITY, New Jersey, U.S.

SPEKULA, Finnish scientific publication

SHOAL BAY PRESS, New Zealand publishing house

SKIDMORE COLLEGE, Saratoga Springs, New York, U.S.

STURMEY ARCHER, Original bicycle three-speed gearing, U.K.

UCLA, University of California at Los Angeles, U.S.
UNIVERSITY OF IOWA, American university
UNITED BALTIC CORPORATION LTD., London ship-owning
    company,
UNITED DAIRIES, Dairy products, U.K.
VERICHROME, Film and photographic products
THE WASHINGTON POST, American newspaper
THE WASHINGTON TIMES, American newspaper
WHITE CASTLE, Fast food chain, 1940's drive-in restaurant, U.S.
WILLIAMS COLLEGE, Williamstown, Massachusetts, U.S.

BIBLIOGRAPHY

1. *The People's War*. Angus Calder

2. *Five Days In London–May, 1940*. John Lukacs

3. *The Duel–Hitler vs Churchill. 10 May–31 July 1940*. John Lukacs

4. *Winston Churchill–The Era & The Man*. Virginia Cowles

5. *The Children's War*. Ruth Inglis

6. *Children Of Europe*. Dorothy McCordle

7. *A History of the American People*. Paul Johnson

8. *The Lost Continent*. Bill Bryson

9. *Old New World*. Lucinda Lambton

10. *Leading The Cheers*. Justin Cartwright

11. *Home Front*. Fiona Reynoldson

12. *Strawberries with the Führer*. Helga Tiscenko

13. *Within These Halls (History–Montclair Academy)*. Robert D.B.
    Carlisle

14. *Dunkirk*. Lt. Colonel Ewan Butler & Major J.S. Bradford MBE,
    MC

15. *Alistair Cooke–The Biography*. Nick Clarke

PRESS ARTICLES–ORGANISATIONS–PERSONAL INTER-
VIEWS:

16. "Another Country" (A *London Times* article, 1998). Justin Cartwright

17. "And You'll Be A Man My Son" (A *London Times* report on English boarding schools). Alan Franks

18. "Branded By The Swastika" (A *New Zealand Herald* report on"Abba" music group's singing star, Anni-Frid Lyngstad). Kate Connolly

19. "A Schizoid Nation" (London *Daily Mail* article). Paul Johnson

20. "United States of America, Global Ratings." *N.Z. Herald*

21. "The British Are Coming" (Westport, Ct., Historical Society. A year, 2002 commemoration report). Margaret Feczko, President

22. *New York Times* review of book: *The Peculiar Memories of Thomas Penman* (by Bruce Robinson) on, adolescent, sexual bewilderment. Patrick McGrath. Review of book: *Martyred Village, Massacre at Oradour-sur-Glane, France*. Alan Riding

23. Chelsea Military Antiques, London. Richard Black

24. Accredited Scientific Papers & Publications on the electromagnetic and radio wave effects on the human brain and intellect made specially available by Leon Langerak

25 *The Montclair News* 1940's, student-produced newspaper of Montclair Academy, New Jersey, U.S.

26. *The Octopus* - 1942 edition. Montclair Academy's school year book

27. "New England Scene" (Vermont) quote by Sinclair Lewis

28. Royal Liver Assurance Ltd. (Pronounced (L-y-ver). Ms Kate Bolland

29. Correspondence and interviews with private individuals.

Index

Index

For sales, editorial information, subsidiary rights information
or a catalog, please write or phone or e-mail
Brick Tower Press
1230 Park Avenue
New York, NY 10128, U.S.
Sales: 1-800-68-BRICK
Tel: 212-427-7139 Fax: 212-860-8852
www.BrickTowerPress.com
www.bookmanuscript.com
email: bricktower@aol.com.

For Canadian sales please contact our distributor,
Vanwell Publishing Ltd.
1 Northrup Crescent, Box 2131
St. Catharines, ON L2R 7S2
Tel: 905-937-3100

For sales in the U.K. and Europe please contact our distributor,
Gazelle Book Services
Falcon House, Queens Square
Lancaster, LA1 1RN, U.K.
Tel: (01524) 68765 Fax: (01524) 63232
email: gazelle4go@aol.com.

For Australian and New Zealand sales please contact
INT Press Distribution Pyt. Ltd.
386 Mt. Alexander Road
Ascot Vale, VIC 3032, Australia
Tel: 61-3-9326 2416 Fax: 61-3-9326 2413
email: sales@intpress.com.au.